More Fool Me

Stephen Fry is a leading light in film, theatre, radio and television the world over, receiving accolades in spades and plaudits by the shovel. As a writer, producer, director, actor and presenter he has featured in works as varied and adored as the movie *Wilde*, the TV series *Blackadder* and *Jeeves and Wooster*, the sketch show *A Bit of Fry and Laurie*, the panel game *QI*, the radio series *Fry's English Delight*, Shakespeare's Globe's celebrated 2012 production of *Twelfth Night* (as Malvolio) and documentaries on countless subjects very close to his heart.

He is also the bestselling author of four novels – *The Stars' Tennis Balls*, *Making History*, *The Hippopotamus* (the writing of which is described herein) and *The Liar* – as well as two volumes of autobiography – *Moab is My Washpot* and *The Fry Chronicles*, publishing in five unique editions, which combined to sell over a million copies.

More Fool Me

STEPHEN FRY

MICHAEL JOSEPH
an imprint of
PENGUIN BOOKS

MICHAEL JOSEPH

Published by the Penguin Group
Penguin Books Ltd, 80 Strand, London WC2R ORL, England
Penguin Group (USA) Inc., 375 Hudson Street, New York, New York 10014, USA
Penguin Group (Canada), 90 Eglinton Avenue East, Suite 700, Toronto, Ontario, Canada M4P 2Y3
(a division of Pearson Penguin Canada Inc.)
Penguin Ireland, 25 St Stephen's Green, Dublin 2, Ireland (a division of Penguin Books Ltd)
Penguin Group (Australia), 707 Collins Street, Melbourne,
Victoria 3008, Australia (a division of Pearson Australia Group Pty Ltd)
Penguin Books India Pvt Ltd, 11 Community Centre,
Panchsheel Park, New Delhi – 110 017, India
Penguin Group (NZ), 67 Apollo Drive, Rosedale, Auckland 0632, New Zealand
(a division of Pearson New Zealand Ltd)
Penguin Books (South Africa) (Pty) Ltd, Block D, Rosebank Office Park,
181 Jan Smuts Avenue, Parktown North, Gauteng 2193, South Africa

Penguin Books Ltd, Registered Offices: 80 Strand, London WC2R ORL, England

www.penguin.com

First published 2014
001

Typeset in 13.75/16.25 pt Garamond MT Std by Palimpsest Book Production Ltd, Falkirk, Stirlingshire

Printed in Great Britain by Clays Ltd, St Ives plc

A CIP catalogue record for this book is available from the British Library

HARDBACK ISBN: 978–0–718–17978–6
TRADE PAPERBACK ISBN: 978–0–718–17979–3

www.greenpenguin.co.uk

Dedicated to Jo, my Personal AsSister and subject of
'simply the best decision I ever made in my entire life'.
In grateful thanks and with profuse apologies for all the
extra work that this will bring . . .

The fool doth think he is wise, yet it is the wise man that knows himself to be the fool

As You Like It, Act 5, Scene 1

The past won't sit still for a moment

Jonathan Meades, 2014

Contents

More Fool Me

Chapter One

There is nothing very appealing about showbusiness memoirs. A linear chronology of successes, failures and blind ventures into new fields is dull enough. And then there is the problem of how to approach descriptions of collaborators and contemporaries:

'She was *adorable* to work with, *incredibly* funny and always intensely cheerful and considerate. To know her was to *worship* her.'

'I was captivated by his talent, how *marvellously* he shone in everything he did. There was a luminosity, a kind of transcendence.'

'She always had time for her fans, no matter how persistent they were.'

'What a *perfect* marriage they had, and what *ideal* parents they were. A golden couple.'

I could there be describing actors, TV show presenters or producers with total accuracy, leaving out only their serial polygamies, chronic domestic abuse, violent orgiastic fetishes and breathtaking assaults on the bottle, the powders and the pills.

Is it right of me to be searingly, bruisingly honest about the lives of others? I am quite prepared to be searingly, bruisingly honest about my own, but I just don't have it in me to reveal to the world that, for example, producer Ariadne Bristowe is an aggressively vile, treacherous bitch who regularly fires innocent assistants just for looking at her the wrong way; or that Mike G. Wilbraham has to give a blow-job to the boom operator while finger-banging the assistant cameraman before he is prepared so much as to think about preparing for a scene. All these things are true, of course, but fortunately Ariadne Bristowe doesn't exist and neither does Mike G. Wilbraham. *OR DO THEY?*

The actor Rupert Everett in his autobiographical writings manages to be caustic in what you might call a Two Species manner: bitchy and catty. The results are hilarious, but I am far too afraid of how people view me to be able to write like that. Very happy to recommend both his volumes of autobiography/memoir to you, however: *Red Carpets and Other Banana Skins* and *The Vanished Years*. Ideal holiday or Christmas reading.

So I now must consider how to present to you this third edition of my life. It must be confessed that this book is an act as vain and narcissistic as can be imagined: the *third* volume of my life story? There are plenty of wholly serviceable single-volume lives of Napoleon, Socrates, Jesus Christ, Churchill and even Katie Price. So by what panty-dribbling right do I present a weary public with yet another stream of anecdote, autobiography and confessional? The first I wrote was a memoir

4

of childhood, the second a chronicle of university and the lucky concatenation of circumstances that led to my being able to pursue a career in performing, writing and broadcasting. Between the end of that second book and this very minute, the minute now that I am using to type this sentence, lies over a quarter of a century of my milling about on television, in films, on radio, writing here and there, getting myself into trouble one way or another, becoming a representative of madness, Twitter, homosexuality, atheism, annoying ubiquity and whatever other kinds of activity you might choose to associate with me.

I am making the assumption that in picking up this book you know more or less who I am. I am keenly aware – how could I not be? – that if one is in the public eye then people will have some sort of view. There are those who thoroughly loathe me. Even though I don't read newspapers or receive violent abuse in the street, I know well enough that there are many members of the British public, and I daresay the publics of other countries, who think me smug, attention-seeking, false, complacent, self-regarding, pseudo-intellectual and unbearably irritating: diabolical. I can quite see why they would. There are others who embarrass me charmingly by their wild enthusiasm; they shower me with praise and attribute qualities to me that seem almost to verge on the divine.

I don't want this book to be riddled with too much self-consciousness. There is a lot to say about the end of

the 1980s and early 1990s, and you may find the way I go
about it to be meandering. I hope a chronology of sorts
will emerge as I bounce from theme to theme. There will
inevitably be anecdotes of one kind or another, but it is
not my business to tell you about the private lives of
others, only of my own. I consider myself incompetent
when it comes to the business of living life. Maybe that is
why I am committing the inexcusable hubris of offering
the world a third written autobiography. Maybe here is
where I will *find* my life, in this thicket of words, in a way
that I never seem to be able to do outside the bubble I
am in now as I write. Me, a keyboard, a mouse, a screen
and nothing else. Just loo breaks, black coffees and an
occasional glance at my Twitter and email accounts. I
can do this for hours all on my own. So on my own that
if I have to use the phone my voice is often hoarse and
croaky because days will have passed without me speaking to a single soul.

So where do we go from here?

Let's find out.

Catch-up

I have a recurring dream. The doorbell sounds at three in the morning. I struggle out of bed and press the entry-phone button.

'Police, sir. May we come in?'

'Of course, of course.' I buzz them in. A series of charges that I cannot quite make out are chanted at me like psalms. I am arrested and cuffed. It is all very hurried and sudden but entirely good-natured. One of the police-men asks for a photograph with me.

We cut, as dreams so cinematically do, to a courtroom, where a much less sympathetic judge sentences me to six months' imprisonment with hard labour. He is disgusted that someone who should know so much better could have committed so foolish a crime and present so ignoble an example to the young, impressionable people who might errantly look up to him. The judge wishes the sentence could be longer but he must abide by the guide-lines laid down by statute.

To the sound of mingled cheers and jeers I am con-ducted down to the police cells and into the back of a van, which is delightfully decorated and exquisitely supplied with crystal, ice buckets and an amazing array of alcoholic drinks.

'Might as well get lashed, Stephen. Last drinks you're going to have for some while.'

I'm at the prison. All the convicts have turned out to greet me. Their welcome is deafening and not in the least threatening.

A vast dining hall. I sit to eat in a huge wide shot like Cody Jarrett as played by James Cagney in *White Heat*. And then we see me in mid-shot, as cool and unruffled as Tim Robbins's ageless Andy Dufresne, taking my tray to the table.

It is clear that I am not in the joint for some appalling sexual or financial misdemeanour that will cause me to be beaten and tormented by my fellow convicts. I have done something that is wrong, that is disapproved of by 'society' yet which is tolerated with amusement by criminals and even police officers.

Nobody lets me see the newspapers. They will only upset me, I am told. It is all very strange.

Friends visit me. Always staying the other side of the bars. Hugh and Jo Laurie. Kim Harris, my first lover. My literary agent Anthony and my theatrical agent Christian. My sister and PA Jo. There is something they are not telling me, but I am comfortable in prison and feel sorry for them, having to leave and return to the world of bustle and business.

I am in the corridor cleaning the floor with an electric

polisher. It has two rotating discs with gently abrasive pads press-studded to the base, and I enjoy holding it like a pneumatic drill, feeling its power under me, how I have to keep it from flying free of my grip as it pulls like an eager dog at the leash. The floor comes up in a glossy shine. This is the life.

An old lag walks up to me, coughing on his tightly rolled-up cigarette, which wags up and down as he speaks. He has seen a letter in the governor's office, which he Pledges and tidies daily. My sentence is to be extended. I will never leave.

I take the news well. Very well.

I wake up, or the dream peters out or merges into something strange and silly and different.

It is easy to attempt a little oneiromancy here. My real life is a prison, so a real prison would be an escape. That would be the one-line pitch, as they say in Hollywood. I am one who, like so many Britons of a certain class and era, was born to institutions. School houses merge into Oxbridge colleges which merge into Inns of Court or the BBC as it was or into regiments or ships of the line or into one of the two Houses of Parliament or into the Royal Palaces or into Albany or the clubs of Pall Mall and St James's. All very male, all very Anglo-Saxon (a few Jews allowed from time to time – it is vulgar to be racially obsessed), all very cosy, absurd and out of date. If you really want to have a look at this world in its last hurrah just before I was born then you should read the first eight

9

or nine chapters of *Moonraker*, a Bond novel, but with an opening that is simultaneously hilarious, fantastically observed, drool-worthily aspirational and skin-pricklingly suspenseful.

I observed of myself in my second book of memoirs, *The Fry Chronicles*, and earlier in my first, *Moab is My Washpot*, that I seem always to be obsessed with belonging. Half of me, I wrote in *Moab*, yearns to be part of the tribe; the other half yearns to be apart *from* the tribe. All the clubs I belong to – six so-called gentleman's clubs and goodness knows how many more Soho-style media watering-holes – are vivid testament to a soul searching for his place in British society. Maybe prison is the ultimate club for people like me.

'That's institootionalized,' as Morgan Freeman's Red puts it in *The Shawshank Redemption*, the world's favourite film.

I am wary of interpretations. I refuse to interpret my life and its motives because I am not qualified. You may choose to do so. You may find me and my history repugnant, fascinating, indicative of an age now long gone, typical of a breed whose time is up. There are all kinds of ways of looking at me and my story.

If you want to bore someone, tell them your dreams. I seem to have got off on the wrong foot. I plead forgiveness for, while I would not claim that there is anything experimental about this memoir, I would ask you to be ready for a flitting backwards and forwards in time. The experience of writing about this period in my life has had some of the qualities of a dream: unexpected, freakish, disgusting, frightening, incredible and at one and the same time crystal clear and maddeningly occluded. It is my job, I suppose in this far from divine comedy, to be Virgil to your Dante, guiding you as straightforwardly and tenderly as I can through the circles of my particular hell, purgatory and heaven. In the following pages I will try to be as truthful as I can; I will leave interpretation and, generally speaking, motivation, to you.

Very Naughty, but . . . in the Right Spirit

Aside from anything else, there is the problem of plunging in as if you already know my past. . .

Bertie Wooster, the hero and first-person narrator of P. G. Wodehouse's Jeeves stories, used to say to his readers at the beginning of each new book something along the lines of 'If you're one of the old faithfuls familiar with previous episodes of my life as given to the world in the volumes *Moab is My Washpot* and *The Fry Chronicles*, now would be a good time to get on with a few odd jobs around the house – go for a walk, wash the cat, get on top of the backlog in your email inbox and so forth – while I fill in newcomers with the story so far . . .' only, of course, he would be referring not to *Moab* or *The Chronicles*, but to *The Code of the Woosters*, say, or *Right Ho, Jeeves*. And it is most unlikely that he would make any reference to inboxes. But you see the point.

There is a faint chance that you might have come across the two predecessors of the memoir you are now holding in your hands, in which case I can imagine you tapping your foot with impatience when it comes to my ushering the uninitiated down old and well-trodden pathways. 'Yes, yes, we know all that, get *on* with it, man,' I seem to hear you mutter from far away. 'Let's come to the new stuff. The juicy bits. Scandal. Showbiz. Drugs. Suicide. Gossip.'

On several occasions, as I meet someone in that embarrassed wine-sipping huddle that always occurs before a dinner party, for example, they might tell me how much they thoroughly enjoyed such and such a book of mine. All fine and charming, if a little embarrassing: 'One never knows what to *say*,' as Agatha Christie's alter ego, the popular author Ariadne Oliver (so splendidly played by Zoë Wanamaker in the television adaptations), often remarks. Anyway, an hour or so in, internally warmed by vinous glassfuls, I might tell, as one does around the dinner table, a story of some kind. I will notice the very person who confessed to admiring my book laughing heartily and whooping in surprise at the punchline. As they wipe the tears of infatuated merriment from their eyes, I will think to myself, '*Hang on!* That *exact* story is told, word for word, in the book they just assured me they liked so much!' Either, therefore, they were lying about having read the book in the first place, which, let's face it, we've all done – so much easier *not* to read books, especially the books of one's friends – *or*, which is in fact quite as likely if not more so, they *have* read it and simply forgotten just about every detail.

What remains, as one ages, of a book, is a smell, a flavour, a fleeting parade of sense-images and characters, pleasing or otherwise. So I have learned not to be offended. One does not write expecting every sentence to be permanently branded into the memory of the reader.

Far from being a curse, such memory leakages are actually rather a blessing. We all become, as readers, a little like the Guy Pearce character in the film *Memento*, only without the attendant physical jeopardies. Every day a new adventure. Every rereading a first reading. That is true at least of *recently* read books. I can recount almost word for word the Sherlock Holmes, Wodehouse, Wilde and Waugh that were the infatuations of my childhood (not to mention the Biggles, Enid Blyton and Georgette Heyer), but don't ask me to repeat the plot of the last novel I read. And it was a really good one too, *The Finkler Question*, by Howard Jacobson, which won a Booker Prize. I should have read it two or three years ago when it came out, but I am hopelessly behind with contemporary fiction. Almost everything I read these days is history, biography or popular science. I laid *The Finkler Question* down, finished from end to end about three months ago, thoroughly satisfied. I remember laughing a lot, there was a (racist?) mugging and a lot of very clever and compelling writing about anti-Semitism and all kinds of other delicious and wildly intelligent prose. But apart from the name Finkler and that incident I honestly don't think I could tell you what happened in the book, only that I loved it. I am way past the age when stories and even exact phrases and speeches stick.

There are seventeen steps up from pavement level to

Holmes and Watson's 221B Baker Street rooms; the Edict of Nantes was revoked in 1685; and the Battle of Crécy was fought on 26 August 1346 (the precise day isn't that hard to fix in my brain as it is my father's birthday). These and all *kinds* of irrelevant nonsenses I can reel off without recourse to Wikipedia. Exact phrases from Holmes, Jeeves, Mr Micawber and Gimlet (Biggles's commando equivalent) come pouring back to me, especially French Canadian Private 'Trapper' Troublay's habit of hissing *sapristi!* whenever he was perturbed.

I actually have a collection at home still of most of the works of Captain W. E. Johns, creator of Biggles and Gimlet (and of their female equivalent, the hearty and heroic 'Worrals of the WAAF'). In a satisfactory row (on my shelf at least, if not in publishing order), three of the Gimlet books are *Gimlet Lends a Hand, Gimlet Bores In* and *Gimlet Mops Up*. Gay innuendo simply rocks. Even Monty Python couldn't do better than that, although their *Biggles Flies Undone* parody made me laugh so much when I first read it in one of the Python books it gave me a serious asthma attack. True. It was the fact that they had so clearly read the books themselves with exactly the same attention to style and mannerism that I had that made me rock backwards, kicking my legs in the air in delight and wheezing like a dying emphysemiac. The point I suppose I am trying to make is that I will have the enormous pleasure of reading Howard Jacobson's book again in a year or so as a fresh and new surprise.

A friend of mine pointed out recently how absurd it was that people reread so little: do you only listen to a piece of music that you love once? Anyway, shush. You're distracting me. The whole point of this opening section is to fill in the newcomers on the subject of *La Vie Fryesque*. And if you are reading this and have also read my previous stabs at autobiography you have been warned: there will be repetition, and possibly even self-contradiction. What I remember now may differ from what I remembered five or ten years ago. But if you feel you know my life up until the ending of *The Fry Chronicles* and have no yearning for a redux reduction, you may happily jump from black arrow to black arrow or pop off and get on with your little tasks about the home, maybe settle into that TV box-set you've always meant to get around to because everyone else seems to have watched it but yourself. Let me try meanwhile to run by the relevant earlier history of my life as briskly as I can.

There is always the opportunity, I might add, for you to put this book down right this very minute and immediately download or buy in hard copy *Moab is My Washpot* and *The Fry Chronicles*, consume them in that order and save both of us all this repetition, but I wouldn't like to come over as greedy for sales. We're all above that kind of unpleasant mercantilism.

So where do I pick the story up from? From whence do I pick up the story? Whence do I pick up the story? Alistair Cooke, the British journalist best known for his broadcasts from America for the BBC, once told me that when he was a very young man contributing material for the legendary C. P. Scott of the *Manchester Guardian* he had submitted a piece of copy which included the phrase 'from whence'.

'Tell me, laddie,' Scott had asked, tapping an angry pair of fingers on the offending phrase, 'what does the word "whence" mean?'

'Er . . . "from where"?'

'Exactly! So you've just written "from from where" – tautology: go and correct it.'

Cooke was foolish enough to stand up for himself. 'Shakespeare and Fielding both frequently used "from whence".'

'Well, they wouldn't have done if they'd written for the *Manchester* fucking *Guardian*,' said Scott.

So. While the others are still at their chores, let me pick the story up for the new arrivals. The others can pick it up whence I dropped it. Doesn't sound right to me, but there we are, Scott must have known what he was talking about.

Our hero, after multiple scholastic expulsions (this is me I'm referring to now, not Alistair Cooke or C. P. Scott – I'm attempting a paragraph of that Christopher Isherwood/Salman Rushdie kind, where I refer to myself in the third person: it won't last long, I promise), after an adolescence steeped in folly, misery, heart-shredding mooncalf romance and a short lifetime of wayward self-delusion and multiple crookedness, a sly, cocky, guileful and self-fantasizing fool, found himself imprisoned for credit-card fraud and – still a teenager – on the brink of a life of permanent failure, incarceration, familial exile and squalid ignominy. He managed somehow to extricate himself from all this and acquire academic qualifications and a scholarship to Cambridge University. Well, he did not 'manage somehow', but broke through thanks to the combined wonders of flawlessly kind parents and his own late discovery that he enjoyed academic work very, very much and could not bear the idea of missing out on a real education, especially amongst the stones and towers and courts of Cambridge, where heroes like E. M. Forster, Bertrand Russell, G. E. Moore, Ludwig Wittgenstein, Alfred Tennyson and William Wordsworth had pursued their silly games, rigorous work, lyrical sodalities, sentimental friendships and semi-serious *sacra conversazione* – reading earnest and intellectually powerful papers from hearthrugs while nibbling anchovies or sardines on toast and being touched up by dons recruiting for MI6 or the KGB.

That Jonathan Miller and Peter Cook of *Beyond the Fringe* and John Cleese, Graham Chapman and Eric Idle of *Monty Python* and Tim Brooke-Taylor, Graeme Garden and Bill Oddie of *The Goodies*, let alone Germaine

Greer, Clive James, Douglas Adams, Derek Jacobi, Ian McKellen, Peter Hall, Richard Eyre, Nicholas Hytner and so on, had also been at that same university, eating up the stage generations before me, was a less self-conscious inducement, although I suppose if I am honest, a small part inside of me did somewhere dream of fame and recognition in an as yet inchoate form.

You do not, I believe, grow up, even if you are Stanislavsky, Brando or Olivier, knowing that you are a great actor. Much less do you grow up believing that you have it in you to make *any* kind of a career out of performance on stage or screen. Everyone has always known that it's 'an overcrowded profession'. We are most of us these days I suppose familiar with the tenets of Malcolm Gladwell's *Outliers: The Story of Success*, which quite cogently argues that no one ever made a success of themselves without having put in at least 10,000 hours of practice before breaking through. No one, not Mozart, not Dickens, not Bill Gates, not The Beatles. Most of us have instead put in 10,000 hours of wishing, and certainly as far as acting was concerned I had long thought I would *like* to take a stab at it but hadn't gone much further than that. I think my first print review, 'Young Stephen Fry as Mrs Higgins would grace any Belgravia drawing-room', went to my head when I was about eleven years old.

'Oooh,' whistling intakes of breath. 'Nine hundred and ninety-nine actors unemployed for every one with a job, young fellow.' How often would I hear this at drinks parties when I was a boy, such remarks always accompanied by the merest flash of a look acutely designed to assure me that with a face and string-bean body like mine I would never make a handsome leading man and should perhaps think of some other career.

'Being a barrister is a little like being an actor,' became my beaming mother's comforting and hopeful mantra. For a while I went along with this and between the ages of twelve and fifteen would tell the Norfolk landowners and their wives to whose parties we came and went that I was all set to make it to the Bar. Norman Birkett's *Six Great Advocates* was now my constant companion, and with all the repulsive self-confidence of the lonely geek I would bore my family with stories of the great forensic triumphs of Marshall Hall (my especial hero) and Rufus Isaacs, a great role model for any Jewish boy, since he rose to become Marquess of Reading and Viceroy of India. From a fruit market in Spitalfields to being curtseyed and bowed at and called Your Highness in the viceregal Palace of New Delhi. Imagine! And unlike Disraeli, a *practising* Jew. Not that I was ever that; nor were any of my mother's immediate family. We were, in Jonathan Miller's immortal words, not Jews, just Jew-*ish*. Not the whole hog. But then, as the Nazis showed, you don't have to practise (even for 10,000 hours) at being Jewish to be beaten, exiled, tortured, enslaved or killed for it, so one might as well embrace the identity with pride. The rituals, genital mutilations and avoidance of oysters and bacon can go hang, as can the behaviour of any given Israeli government, but otherwise consider me a proud Jew.

My background and upbringing in rural Norfolk seem, from a twenty-first-century perspective, a bizarre throwback. I think our way of life was in fact old-fashioned even in its own time. A fish man every Wednesday clopping in by horse and cart, coal trucks, butcher's, grocer's and bread vans arriving to deliver whatever provender that wasn't brought up to the back door by the gardeners for the cook, whose sister-in-law scrubbed floors on her knees three times a week. No central heating, no mains water, just coal or wood fires and a Victorian pump-house to draw up water, one source being a cistern reliant on soft rainwater which filled the tank that fed all the baths and wash basins with soft but rusty-brown bathwater, the other source drawn up from a groundwater aquifer which supplied the house's single drinking-water tap, fixed low down over a wooden bucket in a vast Victorian kitchen warmed only by a coke-fed Aga. There was a china-pantry, a food-pantry, larders, sculleries and an outer-scullery with a huge butler's sink that could only be filled from a grand brass hand pump. Outside the china-pantry, just by the door to the cellar stairs, hung a long rope which ended in a bulging red, white and blue sally. If any of us children were out in the garden and were needed, the rope would be pulled. The clang of the bell could be heard half a mile away at the local pig farm, where I sometimes liked to spend my time ogling piglets. Every time I heard that bell, my stomach seemed to fill with lead, for unless it was lunch or supper time it nearly always meant Trouble. It clanged the news that somehow I had been Found Out and was required to stand on the carpet in front of the desk in my father's study and Explain Myself.

Back inside again, on the wall next to the sally, was the predictable bell panel, which would have told servants from a previous era into which room to scuttle, bow and bob for instructions. Instead of the pulled-by-wire shaking bells so familiar from today's country house films or television series, ours – being an in-its-day modern Victorian house – took the form of a wooden framed box. Each room's name was printed beneath a red star in a white circle which oscillated when an electric bell was pressed. It was said that my parents' house was one of the first in its part of Norfolk to be thoroughly 'on the electric'. I am sure the circuitry was never upgraded from the time of its building in the 1880s until my mother and father finally sold the place nearly a century and a half later. The ceramic fuse boxes, the solid bakelite and brass three- or two-pin plugs were at least eighty years old when I was a boy in the 1960s and I was always astonished by the eye-achingly dazzling white three-pin plugs I saw in friends' houses, just as I was astonished by, and more than passingly envious of, the wall-to-wall carpeting, colour televisions and warm radiators that my friends took for granted. Not to mention their easy access to cinemas, shops and coffee bars. Such ordinary, modern households as theirs may not have had trained plum and pear trees stapled to the gable-ends of their outbuildings, nor could they boast built-in hand-carved linenfold cupboards that a contemporary antiquarian would orgasm over, but they were, to my restless rusticated brain, as *exciting* as my life and household were *dull*.

We move along, as an estate agent would say, from the pantries and cellar door, past the bell panel and rope and encounter an always closed studded baize door which leads through to the house proper. There, hallways, dining room, drawing room, great front stairs and my father's study could be found. Forbidden territory. Next to the baize door were the *back* stairs, which led to our domain.

On the third floor of the house my brother and I each occupied a huge bedroom, leaving the others (one of which was already divided into two rooms) for furniture overspill, spare rooms and attic space. These unfeasibly proportioned rooms, a little William Morris wallpaper still showing through in one of them, had originally been designed as dormitories for servants. Whitwell Elwin, the architect who built the house, had made the mistake earlier, when building his own Victorian rectory in the same village, of providing small individual rooms for his staff. It seems that in these narrow rooms they had suffered acutely from homesickness and loneliness and thus, given

a second chance at domestic architecture, Elwin had created in our house enormous servant chambers in which
the maids and footmen (in their ruthlessly segregated
dorms, naturally) could chatter and console each other
through the night.

Elwin's finest work of architecture was neither the rectory nor our house, but the village church. Booton church
is worth travelling *miles* to see. 'The cathedral of the vil-
lages' it has been called. Sir Nikolaus Pevsner, the great
master registrar of Britain's architecture, who visited
every county and chronicled any building of worth in the
United Kingdom, gave this chapter of my book its sub-
heading when he described St Michael the Archangel's in
Booton as 'very naughty, but built in the right spirit'. I
remember quoting this observation of Pevsner's to John
Betjeman when he came down to the church with a camera crew and some of his Victorian Society friends during
one of my school holidays or rustication (temporary
punishment suspension) periods. I had been given the
exciting job of escorting this distinguished party around,
the self-appointed local expert, and telling them about
the Bath stone, the knapped flint, the crocketed pinna-
cles, chamfering and idiomatic Gothic influences and any
other such pretentious guff as my mind (stuffed as it then
was with prized Banister Fletcher jargonese) could come
up with: 'note the influence of the Cluniac revival' – that
sort of gobshite, as if they didn't know all that without
the cocky pipings of a twelve-year-old who behaved as if

he was the Professor of Architecture at the Courtauld. The great Poet Laureate (or were those years still ahead of him?) was very friendly and patient about all this, but it was only years later that I learned that Betjeman and Pevsner were not on the most cordial of terms, despite each of them so valuing, and indeed so *raising* the value of, architecture in Britain; perhaps therefore my quoting of Sir Nikolaus had been injudicious. I spent the rest of the day, I remember, as a guest of the Victorian Society's formidably knowledgeable and likeable Hermione Hobhouse, diving in on unsuspecting Pugin and Gilbert Scott mini-masterpieces around the county.

Whitwell Elwin may have created an astonishing church, but his major interest (outside, one presumes, his fifty-one-year ministry at Booton) was his editorship of the *Quarterly Review*, his querulous correspondence with fellow Victorian greats like Darwin and Gladstone and his somewhat 'inappropriate' relationships with a series of young girls, the most prominent of whom was his 'blessed girl', Lady Emily Bulwer-Lytton, a viceroy's daughter who later went on to marry the truly great architect Edwin Lutyens, best known for his creation of colonial New Delhi and his collaborations with the horti-culturalist Gertrude Jekyll. Lutyens also designed Booton Manor, an 'averagely fine' example of his work. After building Booton church and its rectory (envious of Lutyens' superior talent as well as jealous of his snaffling the beloved Emily, one supposes), Whitwell Elwin built our house as a thank you to the spinster sisters who had bankrolled his magnificent ecclesiastical folly.

Just to drive home to you how preposterously old-fashioned a dwelling ours was, I should tell you that the lavatories were the boxed-in kind with a high up cistern. Instead of the later decorated china 'pull me' chain, there had originally been a handle next to the bowl which you pulled *up* to flush. The wash basin in the lavatory's ante-room didn't have a plughole. You pulled on a sprung tap to fill it, washed and rinsed your hands, tipped up a lip in the basin which also served as the overflow slit, and the bowl pivoted to empty its water underneath before swinging back to its original position. You probably can't picture it, and I am dissatisfied with my ability to convey its workings succinctly and clearly. Never mind. Similarly, the bathtub upstairs, with its great lion's claw feet, had a long cylindrical ceramic pole that you twisted and let down to seal the plug hole. It was also one of the few bathrooms I have ever known to possess a fireplace.

My brother and I were only ever allowed to have a fire lit in our bedrooms if we were ill. I cannot overstate the pleasure of waking on a dark winter's morning and seeing the embers still glowing in the grate. Otherwise in winter, one relied for warmth on a mountain of eiderdowns and blankets or the company in bed of a cat or two. I had never even heard of a duvet or quilt.

I once found a thin Dimplex electric radiator in an attic and brought it into my room. When my father discovered

I had kept it, dialled up to maximum heat for three days in a row (the breath steaming from my mouth and nostrils was nonetheless visible), he made me sit down and work out, given the price of kilowatt hours, how much my profligacy had cost him. This was an arithmetical problem, of course, wildly beyond my competence. The radiator disappeared, and my fear of mathematics grew that much greater.

Outside, the gardeners provided what the grocer, butcher, bread man and fish man could not supply with their weekly van visits. Apples, pears and potatoes were stored in outhouses over the winter; jams, pickles and chutneys were prepared in the autumn by the cook, Mrs Riseborough. Lettuces, tomatoes, cucumbers, scarlet runner beans, broad beans, peas, marrows, asparagus in raised beds, figs, damsons, plums, cherries, greengages, strawberries, rhubarb, raspberry and blackcurrant canes and the whole rich bounty of the garden supplied us all. Milk was delivered daily in wax cartons which, when dried, we used as kindling for the fireplaces; a local farm provided eggs and dark-yellow butter patted with carved wooden paddles and wrapped in greaseproof paper. I had never heard of or been into a supermarket before I was . . . I can't even guess what age. If we needed brambles for one of Mrs Riseborough's blackberry and apple pies, I would take my baby sister Jo in her pushchair along a bridle path and pick the fruit by hand. The October mixing of the Christmas puddings and the pouring of the apple jelly . . . I am sure that plenty of people still do this every year – more than *ever* before perhaps, thanks to all the Take-offs of the Bake-offs and Cake-offs that now take up most of our television schedules. Cream of tartar and crystallized angelica have never had it so good. Men and women the length of the land still grow vegetables, apples, pears and soft fruits too; I am not, I hope, over-misting my own childhood idyll. Not that for me it was anything close to idyllic, much as it might and ought to appear to have been from this great distance in time and manners.

A grass tennis court and even a badminton lawn were at our disposal; for whatever reason we didn't use them much, only when American cousins visited.

Behind the stable-block was a cottage and separate garden, where a couple who worked for my father lived, and next to that a paddock filled with noisy geese. I used to brave these hissingly aggressive birds to get to a walnut tree around which they honked and flapped as if it were a sacred temple being vandalized by heathens. Despite growing up in the country, I have never been fully at ease with wild animals.

In the garden's overgrown old pigsty and hidden in a hedged area filled with broken sundials and choked ponds my sister Jo and I found, tamed and finally domesticated feral cats and kittens which had been let loose from the almost incredibly eccentric rector of the village church, who didn't, of course, as a high religionist, believe that animals possessed souls, and so they could therefore happily be thrown away like so much litter. Horses we did not have, for over the way my father had converted the monumentally solid stable block into a laboratory. He was a kind of designer, physicist and electronics engineer, impossible exactly to categorize. The stable mangers were filled with tools, the stalls with lathes, mills and other machinery; the vast upper rooms where the grooms might have slept housed oscilloscopes, ammeters and circuitry of the most curious and impenetrable kind. After ten or twenty years of his work there, the smell of solder, Swarfega and freon finally overcame decades of dung, straw and saddle soap.

Reepham, the nearest village to have proper shops and pubs, was over three miles away, and the inhabitants thought of my father, on the very rare occasions they caught sight of him, as the Mad Inventor. If for some reason he had to go in for a supply of tobacco – my mother having succumbed perhaps to a rare bout of influenza – he would stand in the post office, forlornly holding out money in the palm of his hand like a foreign tourist, allowing the correct amount to be picked out. I think he frightened the villagers a little and that Wordsworth's real world of 'getting and spending' frightened him too.

Nothing like as much as he frightened me, however. In my mind he was a compound of Mr Murdstone and Sherlock Holmes, with an element of *The Famous Five*'s Uncle Quentin thrown in. Certainly he had the sinister saturnine features and snarling intolerance of children that marked out the latter and the almost inhuman brilliance and pipe-smoking gauntness of the great detective. It was Holmes himself who observed that genius was an infinite capacity for taking pains and, awestruck and often filled with rage and hatred against him as I was, there was never a time that I didn't think my father an authentic genius. I still do. Between the ages of seven and nineteen, however, I am not sure I was ever able to look him in the eye, or to hear his disgruntled snorts and growls and sighs, without wanting to wet myself or to fly from him in tears of humiliation and misery. Now in his eighties, he is building, from scratch, to his own design, a 3D printer. I know him enough to be absolutely certain that when he has finished it will be more reliable and more elegantly designed than any other that currently exists on the market.

My mother was and remains the warmest and kindest person you could know. Her first love and duty, however, was, and will always be, to my father. And *vice versa*. Which is as it should be. Their marriage always seemed to me to be so ideal that I often wonder if it completely spoiled my chances of achieving a relationship anything like as perfect. Which must be nonsense, since my brother and sister are both blissfully married. We will come to the squashier bogs, the more mephitically foul marshes of my useless and repulsive private life later in this book if you have the patience. Meanwhile, it is still catch-up time.

*

One marvellous favour J. K. Rowling has done all English writers of a certain generation is to clarify this business of being sent off to school. No Hogwarts Express for the seven-year-old Stephen, of course, no Butter Beers or magical chocolate frogs, but all in all a really very similar affair otherwise. Boaters at the school end of the train were crammed on the heads or waved airily by impossibly mature-looking twelve-year-olds; we new boys braced like mules and clutched on to our mothers as the prospect of months of separation in the company of these frightening-looking seniors approached. 'They'll think I look stupid.' 'They'll think I look weedy.' 'They'll think I look common.' All kinds of immature waves of inadequacy rolled over me. I am not even sure that I knew what 'common' meant. It was two years later, reading Nancy Mitford's indispensable *Noblesse Oblige*, that I discovered it turned out to be a word only ever used by 'common' people in the first place, which is rather a lowering thought.

Before Paddington station was finally cleaned, rejigged and renovated ten or so years ago, complete with the statue of its famous and noble bear, I could never go near the place without my bowels turning to water.

Everybody else new you ever meet, and this continues throughout life, is stronger than you are, knows the system better and sees right through to the back of your brain and finds what they see there to be wholly inadequate. Everyone you encounter carries, as it were, a huge club behind their back, while all you hold behind yours is a weedy cotton-bud. I think I may have written this before, or possibly stolen it from someone else: it is, in any case, hardly a fresh observation, and I should be very surprised if it does not strike home with you. The rest of the world was at That Lesson, the one we missed because of a toothache or diarrhoea, the one where *they* – the rest of the school – were told how the world works and how to comport themselves with confidence and ease. *We* all missed it and have felt insecure ever since. *Other people* know some secret thing, and no other people know more than children who are just a few years older than you are.

To go to a prep school 200 miles away at the age of seven seems, like the fish-cart, the 1880s servants' bells or the cook receiving vegetables from cap-doffing garden-ers, madly silly, English, grand and old-fashioned.

You should know, then, before I go any further, that, contrary to the implication of all that has gone before, we were *poor*. Not dirt poor, not peasant poor obviously, just poor compared to all the kinds of people who sent their sons to the same kinds of schools, poor compared to the kinds of people my parents had to dinner parties. Yes, dinner parties where the men wore black tie and the women 'withdrew' from the dining room to the drawing room after the cheese to allow the men time for strong talk, cigars and port. My mother confided in me her prob-ably accurate opinion that this old and now defunct ritual (defunct even in Royal Palaces I am able to tell you – more of that later too) was in fact a way of allowing women to go to bathrooms together without drawing to the attention of their men that the sweet creatures possessed such things as bladders which needed voiding just as much as any man's or horse's did.

We were poor in that my mother drove an ancient Austin A35 with flicky-uppy indicators and my father an Austin 1800 from the heyday of British motoring incompetence (after he had driven an old Rover 90 into desuetude). We never went on holidays, and every time my mother and I went into a shoe or clothing shop throughout my childhood and adolescence I remember squirming and writhing with embarrassment as she complained (very loudly to my ears) that such and such a pair of shoes were 'shatteringly expensive' and that she 'couldn't *possibly* afford' those trousers. I did grow very fast, of course, and she had a small budget from which to buy anything. The school fees themselves (somehow we found ourselves, my brother and I, going to two not wildly grand private schools that were nonetheless just about the most expensive of any in England) were paid for, I am certain, by my mother's father, the beloved Jewish immigrant who died when I was about ten and whom I wish, greatly wish, I had known better. But I grew up with a quite illusory – 'entitled', as we would now say – sense of aggrieved deprivation. To confess this is deeply embarrassing; how could I possibly feel deprived? Just how cheap must I have been to think a country house with servants and grand rooms was horrible and that a modern house with colour televisions, gas ovens, freezer-cabinets, carpets and central heating was a lost dream of luxury?

There we are, then. Off to a prep school in Gloucestershire, far from Norfolk, but beautiful too in its own way. I wrote in *The Fry Chronicles* about my insatiable appetite for sweets. I devoted pagefuls of panegyrics to the tuck shop and provided pagefuls too of self-reproach for the thieving and sly manipulations that my addiction to all things sugary led me to. I suppose they themselves derived from this sense of being hard done by, wherever the hell that came from. Maybe sugar stood in for a parental love or the domestic prosperity that I felt deprived of. Perhaps I was born with one of those narcissistic fantasy minds. The kind that believes they are really the abandoned son of a duke, or that a solicitor's letter will one day arrive informing them of an unknown cousin's fabulous will, of which they are to be sole benefactor. The crown courts are daily full of such sad people. I happen to be that rare thing – rarer than a straight man in a Hollister T-shirt – a fantasist whose fantasies came true, it would seem. A lot of celeb haters would say that most celebs are narcissists. It could be that they are right. Counterintuitively, self-hatred is one of the leading symptoms of clinical narcissism. Only by telling yourself and the world how much you hate yourself can you receive the reliable shower of praise and admiration in response that you feel you deserve . . . or so at least the theory runs.

I survived prep school – *just*. Stout's Hill School, now a holiday resort, was a marvellous mid-eighteenth-century Strawberry Hill Gothic Revival rococo (if you can have such a mixture) castellated fantasy, complete with catacombs and crenellations, a butler (Mr Dealey) and entirely strange characters, such as a Mr Sawdon, whose hands shook uncontrollably and whom we imitated without mercy.

It was only in my last year that one of the masters told me that Sawdon had been a brilliant youth, an authentic war hero, his mind shattered by shell shock in the trenches of Flanders, an experience from which he had never recovered. If I think now of the ho-ho number of times I would creep behind him, imitating his flicking, quivering hands, his slack jaw, his drivelling mutters, his drooling and his weaving, dipping gait, him all unaware, the boys in front watching me over his shoulder and squealing with laughter . . . if I think of that now I want to stick a pen through my throat in shame. What made it all the worse was the memory I have that his face would light up whenever he saw laughter. He believed, I suppose, that he was looking at affection and pleasure, and some distant image stirred in him of a happy life of laughter and friendship before the bone-splintering, mind-ravaging war that destroyed everything he had been. Just about 99 per cent of the times that he saw a smiling face, he wasn't looking at the smiles of friends, he was peering unawares at the mocking grins of young fiends who thought him weird and retarded and worthy of nothing but contempt. All the time I was there he was deliberately tormented, impersonated and cruelly teased almost daily. It is no use my apologizing now. He would be 120 were he still alive, I expect, but I weep as I write this. Weep at my own callous, ignorant and ostentatious viciousness, and weep for the hundreds and thousands of Sawdons who didn't even have the shelter of a school folded in the soft green wolds of Gloucestershire to give them a home.

Mr Sawdon was, I think, somehow related by marriage to the founder and headmaster of the school, Robert Angus. Angus had three daughters, each of whom was more or less nutty about horses, especially Jane, the youngest. Our star alumnus had been Mark Phillips, already in training for the Mexico Olympics as an equestrian and later to marry Princess Anne. Riding at Stout's Hill was not an 'extra' like bassoon lessons or fencing, but part of the everyday curriculum. One would descend from a double Latin class to the stables for an equally serious (and to me much duller) lesson in the arcana of equestrianism. I can still recite the pommels, martingales, snaffles, pelhams, gags, Kimblewick and Liverpool bits (even something called a Chifney anti-rearing bit, if I recall correctly), girth-straps and curry-combs whose every detail and proper use we had to master before we were ever allowed so much as to mount a pony. The smell of saddle soap and dubbin, rarely encountered by me these days, is as intense and evocative as the smell of creosote, cloves or candyfloss. I think of myself – despite an assumption amongst some that I am intellectual, rationalist and almost coldly logical – as an emotional, sensual being, led far more by the heart and other organs than by the brain. Smell, as we all know, evokes the past more immediately than any of the other four senses. Where the aroma of saddle soap takes me, your grandmother's lily-of-the-valley hand lotion or the sweat-and-mud reek of the school changing rooms might take you.

In 2009 I swore, not in the sense of using foul language (although I had muttered plenty of that off-camera), that the day I was nearly thrown by a skittering Tennessee walking horse would be the last time anyone would ever, *ever* see me on top of a horse until my dying day. This incident had taken place while filming a documentary series in which I visited each state of the American union.

The humiliation of arranging the title sequence of *Blackadder Goes Forth* had already more or less determined me never to sit atop an equine again. We had shot the sequence down at the Royal Anglian Regiment's HQ in Colchester, and the idea was I, as the blithering General Melchett, would bestride my mount and take salute while the band led by Captain Blackadder and attended by poor old Private Baldrick, along with Hugh Laurie's nobly asinine Lieutenant George and Tim McInnerny's twitchy Captain Darling, marched past, eyes right, to the stirring march 'The British Grenadiers', which then morphed into Howard Goodall's *Blackadder* theme tune. For practice I got my foot into the stirrup of the colonel's mount, whose name I think was – and this should have warned me – Thunderbolt, swung into the saddle and walked experimentally forwards, clucking and tchitching in a way that would have built up confidence and amiability in a tyrannosaurus who had just heard bad news from his bank. I had walked about the whole parade ground feeling more or less confident, cooing Thunderbolt's name, stroking his muzzle, softly patting his flanks and giving him the news that he was safe and that I loved him.

Thunderbolt and I now stood peacefully awaiting the moment. Cameras, action and . . . cue music. The moment the first blare of the trumpet sounded Thunderbolt reared, neighed like a banshee, pawed the air and galloped around the parade ground as if stung by a gadfly. None of this was helped by Hugh all but falling to the ground heaving with such uncontrollable laughter that he could scarcely breathe. I was eight and a half feet at least from solid concrete, holding on for dear life, and my friend thought it was the funniest thing he had ever seen in his life. Men.

So you may well imagine that twenty years later in the Southern states of America the prospect of heaving my carcass on a Tennessee walking horse was causing me a little perturbation. It was Georgia we were investigating at this stage of our documentary series on the fifty states, and we were the guests of a very kind family who lived in a plantation house that didn't seem to have changed since the days of Scarlett O'Hara. It was clear that my discomfort in the presence of horses transmitted itself.

'Now don't you go worrying about her,' my amiable hostess had reassured me with a delicious high-class Southern drawl. 'There never was born a horse so docile . . .' that last word pronounced, of course, in the American way, as if to rhyme with 'fossil' or that turdine melodic songbird, the throstle. Yes, isn't turdine a splendid word? Anyway, back to that docile animal.

'That's all very well,' I remember gasping, as I tried to heave my bulk on to its back, 'but horses and I never get on, which is why I never get on horses. They know that I don't like them and they always panic.' Even at my initial gentle, reasonable, unhurried, clucking, apple-offering, muzzle-nuzzling approach the beast's ears had instantly drawn back, the flanks had pricked and twitched, and the hooves had stamped as if it had detected Satan in me.

'Not this one, hun . . .' came the complacent, murmured reply.

Five minutes later, just in time for the camera to catch my humiliation, the 'walking horse' freaked out at the horror of having me astride it or possibly (like every fucking horse ever fucking born) became utterly spooked by the astounding existence of such wholly unexpected and terrifying phenomena as wind, trees, sky, a bird gliding in the distance, a chicken, a hedge, a leaf whirling in the wind, a butterfly – you name it – and galloped off, bursting through the corral fence, while I screamed and juddered in the saddle, incompetently trying to operate the brakes.

'Well, I declare she's never done that in her *life* . . .'

You would think a prep school laid out in idyllic countryside, with a lake, woods, spinneys and rolling parkland, and where the riding of biddable and patient ponies was compulsory, might have prepared me for at least normal human competence on horseback. The school achieved this for me no more than it prepared me for normal human competence at life. Just as I can't and never could ride horses, I can't and never could live. At least, I have never felt I could.

So (this is still for the new subscribers, I should warn) I survived six years of prep school and moved at the age of thirteen to Uppingham, an old-fashioned public school set in the glorious county of Rutland. It was here that, to contradict Philip Larkin, love fell on me like an enormous No. Most of my life since has been a response to that. Fortunately, however, there had been books.

I will leap backwards a little to Booton and myself at an earlier age just to explain the effect that books had had on me by the time I arrived at Big School. I relish all things digital, but if I had been born twenty-five years later I dread to think of how little I would know about the written word.

I am not so foolish as to join myself with those heralds of doom who claim that the internet and social networking will inevitably spell the death of literacy, literature, focus, concentration span or 'real' human interaction. When moving-type printing was invented it was damned as a technology that would rot the mind. No longer would a scholar have to know everything, they could just 'look it up'. When the novel arrived it was damned as destructive, escapist, shallow and detrimental to morals. The same howls of protest were screeched at popular theatre, music hall, cinema, then television, video-gaming and now social networking. Human teenagers in particular are tougher than their elders will ever believe. The bullying, abuse and trolling is, of course, horrific, but believe me, a teenager has a better life of it now than he or she ever did a hundred years ago, when physical punishment, cruel sadistic beatings and sexual abuse went unquestioned in schools and in the home.

As it was, my father, who was from the radio (or wireless as it was then called) generation, thought televisions were perhaps permissible for showing events like Churchill's funeral, moon-landings or serious news stories, but otherwise our little black-and-white set at home was relegated to the corner of the kitchen, its aerial being just a wire poked in the rear antenna socket and Blu-Tacked to the wall. My mother pasted a cutout newspaper cartoon on the television's side: a housewife is explaining to her friend, 'Oh, we had one of the very first colour sets, but the colours have faded now.'

Insomnia, especially on hot nights, was one of the chief miseries of my childhood and youth. The only answer therefore was to read, which in itself presented an absurd problem. If I opened the windows to cool the room it would soon fill with huge moths, May-bugs, June-bugs and all kinds of simply terrifying arthropods peculiar to Norfolk which, like crazed winged lobsters, would carom and careen straight to my bedside lamp and flicker, bang and buzz about inside the shade. I happen to be horribly afraid of moths – an utterly irrational fear, I am quite aware, but agonizingly real.

Somehow I managed, despite these abhorred fluttering distractions, to get through hundreds of books a year. My parents had many of their own, most of which I had soon consumed more than once. I further supplemented my reading matter at first from a large grey mobile library which arrived every other Thursday at the corner of two lanes not far from the house. I am not sure such services still operate; it seems doubtful – councils these days seem disobliged so much as to resurface a road, educate a child or empty a dustbin.

One Sunday afternoon, aged twelve, while my father was safely at work in the stable block 'over the way', I watched on the little television Anthony Asquith's film version of *The Importance of Being Earnest*. I vividly recall sitting on an uncushioned wooden kitchen chair, face flushed, mouth half-open, simply astonished at what I was watching and, most especially, *hearing*. I had had simply no idea that language could do this. That it could dance and trip and tickle, cavort, swirl, beguile and seduce,

43

that its rhythms, subclauses, repetitions, *clausulae* and colours could excite quite as much as music.

When Algernon says to Cecily, 'I hope, Cecily, I shall not offend you if I state quite frankly and openly that you seem to me to be in every way the visible personification of absolute perfection?' I wriggled and giggled and repeated the phrase to myself in disbelieving bliss. Enough times to commit it to memory there and then. I would repeat it solemnly to the (faintly bewildered) Mrs Riseborough.

'Oh, you do go on with your nonsense. How that drives Nanny crazy.'

By this time Mrs Riseborough had been promoted to the role of nanny to my sister, something she considered a great advancement (although she still cooked, ironed and performed innumerable other jobs around the house), and thenceforth would much rather be called Nanny Riseborough than Mrs Riseborough. Her Christian name, Dolly, was used only by her immediate family, although her husband Tom, who had after all given her the name, preferred to call her in Janeite, Dickensian fashion 'Mrs Riseborough'. She died only last year, aged almost a hundred. I had visited her a few times over the years but deeply regret missing her funeral. I am not sure that such combinations of independence, strength and unquestioning service still exist. Her son Peter came to own a very successful and popular Norfolk gastropub called The Ratcatchers. Rather than sitting at a table and enjoying a little sip or a well-earned bowl of soup, his mother would insist on washing up in the kitchen behind the bar, right through into her nineties.

That day years before, my repeatedly telling her that I hoped I would not offend her if I stated quite frankly and openly that she seemed to me to be in every way the visible personification of absolute perfection might have flustered her a little, but she was used to my behaviour, which was at times so frantic, fanciful and foolish that it would today quite certainly be diagnosed as Attention Deficit Hyperactivity Disorder.

Wilde's phrase, and many others from the film – 'Cecily, you will read your Political Economy in my absence. The chapter on the Fall of the Rupee you may omit. It is somewhat too sensational' – took hold of me completely. In an age before video recording, the best I could do was imagine myself inside the world of this extraordinary motion picture, which turned out, my mother told me (after of course patiently enduring the matter of her too being the visible personification of absolute perfection), to have been based on a play, a copy of which she was sorry to say was not in the house.

The following Thursday I stood then, the only customer (lender? user? what was the word then?), fretfully at the corner of the lanes, waiting for the battleship-grey mobile library to hove into view. The driver lurched the van, of the kind that I think used to be called a pantechnicon, to a halt, came round to open the door and lower the steps and tousled my hair and patted my bum as I ascended (as adults were quite rightly allowed to do in those days without being hauled up before the courts and having their houses set fire to). The librarian, a be-cardiganed, multi-beaded old dear, was also apt to ruffle my hair. She often told me that I read so many books I would soon grow into one. For a child to read books, especially in the summer, was looked on as very peculiar and, of course, unhealthy, something I had always been used to being considered on account of my loathing of all forms of organized games and sports.

'Have you,' I asked her breathlessly, 'ever heard of a play called *The Importance of Being Earnest*?'

'Why yes, my love, that's just up there, I think.'

It was far from the largest drama section you have ever seen in a library. A smattering of Shaw, Priestley and Shakespeare, but also – marvellously – the collected comedies of Oscar Wilde. She stamped the book out with that splendid springing, spanking sound that will never be heard on these shores again. It had last been lent, the previous stamp showed me, in 1959. I thanked her, dismounted in a bound, flew up the lane, round the rear of the house, up the back stairs and into my bedroom.

Lady Windermere's Fan, A Woman of No Importance, An Ideal Husband, The Importance of Being Earnest. I read them all again and again and again until a fortnight later, when I found myself once more restlessly pacing the corner of the two lanes.

'Have you anything else by Oscar Wilde?'

'Well, now, I aren't rightly sure . . .' she lifted her reading glasses from the delicately linked silver chain that hung round her neck, pushed them to her nose and came around the desk to inspect the shelves as if for the first time. 'Ah, now, there you go.'

The Complete Works of Oscar Wilde. This was more, so much more than I could possibly have hoped for. Once again I flung myself on my bed and started to read. Some of the dialogues written in the Socratic style in essays like 'The Decay of Lying' and 'The Critic as Artist' confused me a little, and parts of 'The Soul of Man Under Socialism' were quite beyond me. The poems I frankly disliked, save for 'The Ballad of Reading Gaol', which seemed an odd subject for such a glamorous and flowing lord of language to have chosen. The stories for children made me weep, as they do to this day, and *The Picture of Dorian Gray* touched a part of me that I couldn't quite define but disturbed and excited me very deeply indeed. 'De Profundis', too, I found beautiful, but puzzling. I wasn't sure what the allusions to 'prison' and 'shame' and 'scandal' and so on were supposed to mean. Indeed, I assumed the letter to be a work of fiction that held some allegorical meaning beyond my reach.

I kept this collection for four weeks, and the cosily obliging librarian waived the late return penalty of sixpence when I at last brought it back to the mobile library. I asked if she had anything else by this Oscar Wilde.

She pointed at the book. 'If that says "The Complete Works", then I should think that's the complete works, wouldn't you, young man?'

'Hm.' It was hard not to see the justice of this. 'Well, do you have anything *about* him, perhaps?'

Her soft, powdered cheeks pinkened a little, and in a rather quavery voice she asked me how old I was.

'Oh, I'm a very advanced reader,' I assured her. Being tall and with a voice that never broke but slowly deepened, I could usually pass as older than my real age; at this time, unless memory plays me false, I had just turned thirteen.

'We-ell . . .' she fossicked about the lower shelves and came up with a book called *The Trials of Oscar Wilde* by an author called H. Montgomery Hyde.

The book was like a kick in the teeth. A kick in the gut. A kick in the groin. A kick most especially in the heart. After reading about the character of this brilliant, engaging, gentle, exceptionally kind and quite remarkably gifted Irishman, to discover the truth of the sudden and calamitous third act of his life, the three trials (it is often forgotten that following the legal action he foolishly took against the Marquess of Queensberry, there were not one, but two criminal trials against him, after the first ended in a deadlocked jury), the exile and the squalid and unhappy travels and subsequent penurious death in Paris, all this was almost more than I could bear.

Yet.

Yet it also confirmed in my deepest heart something

that I had always known. That he and I shared a similar 'nature', as he would say, or 'sexuality' as we would call it today.

My heart was wrenched by the story of Oscar. The mobile library was no longer enough. The only place for me now was Norwich City Library, twelve miles away. Sometimes I had the energy to bicycle, sometimes I took the daily coach that stopped at that same meeting of lanes at twenty to seven every weekday morning.

Before the internet and Berners-Lee's miraculous World Wide Web, the closest you came to metadata or hyperlinks were the bibliography and the index cards in the wooden drawers of a library catalogue.

I started by seeing what else this Montgomery Hyde had written. *The Love That Dared Not Speak Its Name* was one book. *The Other Love* was even more astonishing. I found myself endlessly in Norwich City Library, scribbling down names from the bibliographies at the end of each non-fiction book (bibliographies are the lists of titles and writers that the author has used as sources) and then haring to the catalogues to see if the library might hold a copy of anything related to a newly acquired lead to the world of forbidden love. Through such means I learned about the infamous Baron Corvo, aka William Rolfe, and his eye-popping, trouser-shifting 'Venice Letters', Norman Douglas, T. C. Worsley, 'Y' (an anonymous gay autobiographer), Robin Maugham, Angus Stewart, the scandalous Michael Davidson, Roger Peyrefitte,

Henry de Montherlant, Jean Genet, William Burroughs, Gore Vidal, John Rechy and dozens and dozens of others. It was the equivalent of clicking on web links, more cumbersome and time-consuming, of course, but breathlessly exciting. Along the way, as a happy accident, I acquired a kind of alternative literary education that ran in parallel to the one I was receiving at school. You cannot read Genet or about him without encountering (the entirely heterosexual so far as we know) Jean-Paul Sartre, and you cannot brush up against Robin Maugham without making the acquaintance of Paul Bowles and the Tangier set. Burroughs leads to Denton Welch, Corvo to the Bensons, Ronald Firbank, Stephen Tennant, Harold Acton and so on until by fortuitous and serendipitous circumstances, fuelled by inner erotic curiosity and stimulation, I found a world of artists and writers, straight and gay, who were their own reward.

Suppose I had been born in the 1980s? All the vindication and support I might ever have needed to make me comfortable about my sexuality could have been found in television programmes like *Queer as Folk*, by the pioneering gay kisses on *EastEnders* and *Brookside*, in Pride marches along the streets of London and in the billions of pathways, savoury and unsavoury, offered by the internet. The fact that my childhood, youth and early manhood preceded all of this diversity, freedom, tolerance and openness I, of course, regret to some degree – the brave new gay world would have saved me the doomed feeling I had that my life was inevitably to be one of secrecy, exile, seedy sex shops and the police courts – but I am very, very glad that the only available route to a proud acceptance and endorsement of my gay nature should have come through literature. I think I would always have loved Shakespeare, Keats, Austen, Dickens, Tennyson, Browning, Forster, Joyce, Fitzgerald, what the bluff English master of one of the private schools I attended called 'the big hitters', but I cannot thank my sexuality enough for giving me, in my particular case, a love of all reading and an introduction to the gay identity which offered so much more than gaytube and xhamster.com.

So, here I am now at Uppingham School, knowing that I was technically one of a despised and secretly special tribe, but little suspecting that the big issue in life was never going to be the gender one masturbated over; that was small potatoes. What smacked me amidships, holed me below the waterline and sent me bubbling to the bottom of the ocean was love. Love made a wreck of me. Love, the silly word that lyric writers and pop songs endlessly overused; love, the subject of so many plays and poems and films; love, that soppy plotline that got in the way of a good story. Love came up and punched me so hard in the face that I have been giddy and brain-softened ever since. I'm flattened on the canvas, towel thrown in and having barnacles affix themselves to my rotting decks on the sea bed, if we are to allow me to mix metaphors.

The fact is, real life is sometimes so complicated that a pure unmixed metaphor would be unconvincing. And the truth about love . . . well, as Auden wondered:

> Will it come like a change in the weather?
> Will its greeting be courteous or rough?
> Will it alter my life altogether?
> O tell me the truth about love.

The third line was answered by an emphatic 'yes'. Add together a manic and disruptive nature in the classroom, an addiction to sweets (as covered in loving, meticulous detail in *The Fry Chronicles*), a fear and hatred of compulsory games (absurdly replaced today by a love of almost *all* sport) and this new heart-pounding, soul-lacerating feeling that consumed my every waking hour, and a Stephen emerges who is simply too hot to be handled by any school, teacher or parent, let alone by himself.

I was finally expelled from Uppingham School in my first term in the lower sixth form, just as I was embarking on a two-year course of A levels. I had taken all my O levels when I was fourteen, a normal procedure then: if they thought you could get them, they put you in for them. I may have been academically mature but I was as physically and emotionally mature as a newborn puppy. And so much less adorable.

Why was I expelled? Some fraction of you reading this will want to know, another (perhaps larger) will be really seething now. 'This isn't a book, it's a retread!' they'll be shouting. On the other hand, it seems so rude to gloss over the whole episode as if expecting those in the dark to guess or spend money on a previous autobiography. So once again, I will remind those who don't want to watch a repeat that they can change channels, mix themselves a liver-and-whey protein shake, knit a smartphone-cosy or simply take a nap.

I was sacked from school because I had received permission from my housemaster to go to London for a meeting of the Sherlock Holmes Society of London, of which I was, at the time, the youngest member. I was to deliver a paper on T. S. Eliot's metrification of Sherlock Holmes's description to Doctor Watson of the life, appearance and habits of Professor Moriarty, who, in Eliot's *Old Possum's Book of Practical Cats*, becomes Macavity the Mystery Cat. The idea was to do the evening, which was on a Saturday, be free in London for Sunday *and* the following Monday, which was a public holiday to celebrate the Queen and Prince Philip's silver wedding, and return by the last train that day. As it is, I (and my friend Jo Wood, who was not so natural a law-breaker, but loyally attended me) were suddenly gripped by cinemania. We saw *Fritz the Cat*, *A Clockwork Orange*, *Cabaret*, *The Godfather*, all of them, time after time after time, as they ran and ran repeatedly on all-day programmes in the major West End cinemas. By the time we woke up from our binge it was Wednesday.

Sheepishly we returned and wolfishly we were devoured. Jo, having no form, was rusticated until the end of the term. I was shown the full red card.

My parents tried another seat of learning, the Paston School, a local direct-grant grammar with the distinction of having educated the young Horatio Nelson. Its allure was lost on me, and I developed the habit of hopping off the bus that took me there in the small town of Aylsham, halfway between my house and the school in North Walsham, and spending all day and all the spare money I had managed to find in my mother's handbag on pinball, cigarettes and Fanta. Before long the Paston had had enough of me too. For one thing they had wanted to put me on a course of O levels. I indignantly (and I daresay defiantly and arrogantly) declared that I had a very good set of O levels already and had been expelled from Uppingham while in the sixth form half a term into an A level course. Why should I have to sink down to the fourth form again? 'Because we do things by age here,' was the unsatisfactory reply. Or possibly they sensed that I was all show and no substance. At any rate I was slowly turning into one of those sneering, 'I've had it up to here with edu-bloody-cation' teenagers. Pinball and smoking were my highest ambitions.

To pursue even these minor pastimes I needed money, however, and when the Paston had hurled me out on my ear, my parents sent me as a last resort to NORCAT, the Norfolk College of Arts and Technology in King's Lynn. Here I developed the even more expensive habit

Chelsea. Oh dear.

Chelsea – seems a waste of time to take trouble over tying a bow tie but neglecting
to shave properly . . .

Kim Harris,
Chelsea.

Kim in Draycott Place, taken
by self (I solved that Rubik's Cube
too, but months after my father
cracked it).

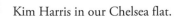

Kim Harris in our Chelsea flat.

My beloved parents . . .

My Personal AsSister doing what she does better than anyone.

In 1986, I spotted a house for sale in classic west Norfolk brick. Reader, I bought it.

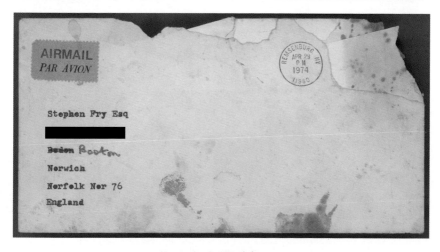

Remsenburg N.Y.
April 30.1974

Dear Mr Fry.

Many thanks for your letter.   Much
appreciated.

I found what you told me about yourself very
interesting. Here is a little about myself. I
have been living in this hamlet, eighty miles from
New York. for twenty years with a wife, a sister
in law, two dogs and six cats. I am a terrific
enthusiast on baseball, never missing a New York
Mets game on TV. My legs having gone back on me,
I do nothing these days but read and write. I have
just finished a new Jeeves novel which my London
agent and published think is the best I have done,
and am now trying (vainly at present)to get a plot
for another.

All the best
Yours

P. G. Wodehouse

AIRMAIL
PAR AVION

Stephen Fry Esq

███████████

Booton
Norwich
Norfolk Nor 76
England

From P. G. Wodehouse.

Chelsea: Pipes are hard work. P. G. Wodehouse signed photograph evident.
As is Rubik's Calendar, which is just showing off.

Chelsea flat, at work on something. You can just see the signed photograph
of P. G. Wodehouse on the left.

Rowan's inexplicable ability to find something more interesting than me.

Attempting a carol. Christmas Day, Norfolk, 1987.

Chelsea – damn, I wish I still had that pullover . . .

of gambling. A set of us would smoke and drink beer in a pub called the Woolpack, playing three-card brag for hours on end. I happily fell in with a group of highly literate and fascinating young eccentrics from the town. We met together to talk Baron Corvo, contribute to a strange magazine called the *Failure Press* ('failure' was deliberately misspelled in some way), devise a unique alphabet and arrange Paradox Parties, parties to which you could not be admitted unless you submitted an original paradox. Pretentious, you might think, but to find such a group in King's Lynn was thrilling for me. It was like finding not water in the desert, but a flask of quince, starfruit and lychee juice. Original. Strange. Testing. Provocative. And, as we would say of almost everything we liked, highly conducive.

At least NORCAT let me take A levels. But what with falling for a very lovely and smart girl from that group (yes, I have that 10 or so per cent of me that is entirely capable of being attracted to girls), feeling wholly uninspired by the academic side of life and still burning inside with that desperate first love that had made such a mess of me at Uppingham, I was becoming a less stable, predictable or hopeful entity.

It is a terrible thing to look back and realize that one grew up in a kind of golden age. Tarnished, but golden nonetheless. The 1970s are typically portrayed as grey, hopeless, hyper-inflationary, riddled with failure, strikes and sullen class warfare. Certainly, if you watch an episode of *The Sweeney*, it's hard to square John Thaw's menacing, jaw-crunching, whisky-slugging, cigarette-puffing, convention-defying Flying Squad detective Jack Regan with the unconvincing-Oxford-English-accented, crossword-solving, classical-music-loving, vintage-Jaguar-driving, tweed-jacketed Inspector Morse, who appeared a generation later. The brutal realism of the one contrasted with the cosy nonsense of the other is revealing. Similarly, the excellent balance of *Upstairs Downstairs* stands up very well against the ghastly snobbery and tacked-on *noblesse oblige* of that horrible Abbey programme. I say this guiltily, having actor friends I like very much who play in it, and play excellently, but truth must out.

Musically the 1970s were astonishing, even for someone like me, who is not especially attracted to pop or rock. You can distinguish early 1973, for example, from late 1973 in terms of both musical and fashion styles. Loons came in and bellbottoms bowed out. Every week you could see the young Elton John, David Bowie or Marc Bolan on *Top of the Pops* (admittedly Gary Glitter and Jimmy Savile too), not to mention Mud, Slade, Wizzard, Roxy Music and a myriad of freakish novelty songs and eclectic mixes. Meanwhile Led Zeppelin, The Rolling Stones, The Who, Pink Floyd, Genesis, Yes ... giant album artists were dominating the world. A few years later punk exploded – all this a heartbeat away from the dissolution of The Beatles. Music, unless my ear is staggeringly dysfunctional, hasn't undergone anything like such re-markably swift, imaginative, colourful and fundamental changes of style in the twenty-five years between the arrival of rap and now. Bits of acid house, trance, garage and other electronic dance music seem to have coincided with hip-hop in a more or less unbroken line. A photo-graph of an eighteen-year-old in 1990s clothes looks exactly like a photograph of an eighteen-year-old in twenty-first-century clothes.

But that is not the point, not the point at all. We moan about the sense of entitlement the young are said to have today. I think it is nonsense. It is simply that they are aware of the *actual* entitlement my generation enjoyed. Despite coming from a comfortably off household, since expulsion from private school all my education was at the expense of the state. Grants to cover living costs, tuition fees, everything. I even, while I was in debt to a bookshop at Cambridge, had the cheek to send a photocopy of their bill for the due sum of four hundred or so pounds (the equivalent of well over a thousand now) to the Norfolk and Norwich Local Education Authority. A tutor had added a paragraph to say that, as a scholar and potential academic of the future, these books were necessary to me. A cheque to cover the bill was immediately sent. I tell stories like that to my godchildren and nephews, who are just emerging from their university careers, burdened with debt, and I can see them wanting to punch me in the face. Hard.

I left university and shared a flat with my friend and Cambridge lover Kim in Chelsea, and life seemed infinitely interesting and straightforward. For the emerging graduate today there seems to be little on offer but a McJob, endless unpaid internships (only then if you know the right people) and a first rung on the property ladder that is higher and less attainable than the middle rung was in my early days.

But wait a minute – you've made me leap ahead of myself again. So, NORCAT. Three-card brag, beer, a girl, absolutely no interest in the curriculum and . . . a disappearance.

My memory cannot quite summon up the absolute circumstances of the First Great Escape. I was seventeen, it was 1974, I think I had agreed to go to some kind of musical festival and meet up with my friend Jo Wood. To cut a long (well it's fairly long in *Moab is My Washpot*) story short, some credit cards fell into my possession. Which is to say that I stole them. The short arm of the law had been reaching out feebly for three months or so before I was finally apprehended at the Hotel Wiltshire in Swindon, which stood, conveniently, absolutely opposite the police station.

I refused to give my name. My poor old mother and father had been through enough, surely? A sly officer, who unbeknownst to me had been going through my luggage in another room, returned and slowly whispered names that had been written on the flyleaves of the books

I had been lugging around with me during my adventures. A lot of them had been stolen from libraries, bookshops or friends' shelves, of course, and had all kinds of names scrawled on their title pages. Eventually, as I was being questioned by the detective sergeant in the interview room, I heard 'Stephen Fry?' being said in a low voice behind me. I had swung round and answered 'Yes?' before I was aware of the trap I had fallen into. I was, of course, on a missing persons list, and it was not long before my parents had sorted out a solicitor – my godmother's husband, who lived not far away. The game was up, and the goose cooked.

Some months of custody followed in the delightfully named Pucklechurch Prison. I had declined bail (not that I think my parents would have offered it anyway) and stayed at Pucklechurch for two weeks before another magistrate's appearance in Swindon, at which I was expected to plead. I announced my unquestionable guilt and was sent back on remand while the police took an embarrassingly long time to collect and assimilate the paperwork from the seven counties in which I had fraudulently used the credit cards. Back inside now as a con, as opposed to a non-con, the colour of my uniform changed and I was set to work.

The time passed easily and pleasantly enough. I had spent fourteen years in the private school system for heaven's sake: this was nothing. Other inmates at this young offenders institution, all tougher and mostly older than me, sobbed themselves to sleep. They had never spent a night away from home before.

At my trial, a dear friend of my parents, the imposing Sir Oliver Popplewell, then a noted QC, now a retired judge, represented me. I had worried that his distinguished name and reputation might rile the magistrates, a metropolitan sledgehammer sent to crack a provincial nut could seem offensive to their *amour propre*. I was also concerned that they might have little patience with one who, unlike most young offenders, had been given every opportunity and simply pissed his good fortune against the wall each time. I was guiltily stricken myself by the obvious difference in the 'life chances', as we would say now, of most of my luckless fellows back at Pucklechurch, who had been born into backgrounds of poverty, ignorance, squalor and abuse.

The magisterial bench, however, concluded that, since I had a solid family background (and perhaps came from the same class as them, I crimson at the thought), there was no need for a prison sentence, which would in those days and at my age have taken the form of Home Secretary Roy Jenkins's 'short sharp shock', the notorious detention centre, which was all the rage at the time. I had been dreading this: fellow cons at Pucklechurch told me it was all about running around and gym and weights and eating standing up and running about again like someone in Olympic training. DC provided the world with marvellously fit villains, ideal candidates for posts like nightclub bouncers and drug dealers' debt enforcers. Fortunately for me, taking into account the months I had already served (plus the other possible reasons I have indicated) I found myself sentenced to two years' probation in the care of my parents.

We move then from the image of the wretch lying on the stone flags of the prison cell, shadows of the prison bars cast across his sobbing frame, rats squeaking, gibbering and weeing in the corner, we move from this unhappy (and wholly inaccurate) picture to the solemn silence of the journey home from Swindon Magistrate's Court, father's stern face at the wheel, jaw tightly clamped and eyes sternly on the road ahead.

I seem to be sketching the biography of a Cambridge spy, a whole genre of literature in itself, factual and fictional. But whenever Kim Philby or Guy Burgess and their circle are written about, or (spoiler averted) the mole in Le Carré's *Tinker, Tailor, Soldier, Spy*, for example, there is repeated (to the point of cliché) emphasis on how withdrawal of the parental presence at an early age, the very nature of an old-fashioned classical English education given to a certain kind of person equipped with charm, intelligence, duplicity, guile (I was always called Sly-Fry, from my earliest memories of my very first schools) who had an almost pathological need to prove himself, to *belong*, could provide all the ingredients of a five-star, twenty-four-carat traitor and spy. I was and am neither of course, but had I been at Cambridge in the 'low dishonest decade' of the 1930s, instead of at the beginning of Thatcherism – between the 'Winter of Discontent' and the Falklands War essentially – then perhaps I would have been drawn into the Ring of Five and made it a Ring of Six. I doubt it: I'm not sure that the SIS, or MI6 as it's usually called these days, the most exclusive club there ever was in Great Britain, would have taken a Jew. Victor Rothschild came the closest, being a Cambridge Apostle like Burgess and Blunt, but even he, glamorous first-class cricketer, decorated war hero and Bugatti-riding adventurer that he was, was MI5, not 6. Some people still believe that Rothschild was the fifth man who closed the circle. We will probably never know. But there was a world of difference between the two services: 6 was pukka, 5 much less so. I am sure that is not so today, but what *is* true today is that I possess so many of the similar qualities, right down to a love of cricket, claret and clubland.

An upbringing that might under different circumstances have been used for a complex secret betrayal of my tribe became instead a simple public mockery of it in *Latin!*, my first piece of proper writing, followed by Cambridge Footlights sketches and, in the outside world, *Blackadder*, *Fry and Laurie* and so on. Like the satire of the 1930s Berlin cabarets that, as Peter Cook observed, 'did so very much to prevent the rise of Adolph Hitler', the satire in *A Bit of Fry and Laurie* such as it was – privatization, obsession with the free market and so forth – had the force and effectiveness of a kitten armed with a rubber bayonet, but we never expected anything else. We probably didn't imagine, however, that Old Etonians would still be ruling the country a quarter of a century later. Or indeed that they would be ruling the American TV and movie box office in the form of Damian Lewis, Dominic West, Tom Hiddleston, Eddie Redmayne and – ahem – m'colleague Hugh himself.

Male writers in Britain between the wars, as Martin Green brilliantly observed in *Children of the Sun*, could be divided into two classes: those that went to Eton and wished they hadn't, like George Orwell, and those that hadn't and wished they had, like Evelyn Waugh. I certainly cannot convincingly deny that I fall into the second category. The great advantage of an Oxbridge education is not that some mafia pushes you up the ladder as soon as you leave, nor is it in the education and living standards that you enjoy at either university: the real advantage is that you never have to deal with the fact that you didn't go there. Many genuinely never wanted to, many brush it all off with a 'Yeah, I could have gone, but the course at Warwick was so much better', others simmer in rage at the number of us in comedy, television, the law and all the other establishment trades. As would I, had I not got in. So it is with Eton. It would have been nice to have gone there, but on the other hand I would probably have been expelled even earlier, and who knows what criminal abominations I would have committed with an OE tie and that spy-like deceitful manner?

Where were we? Travelling with my parents in a silent journey from Pucklechurch Prison back home to Norfolk.

The twelve months between 1976 and 1977 followed. My first ever year of self-control. Possibly my first and *only* year of self-control. Every day I worked on the one-year course of A levels that I had managed to persuade Norwich City College to allow me to sit for. Aside from the syllabus, I read every Shakespeare play, writing synopses and notes on each character and scene. I devoured Chaucer, Milton, Spenser, Dryden, Pope and all the literary giants that I supposed I would have to be expert in before Cambridge would even look at me. I read *Ulysses* for the first time, with the help of a reading companion written by Anthony Burgess. I worked part-time in a department store in Norwich. I didn't steal or transgress. I was, it must be said, quite extraordinarily focused, sober, clean and concentrated.

Fortune favoured me, and I won a scholarship to Queens' College to read English Literature. If you have read *The Fry Chronicles*, you shouldn't be here, you should still be descaling the rabbit or tread-milling in the gym to the varied stylings of Jack and Meg White. You already know all of this, so I shall steam through for the others, and you'll find out where to pick up from where I last left off.

I performed in lots of plays when I got to Cambridge.

I fell in love with and shared rooms with a brilliant classicist and chess player (and more importantly wonderful person) called Kim, as in Philby. I produced articles for university magazines. I wrote the aforementioned play *Latin! or Tobacco and Boys*, which was performed at Cambridge and then taken to the Edinburgh Festival. This led to my meeting a tall fellow with a red flush to each cheek and a rather endearing way of saying 'Hullo!' He was James Hugh Calum Laurie, a name which can be convincingly expressed sixteen ways.

'Hi, I'm Calum Laurie Hugh James.'

'Laurie James Hugh Calum, at your service.'

'James Laurie Calum Hugh, how may I help?'

Et cetera. So many permutations, but he chose to call himself Hugh Laurie, which is how the little world of Cambridge then knew him and how the wider world of the . . . er . . . wider world now knows him.

Together with friends Emma Thompson, Tony Slattery, Paul Shearer and Penny Dwyer, we put on a show in our last year. It won a new award called the Perrier Prize, which resulted in us going to perform our show in London, then Australia, before coming back to record it for the BBC.

This is the linear bit and dull even if you haven't read it before. Kim and I shared a flat in Chelsea, while Hugh, Emma, Paul and I started to do a show for Granada Television in Manchester. We were, as it were, boy-banded together with Ben Elton, Siobhan Redmond and Robbie

Coltrane to create a new sketch comedy troupe. The resultant show, *Alfresco*, was not much of a success, but we liked each other's company, and new opportunities arose.

Kim and I drifted apart, but are still the warmest and best of friends. My fifteen years of so-called 'celibacy' began. Work started to come in the form of newspaper and magazine articles, a West End play, a stage run of Alan Bennett's *Forty Years On*, and then *Blackadder II*.

Noel Gay's musical comedy *Me and My Girl* came next. I worked on the 'book', in other words the story, dialogue and some of the lyrics. 'The Sun Has Got His Hat On' was a charming number from Noel Gay's back catalogue, and the director Mike Ockrent and I managed to make it a suitable opener for the second half of the show. The verse

> He's been roasting niggers
> Out in Timbuktu
> Now he's coming back
> To do the same to you

needed a little tweak, one could not but feel.* With pulsating lyrical talent, Gilbertian wit and astounding geographical, agrarian and botanical understanding the verse now became, under my magical weaving fingers,

---

* Since I wrote this passage some poor sod of a local radio DJ was forced into resignation for playing an old recording of the song. Oh lawks.

He's been roasting peanuts
Out in Timbuktu
Now he's coming back
To do the same to you

Nobody seemed to notice. No letters from outraged Malians denying that they had ever roasted a single peanut, not even in fun. No death threats from the guild of professional peanut roasters of Atlanta, Georgia. But the show was a success in the West End and then on Broadway. It made me money. I went mad buying classic cars, a country house, all kinds of things.

I filled every day with writing: book reviews for the now deceased *Listener* magazine, general articles for magazines like *Arena* and radio pieces for any number of programmes hosted by Ned Sherrin.

I became friends with Douglas Adams and began a lifelong love affair with all things to do with computing and the digital world.

In 1986, sharing a house with Hugh and others, just having finished recording the *Blackadder II* series, I was offered by an actor, who for obvious reasons shall remain nameless, a line of the illegal stimulant cocaine.

Right, all those who feel they absorbed *Moab is My Washpot* and *The Fry Chronicles* can come back in now. You will know from the latter that I seemed to have been born with a propensity to become addicted to things beginning with *c*. Sugar (C_{12} H_{22} O_{11}) – in the form of Candy, Confectionery and Chocolates – Cigarettes, Credit Cards (other people's to begin with), Comedy, Cambridge, Classic Cars, Clubs and so on.

But Cocaine. Oh dear. This has to be played delicately. If I go on about it too much it will sound like repellent braggadocio: 'Wow, what a wild crazy-head this guy Steve-o is. Taking blow like a crazy rock star. Cool.'

If I drown myself in pity it's no better: 'I was in the grip of a disease, and the name of that disease was addiction.' There's something po-faced, self-pitying and sanctimonious about that, true interpretation as many would insist that it is.

We have heard it all before. In short-form magazine articles, in long tearful confessionals. It is yesterday's news. Kind of. But it was fifteen years of my life, so it would be wrong of me at least not to – as it were – give you a sniff of the coke years.

Moral or Medical?

The Line-up

- Buckingham Palace
- Windsor Castle
- Sandringham House
- Clarence House
- The House of Lords
- The House of Commons
- The Ritz
- The Savoy
- Claridge's
- The Dorchester
- The Berkeley
- The Connaught
- Grosvenor House
- White's Club
- Brooks's Club
- Boodle's Club
- The Carlton Club
- The United Oxford and Cambridge Club
- The East India, Devonshire, Sports and Public Schools Club
- The Naval and Military Club

- The Reform Club
- The Travellers Club
- The Army and Navy Club
- The Naval and Military Club
- The RAC Club
- The RAF Club
- The Beefsteak Club
- The Garrick Club
- The Savile Club
- The Arts Club
- The Chelsea Arts Club
- The Savage Club
- Soho House
- The Groucho Club
- BBC Television Centre
- Fortnum & Mason
- ITV HQ
- The London Studios/LWT
- Shepperton Studios
- Pinewood Studios
- Elstree Studios
- 20th Century Fox
- *Daily Telegraph* offices
- *The Times* offices
- *Spectator* offices
- *Listener* offices
- *Tatler* – Vogue House
- *Vanity Fair* – Vogue House

I take this opportunity to apologize unreservedly to the owners, managers or representatives of the noble and ignoble premises above and to the hundreds of private homes, offices, car dashboards, tables, mantelpieces and available polished surfaces that could so easily have been added to this list of shame. You may wish to have me struck off, banned, blackballed or in any other way punished for past crimes; surely now is the time to reach for the phone, the police or the club secretary. There is no getting away from it. I am confessing to having broken the law and consumed, in public places, Class A sanctioned drugs. I have brought, you might say, gorgeous palaces, noble properties and elegant honest establishments into squalid disrepute.

That was then, this is now, yet some of you will be reading this in horror, not because you are easily shocked, but because *you thought better of me than this*. You might have children who will read of my pathetic exploits and you fear that they will take them as permission or encouragement to imitate the chopping-out of that long line of cocaine that stretched from 1986 to 2001. Oh Stephen, *how could you?* Such weakness, such feeble-mindedness, such self-indulgence. Such an insult to the efficient and admirable brain with which nature graced you and the warm and loving home in which your parents brought you up with such care.

This is where it all gets damnably difficult. We come to choosing between what we might call the addiction approach and the personal responsibility approach. There are those, there will always be those, who simply do not buy this addiction concept. Most especially they repudiate the premise that addiction is a disease, one that grips you as permanently and assuredly as any chronic affliction such as diabetes or asthma. They only see weakness, lack of grit, absence of will-power and feeble, self-justifying excuses. They hear, most especially, figures in the public eye talking of 'pressure' and 'stress' and they want to puke up. Here are rich, overpaid, over-praised, over-pampered, overindulged 'celebrities' who scrabble and snuffle and snort like rootling truffle pigs at the first bump of naughty powder they are offered and then, after years of careless abuse, when their septum finally surrenders, or their mind turns so paranoid on them that they lose their only true friends, they bleat, 'But I've got a disease! I'm an addictive personality! Help!'

I'm painting it as blackly as I can, yet I know some of you will see the foregoing as the correct, or at least as a convincing, analysis. Addicts are looked at with the same wrinkled-nosed disgust that is directed at the morbidly obese waddling through Target and Walmart stores in the Midwest states of America. Those poor clams can at least claim indigence and ignorance as the root cause of their addiction to the high-fructose corn syrup, ice cream and corn dogs that are slowly killing them. Does a rock star, City whizz-kid, actor, journalistic feature writer, best-selling novelist or comedian have the same excuse?

In the opposite corner there is the straightforward reverse of this pitiless verdict. It argues that addiction is indeed a condition, often inherited or congenital, and that the only way to defeat it even if it is not a 'real' disease is *to treat it as if it is.*

I can quite see how one view speaks to the contempt, envy, resentment, scorn and impatience many in the modern world have for what is so revoltingly called and yet so revoltingly *is* 'celeb culture'. A spoiled minority, to which I find myself belonging willy-nilly,* seem to be encouraged to believe their views on everything from politics, art, religion and society are more valid than that of everyman or -woman. Oh how we oh so modestly and smilingly lord it over the rest of society: unto us is given more than we need by way of freebies, attention and opportunity, while ordinary, *real* people struggle with the daily round, unattended to, unheard, bulldozed or at least elbowed aside by a brutish, shallow culture which values fame even above money.

I have been fairly well known in my own country for a quarter of a century, and beyond, in Russia, Canada, New Zealand and Australia, for perhaps fifteen. My books have been translated into dozens of languages, but mostly I find when wandering in Eastern Europe or South America that I am taken for a strangely morphed compound of Jeremy Clarkson and James May from BBC

* In the *real* sense of willy-nilly. Not in the sense of harum-scarum or all over the place.

73

Television's *Top Gear*. Something to do with being a tall, fleshy Englishman with odd hair who rings a faint bell in the eye of the average Bulgarian or Bolivian, if bells can be rung in eyes, that is.

I remember a marvellous line of Anthony Burgess's when he reviewed, in, I think, the *Observer*, William Goldman's peerless *Adventures in the Screen Trade*. Burgess used the phrase of film stars: 'those irrelevantly endowed with adventitious photogeneity'. Or it may perhaps have been 'those adventitiously endowed with irrelevant photogeneity'. It so happened that I got to know William Goldman well in the early to mid-1990s when John Cleese, in a breathtaking act of generosity, chartered a boat for about thirty to go up the Nile. All we guests had to do was turn up at the Cleesery in London, and the rest was taken care of: carriage to the airport, flights, laundry, food, sight-seeing, informative evening lectures – everything was looked after for us on the floating Claridge's that glided up from Cairo to the Aswan Dam.

One afternoon comes back very clearly to me. We were shading ourselves in the shadow of an ancient pylon in Luxor while our tour guide spoke of hiero-glyphs and higher things. I asked Bill a few questions that I had been too shy to previously. He was hero enough for having written *Adventures in the Screen Trade* and earlier *The Season*, a still perfectly relevant and never less than insanely readable summation of one year in the life of Broadway. But Goldman was the screenwriter who wrote *Butch Cassidy and the Sundance Kid*, *All the President's Men*, *Marathon Man* and *The Princess Bride* and was, even then, chewing over whether he would accept the offer from Rob Reiner and Castle Rock to adapt Stephen King's *Misery*.

Unforgivably gauche as it seems, I found my mouth forming the shy sentence: 'So, er, what's Robert Redford really like?'

'Well,' said Bill, 'tell me what you would be like if for twenty-five years you had never heard the word "no".'

Which is as good an answer as could be given. It is far from necessary and sufficient not to have heard the word 'no' for decades to become a brat, or spoiled or impossible to deal with, but it goes a long way to explaining some of the more painful characteristics of those who are called stars.

It's rather like the argument used to defend those brought up in poverty and abuse, however. It fails to explain those many who, under the same intolerable, horrific circumstances, do *not* become members of gangs or crack-smoking thugs who could remorselessly beat an old man to death for asking them to keep the noise down. There are those who have endured childhoods we can't even imagine who go on to university and lives of fulfilment, kindness and familial bliss. Similarly there are long-established stars, Tom Hanks to pull a random name out of the Starry Sorting Hat, who are as kind, self-deprecating, professional, unspoiled and modest as it is possible to be.

So we return to drugs. How can I explain the extraordinary waste of time and money that went into my fifteen-year habit? Tens if not hundreds of thousands of pounds, and as many hours, sniffing, snorting and tooting away time that could have been employed in writing, performing, thinking, exercising, *living*. I can't begin to explain it, but I can at least attempt to describe it.

The Early Days

The first effect of cocaine is of . . . nothing. You don't get the huge, whooping, rushing high that is said to be the reward of heroin or of crystal meth and crack. I haven't tried any of those because I am a squeamish wimp. Perhaps this denies me any credit as a true addict. Friends like Sebastian Horsley and Russell Brand, the late Philip Seymour Hoffman and all those rock stars of the 1970s who were unafraid to put a flame under a spoon, suck the juice into a syringe, tighten a tie round their biceps with their teeth, pump their fists and tap with two fingers until they found an available vein, whether it be, once the more available ones had hardened into uselessness, a vein in their eyeball or their penis, then plunge the plunger, they were surely the true addicts. I got the word 'squeamish' from an article I read by Aaron Sorkin, the screenwriting phenomenon who gave the world *A Few Good Men, The West Wing, The Social Network* and *The Newsroom*. He was taking a break in rehearsals with Philip Seymour Hoffman and, as an ex-coke fiend, was saying to him that he'd always been too squeamish to inject himself, otherwise he supposed he'd have been a junkie. 'Stay squeamish,' was Hoffman's (typically) curt reply. It wasn't too long after

that that he himself was dead. Twenty-three years 'clean'
and then one back-slide and it was all over. It's rather like
nuclear weaponry: you can never say it is safe because it
has only been safe *up until now*; it needs to be safe for all
time: one moment of not being safe, and the whole game
is up.

So, back now in London in 1986 for my first experience of taking coke. I nervously watch my friend take out
a folded wrap of paper, open it and shake out a heap of
granular white powder on to a metal tray on the table
beside him. He takes out a credit card and with its edge
chops gently until the powder is as fine grained as he can
make it. He uses the edge to sweep this pile into five equal
lines, rolls up a ten-pound note, bends down, applies the
end of the tube to one nostril and the other end to the
first line and with a sharp snort sucks in half of it. He
takes the remaining half of his line up the other nostril
and then passes me the rolled-up tube.

With as much nonchalance as I can muster I reproduce
his actions. My hand is trembling a little, and I am more
than a little anxious not to imitate Woody Allen's notorious sneeze in *Annie Hall*. My bent nose has gifted me a
deviated septum, which means that it is uncommon for
both nostrils to be in full working order at the same time.
I force as much suction as I can on my line with the weak
left nostril and nothing moves. Embarrassed, I take the
whole line up my clear right nostril with one huge snort.
The powder hits the back of my throat and my eyes sting

a little. The other three, also neophytes at this ceremony, take their turns.

I sit back, expecting hallucinations, a trance, bliss, euphoria, ecstasy . . . *something*.

Our host, as is his right, licks his forefinger and sweeps up the residue of powder, pushing it round his gums.

'Er . . .' says one of our number braver than me, 'what are we supposed to feel?'

'You get a bit of a buzz' – the expert claps his hands together and exhales loudly – 'and you feel just . . . good. That's what's so great about coke. It's kind of subtle?'

Up until this time the only illegal drug I had ever tried had been dope, which I had been rather ashamed of strongly disliking. Cannabis, even the milder versions of grass and resin available back then before the age of skunk and buds, was certainly not subtle, neither in effect nor in after-effect. In 1982 I had once vomited all over, around, above and below the lavatory of a friend's house only a few months after coming back from our Footlights tour of Australia. I can't remember any discernible pleasure at any stage and had more or less foresworn the weed. Most people have a drug that suits them, whether it is nicotine (not much of a behavioural modifier), coffee, cannabis, alcohol, ketamine, crystal meth, crack, opium, heroin, speed, MDMA/Ecstasy. I had decided early on that cannabis was not for me, but I hadn't for one second considered replacing it with another one.

Sitting back now and inspecting the effect of the

cocaine, I have to confess to noticing finally a benevolent stimulation. I observe too that we are all inclined to talk a little more. Mostly over each other, without listening, a feature I will soon come to recognize very clearly.

A Brief History of Blow

Cocaine (if you call it 'blow' you sound hipper and cooler), as most people know, derives from the coca plant, indigenous to South America, principally Colombia, Peru and Bolivia. The leaves of the plant are freely and legally available in those countries to chew or to make into a tea known as a *mate* and are said to help humans cope with the fatigue and altitude sickness associated with the high Andes. Ingestion of these leaves or infusions doesn't impart a fraction of any of the euphoria or stimulation associated with cocaine, but they are said to be rich in all kinds of vitamins, minerals and fibre.

When I was in South America in my puffing, wheezing cigarette-smoking days, locals there encouraged me to chew the leaves with lime, or to add lime juice to the *mate*, in order to speed up the (very mild) effect of coca and help me with the exhausting altitude. I suppose the process of adding lime is a gesture towards the acid/base extraction which turns coca into cocaine, the Class A scheduled drug, the billion-dollar industry, the working-class, media-class, rural and urban community must-have weekend companion that has been growing and growing in popularity since the 1970s and still shows no sign of declining. A chief constable told me not long ago that it is easier to score cocaine in a market town in East Anglia than it is in Soho Square. It's Lombard-street to a China orange* that there is more coke consumed on Friday and Saturday nights in Doncaster than in Chelsea. No one can call the substance cheap, but it has held its price pretty steadily over the past decade or so and it is now far from the preserve of the members of 'trendy' – as the word then was – Soho or Mayfair private clubs.

It was in the nineteenth century that the breakthroughs were made that turned this harmless, utterly non-addictive Andean bush-leaf into coca-ine ('-ine' is a suffix chemists give to alkaloids: coffee's alkaloid is caffeine; the alkaloid of *Atropa belladonna*, or deadly nightshade, is atropine; and so on). Heroin, on the other hand, was so called by the Bayer Company of Germany, who gave us aspirin, because it was thought to confer heroic properties on the user.

No less a figure than Sigmund Freud was one of the first major medical figures to write on the properties of cocaine, which was a *rara avis* in the nineteenth century, inasmuch as most major drugs were narcotics, usually derived from the poppy family: morphine, opium, codeine and Queen Victoria's favourite tipple, laudanum, which is

---

*A once common phrase that no one seems to know any more, but is worth looking up.

morphine and alcohol combined: blissikins, as Nancy Mitford used to say. Freud's book *Über Coca* contains some fascinating insights into the effect of this new drug on himself and his patients/volunteers/kidnapped tramps.

> It seems probable, in the light of reports which I shall refer to later, that coca, if used protractedly but in moderation, is not detrimental to the body. Von Anrep treated animals for thirty days with moderate doses of cocaine and detected no detrimental effects on their bodily functions. It seems to me noteworthy – and I discovered this in myself and in other observers who were capable of judging such things – that a first dose or even repeated doses of coca produce no compulsive desire to use the stimulant further; on the contrary, one feels a certain unmotivated aversion to the substance.

As *if* and I wish . . .

> The psychic effect of cocaïnum muriaticum in doses of 0.05–0.10g consists of exhilaration and lasting euphoria, which does not differ in any way from the normal euphoria of a healthy person. The feeling of excitement which accompanies stimulus by alcohol is completely lacking; the characteristic urge for immediate activity which alcohol produces is also absent. One senses an increase of self-control and feels more vigorous and more capable of work; on the other

hand, if one works, one misses that heightening of the mental powers which alcohol, tea, or coffee induce. One is simply normal, and soon finds it difficult to believe that one is under the influence of any drug at all.

Freud *drank* while he worked? Oh, well, that explains everything . . . Just to repeat:

> It seems probable, in the light of reports which I shall refer to later, that coca, if used protractedly but in moderation, is not detrimental to the body.

We'll ignore the happy-sounding 'sudden cardiac death' that today's doctors and rehab clinicians like to harp on about with what I can only call tactless relish.

> Coca is a far more potent and far less harmful stimulant than alcohol, and its widespread utilization is hindered at present only by its high cost.

The cost issue is still true, I suspect, and there are certainly many, many more deaths from alcohol in the world than from cocaine. Even taking into account the wider use, death from sustained cocaine ingestion is, I think, moderately rare, but certainly not unheard of.

> Long-term use of coca is further strongly recommended and allegedly has been tried with success in all diseases which involve degeneration of the tissues, such as anæmia, phthisis, long-lasting febrile diseases, etc.; and

also during recovery from such diseases . . . The natives of South America, who represented their goddess of love with coca leaves in her hand, did not doubt the stimulative effect of coca on the genitalia.

Ask any seasoned cokehead, certainly a male one, and they will probably agree with those lines of the Porter in *Macbeth*, who is discoursing here about alcohol but may as well be referring to Charlie.

> Lechery, sir, it provokes, and unprovokes;
> it provokes the desire, but it takes
> away the performance: therefore, much drink
> may be said to be an equivocator with lechery:
> it makes him, and it mars him; it sets
> him on, and it takes him off; it persuades him,
> and disheartens him; makes him stand to, and
> not stand to; in conclusion, equivocates him
> in a sleep, and, giving him the lie, leaves him.

Save that cocaine doesn't 'equivocate one in a sleep' so much as leave one wide-eyed and drippy-nosed for hours upon end, staring at the ceiling and making promises for the morrow that one knows one will not keep.

Mantegazza confirms that the coqueros sustain a high degree of potency right into old age; he even reports cases of the restoration of potency and the disappearance of functional weaknesses following the use of coca, although he does not believe that coca would produce such an effect in all individuals.

Marvaud emphatically supports the view that coca has a stimulative effect; other writers strongly recommend coca as a remedy for occasional functional weaknesses and temporary exhaustion; and Bentley reports on a case of this type in which coca was responsible for the cure.

Among the persons to whom I have given coca, three reported violent sexual excitement which they unhesitatingly attributed to the coca. A young writer, who was enabled by treatment with coca to resume his work after a longish illness, gave up using the drug because of the undesirable secondary effects which it had on him.

So one patient became so embarrassed by the increased libido of the drug that he discontinued it. 'Undesirable secondary effects', indeed. A Viagra, a workhorse, a cure for numerous debilitating ailments, less dangerous or mind-altering than alcohol, cocaine was welcomed by the late nineteenth century and, as is well known, gave the drink Coca-Cola the first half of its name, although the company dropped it from the list of ingredients in 1929. It was available everywhere legally in pastille, pill or potion form as a tonic and often self-contradictory treatment, being most efficacious in the cure of constipation and magically helpful too for the firming of loose or watery stools. It aided concentration and work rate, it cheered melancholy and in smaller doses was remarkably effective in the calming of recalcitrant children.

This was all during a period known as the Great Binge, roughly designated by social historians as 1870–1914, after which the First World War came and spoiled everything: almost at the sound of the first martial trumpet, beer was weakened, licensing hours were decreased, and, in 1915, the French banned absinthe, the poster child of the Great Binge. In between, during the Binge itself, however, everything was on sale at your local chemist or drug store over the counter, no questions asked. Fortnum & Mason, the elegant and grand Grocers' Royal of St James's, sold tasteful hampers which included silver boxes containing syringes and *étuis* for doting parents to send heroin and cocaine to their sons in the South African War and early years of the Great War. Indeed, Benzedrine, the trade name of a kind of amphetamine or 'speed', was supplied to commandos throughout the Second World War as part of their usual rations. In the Ian Fleming novels, James Bond is hardly ever off the stuff. It was just my luck to be born into an era when virtually anything exciting, beguiling, enchanting, naughty and nice was furiously illegal. Those comedians and actors a generation above me who were worried about their weight would regularly go to their doctors and be prescribed as many 'bennies' as they wanted. Generally speaking, anything that speeds up and stimulates your metabolism will suppress your appetite. Downers like cannabis produce, as is well known, that undignified state known as the munchies. Groups of young men and women invading a twenty-four-hour petrol station loading up on Mars Bars, Doritos and great basketfuls of junk food are as clear a statement of an evening of passing joints around as you could get.

Maybe it is the very illegality of cocaine that drew me to consider becoming a user. Perhaps an echo of Sherlock Holmes and his Seven-Per-Cent Solution resonated in the back of the mind. Perhaps my sexuality, or even my Jewishness, had always made me believe deep down that I would never be *normal*. That I was forever to be an outsider, a transgressor.

Nowadays there is a war of catch-up going on: a running war between the drug enforcement agencies and the enterprising chemists out in the world. Change a molecule here and a molecule there and you've got yourself a 'legal high' – some kind of pill (advertised as not for human consumption but 'for promoting healthy plant leaf shine') which will send you completely wild for about a day and a half. Which is probably overdoing it if you have a schedule like mine.

Here is a truth so obvious that people fail to notice it: *precisely* the same substances may, in fact usually do, have entirely different effects on different people. We see this clearly with allergies: Person A can down a bag of peanuts in one and then, with a satisfied eructation, ask for more, while Person B is on the floor choking to death with anaphylaxis because he took a bite out of an apple that grew on a tree near a factory which ten years previously used nuts in its food processing plant.

We are used to it with alcohol too: we can sit at a table and match a friend glass for glass until that moment, that ghastly moment, mortifying for all, when the friend's eyes will snap down like shutters, he or she will start arguing with the waiters, they will start to repeat themselves, get spoiling for a fight and generally become a foul and unspeakable embarrassment everyone is anxious to be as far away from as possible. They will have had exactly, to the sixteenth of an ounce, the same amount of alcohol in their body as you have, yet you are capable of walking in a straight line, reciting 'Ozymandias', doing the crossword and drinking another four glasses without feeling anything more than a little merry. The number of times I have had to tell friends of mine who have had trouble with the bottle that they just must face up to the fact that they are, unfair as it seems, to all intents and purposes, allergic to it . . . you can't even make a rule out of body size. I have had huge friends who just can't take a drink, and have known dainty girls who can drink continuously without showing any sign of instability, aggression or wobble.

I am very lucky, or perhaps unlucky, in that I have a high tolerance for alcohol myself. Sometimes I've been known to mix it with an injudicious pill and found myself in bed the next morning without the faintest recollection of how I got there or how the whole evening panned out.

Another characteristic that I must be really clear and

straightforward about is that I *hate parties*. I absolutely detest them. I don't think I have ever liked a person as much as I have hated a party. The moment I am there I want to leave. I discount meals around a dinner table in a private house or restaurant. But parties with music, with people standing up, parties with music, parties with buffets or canapé wait- ers, parties with music, bring-a-bottle parties, parties with music, poolside parties ... did I mention music? There's a famous speech in Evelyn Waugh's novel *Vile Bodies*, which I lifted almost whole for a screen adaptation I made in about 2002. 'Oh, Nina, such a lot of parties ... all that succession and repetition of humanity. All those vile bodies.' Waugh was a rude snob, a bully and a rascal, but he wrote like an angel, and he and I (or at least I and Adam Fenwick- Symes, his hero) are as one when it comes to parties.

In the gay community, to which I did not belong, despite the sexual visa issued to me at birth which told the world that I was a citizen, musical comings-together were the least squalid form of finding a partner for the night and – who knows? – for the long term. These com- ings-together were in gay bars that pumped out Donna Summer, Blondie and the Eurythmics or in places like Heaven, down behind Charing Cross, which was sup- posedly the largest disco in Europe. I went to Heaven precisely once and found it hell. The noise, those awful up-and-down raking inspections that greeted you wher- ever you went. I knew that I fell short of the ideal, which in those days seemed to involve string vests or plaid shirts, moustaches, jeans and plenty of muscle. The clone look, as it was known on account of its duplicated prevalence.

That one time I went to Heaven (I know, a clever name for a nightclub one must admit) I saw Kenny Everett dancing frenziedly and happily. He coo-cooed and blew me his special brand of extravagant kiss and threw back his head as if to say 'Dahling!' before being swallowed up in the bopping mass.

I saw too my friend from Cambridge, Oscar Moore. He was to go on to write *A Matter of Life and Sex* under the pseudonym Alec F. Moran (an anagram of *roman à clef*) and to edit the film magazine *Screen International*. Everett continued to be sacked and rehired, sacked and rehired, sacked and rehired every six months or so by the BBC.* Before too long both Moore and Everett would have died painfully and unhappily.

Sex

I do apologize for leaping about like this, but I did warn you. In my mid-twenties a sexual relationship, aside from

---

* After three series a BBC executive eventually cottoned on to the terrible truth that the name of Everett's female vulgarian, Cupid Stunt ('all in the best *possible* taste'), could be crudely spoonerized. She was forbidden from reappearing. A new, seemingly identical, character called Mary Hinge popped up in the next series. 'Now you see that's better,' said the executive. 'You don't need to be smutty to be funny.'

the usual schoolboy larks and nervous cottaging, had come to me but once. It took the shape of my partnership with the aforementioned remarkable, brilliant and loyal friend Kim. We were lovers at Cambridge, and only the necessity of driving weekly up to Manchester to work on my first television series, *Alfresco*, kept us apart. Perhaps too much, for this marvellous lover in one arena loved what I exactly most didn't: the 'scene', those gay clubs and pubs and their music. Conversation was what I adored. Sometimes even other people's. How can you converse with 'Pump Up The Volume' vibrating your tummy and hoarsening your voice to a whisper that wouldn't be heard in a nun's cell?

Well, I returned one weekend to find a Graeco-American young man there, called Steve. In a perfectly happy, loving way I moved to the spare room in the Chelsea flat, while they took the master bedroom. Yes, in those rosy years one could live in a two-bedroomed flat in Chelsea just between the King's Road and Brompton a year after coming down from university. Well, I say 'one' – Kim's parents had money, and not all my contemporaries were as lucky: some had to live as far out as Clapham and Islington. To have been born clutching the coat-tails of the baby-boom was to have drawn first prize in the lottery of life. I am quite sure the young don't want my pity, but they do have my wanted or unwanted sympathy.

Everything continued swimmingly, Steve was very

charming, I didn't feel the least betrayed, and Kim and I have stayed the best of friends ever since.

A perfectly accidental advantage of this celibacy and my loathing of gay clubs and pubs was that at precisely the same time I emerged from university HIV emerged into the world too, although the first name I ever heard it given was GRID – Gay Related Immune Deficiency. By the decade's end I would have sat at the bedsides of many friends and attended the funerals of more. There is no virtue in my having survived the swathe of death that AIDS cut through a whole generation of gay men and intravenous drug users any more than I am prepared to say that there was any vice in the infection and deaths of those who did succumb. Once the facts were out, it was pretty dumb to be caught by the virus, it must be admitted, but my fiercest feelings at the time were for the hysterical untruths and myths perpetuated by the tabloid newspapers. I began to involve myself in Britain's first AIDS charity, the Terrence Higgins Trust, and have worked with them ever since.

We mounted in the late 1980s and early 1990s three or four benefit shows for THT called *Hysteria*, two of which were televised. In one of those Eddie Izzard made his television debut, in another Vic Reeves and Bob Mortimer. At these packed-with-stars benefit evenings the audience will be very stoked up, and when one comes on, as master of ceremonies, to announce, 'And now ladies and gentlemen, loosen your girdles and clamp your thighs, it's . . . Mr . . .

Rowan Atkinson!' or '. . . Miss Jennifer French and Dawn Saunders!' there will be an explosion of cheers and foot-stomping and whistles of joy and welcome that hit you like a force field. Unless the material they perform is entirely astonishing, the sound that accompanies their exit is necessarily a little less wild. That is no sign of failure, naturally. It was then a thrilling pleasure to announce, 'I know you're going to love him, please welcome the extraordinary Eddie Izzard!' There wasn't exactly the lone cough, tolling of a bell and bouncing of tumbleweed so beloved of *Simpsons* scriptwriters and others, but the reception was little more than cheerfully polite. His exit though – oh my word. The audience actually stood as they cheered him off, and I, in the wings, had to push him back on to take another roar of approval. I turned to one of the producers, and we both mouthed simultaneously, 'A star is born.' I know: what a cheesy showbizzy cliché, but you have to accept some.

Weird truth: since I began this paragraph an email just hit my inbox, reminding me of this June's Terrence Higgins Trust Gala Dinner. For the last twenty-odd years I have made a fundraising speech on these occasions and before each I have the same panic attack about what I'm going to say. It becomes harder and harder not to repeat myself. Maybe I'll cheat this year by reading out passages from this book.

A surprising number of you (surprising to me because I think, despite the evidence of my passport, that I still hover somewhere between my mid-twenties and early thirties) won't really know quite how disastrous, ugly, desperate, upsetting and frightening the AIDS epidemic was. The transition from being 'HIV positive' to having 'full-blown AIDS' – always 'full blown', no one ever managed to find another phrase – meant that death was a certainty. Well, not entirely a certainty. I have two friends who were diagnosed early and seem to possess some inbuilt antibody. Naturally, virologists have swarmed all over them, attempting to determine why they are to all intents and purposes immune.

Those dying of AIDS resembled the survivors of Nazi death camps: the gaunt, hollowed cheeks, the total emaciation, the dry, crusted lips, the dull glimmer of fear and pain and hopelessness around the eyes. And always the shallow panting from infected lungs that denied any conversation but the most banal and forcedly cheerful from visitor and visited.

Perhaps the most upsetting sights I ever saw were anxious parents sitting on one side of the bed, looking down at their wasted and withered child, while on the other side sat the (for whatever reason) healthy and uninfected partner. The parents would flash sidelong glances that seemed to say, '*You* did this to our boy. *You* killed him. Why aren't *you* dying too?'

If I had enjoyed the 'gay lifestyle' and cruising and bars and clubs, it is very probable that I would be long dead. Anyone who ever saw someone suffer from AIDS knows it was not the release of death but the agonizingly drawn-out manner of dying that was so cruel and unendurable.

Very often friends of mine had to give their parents two pieces of shattering news in one.

'Mum, Dad, I have something to tell you. I'm gay.'

'What?'

'Yes. And, um, I have AIDS.'

Imagine a family having to deal with that. I met some heroic parents along that troubled fifteen to twenty years, when to test seropositive, as doctors called it, was to receive a certain sentence of death.

Religionists from pulpits and evangelical TV stations announced that this was all God's punishment for the perverted vice of homosexuality, quite failing to explain why this vengeful deity had no interest in visiting plagues and agonized death upon child rapists, torturers, murderers, those who beat up old women for their pension money (or indeed those cheating, thieving, adulterous and hypocritical clerics and preachers who pop up on the news from time to time weeping their repentance), reserving this uniquely foul pestilence only for men who choose to go to bed with each other and addicts careless in the use of their syringes. What a strange divinity. Later he was to take his pleasure, as he still does, on horrifying numbers of women and very young girls raped in sub-Saharan Africa while transmitting his avenging wrath on the unborn children in their wombs. I should be interested to hear from the religious zealots why he is doing this and what kind of a kick he gets out of it. But we are wasting time on those beneath contempt.

I suppose we will return to sex at some later point, but for the moment, where are we? Before you distracted me with your fevered and filthy red herrings and irrelevant erotic diversions, we were examining that first intranasal introduction of cocaine into my system. I wrote that the effect upon me had been between zero and minimal. A slightly increased propensity to talk and a little jigging up and down of the knees. Nonetheless that momentous evening will never leave me. We all had a second line, finishing up our friend's supply – he was only an underpaid actor after all. It was that second line that got hold. Don't misunderstand me, it didn't hook me and turn me instantly into an addict. Just a few smokes or shots of heroin won't make a junkie out of you, even if twenty or more just might. The second line gave me enough of what Freud had called 'euphoria' and enough of a sense of energy and optimism to make me think that this was a drug tailor-made for me.

The strange thing about cocaine is that it is said to cause a *dependency* rather than an addiction. Tallulah Bankhead put it this way: 'Honey, cocaine is not addictive. I should know, I've been taking it for twenty years.' Alcoholics, smokers and junkies are addicts. That is how I looked at it as the habit grew after that first simple encounter. Not one of the others in that room, all close friends, responded in the same way. There was ever something darker, more dangerous and – let's be frank – more stupid about me than about my friends. Socially, psychologically and inwardly stupid. Imbecilic. Self-destructive. More of a fool.

By the end of the 1980s I would no more consider going out in the evening without three or four grams of cocaine safely tucked in my pocket than I would consider going out without my legs.

Yet I was after all able to find it perfectly simple to go to the country and write my first novel, *The Liar*, sitting at the computer in Norfolk for four months without even the *thought* of cocaine crossing my mind; and this was when I must have been already regularly using it for five years. Just about daily.

I dare say cocaine was ready and waiting for me, but the real reason I embraced it is that I found it could give me a second existence. Instead of performing and being in bed with a mug of Horlicks and a P. G. Wodehouse at 11 p.m., coke gave me a whole new lease on nightlife. It made me for the first time in my life actually enjoy parties, though still never parties with music, no matter how wired I was. So long as I had two or three wraps in my pocket and access to a lavatory that wasn't too squalid or have too long and obvious a queue for the stalls, then I was a new, sociable, fun-loving Stephen. No longer the Stakhanovite drudge, producing column after column for magazine after magazine, voice-over after voice-over for face creams and dog biscuits and TV appearance after TV appearance for anyone who asked, I was Stephen the party animal, always to be seen at the now defunct Zanzibar in Great Queen Street, Covent Garden or its famed and 'storied', as Americans would say, successor, the Groucho Club in Dean Street, Soho. Bed by four or five in the morning and then up at ten feeling fine, ready to get through the backlog of magazine articles, reviews, radio scripts and whatever else the day demanded.

There again, I was lucky and unlucky. I know many, many people who profess to liking coke but who just can't recover the next morning and will feel like hell for two days afterwards. For some reason it never had that effect on me. I would awaken with a spring and a bounce and Tigger my way down to the kitchen in search of breakfast, much to the grumpy annoyance of Hugh, with whom I still shared a house at that time, along with his girlfriend and other Cambridge friends. Never the larkiest bird in the morning sky, Hugh, after a day in the gym, bed at 11.30 and not so much as a gin and tonic in between, still managed to feel like hell until mid-afternoon and seven coffees the next day.

I felt blessed. I was meeting new people at all kinds of parties, not just coke parties with fellow cokeheads, but ambassadorial, political, social and geeky-digital parties. I would never have accepted invitations to any kinds of parties like that without the little friend in my wallet.

Paraphernalia

Not the most important issue: if you've got a gram or two about you and any available surface on which the powder won't get trapped or soaked in then frankly a currency note and a credit card will get the job done perfectly adequately. Or you can even transfer by the corner of the card or a pinch of the fingers a 'bump' on to your fingernail or the side of your clenched fist and sniff it in like a Regency snuff-taker. Nothing can keep an addict from his supply. But for a cleaner, neater, altogether *purer* experience I had put together quite the little kit. During my visits to the sound studios of Soho for the purposes of lending my larynx to the allure of L'Oréal or the double-action brilliance of Bold Automatic, I had taken every opportunity to snaffle, when no one was looking, a useful collection of those editor's razor blades with a protective bar on the top that they used for cutting tape back in the days of old analogue reel-to-reels. Whenever I passed a McDonald's I popped in to make another haul. Ronald McDonald's red, white and yellow drinking straws, stored in glass carousel jars by the napkin and ketchup sachets, were the coke sniffer's ideal. Hygienically protected in paper with a wider bore than the average straw, fistfuls could easily be taken home, and each straw neatly snipped in half with scissors to make the best possible sniffing tube. Washable too. I mean, for heaven's sake, when one is generous with one's supply, as I always prided myself on being, who knew what germs lurked within the snotty nostrils of the user to one's left as one passed on the straw?

Storage? I won't believe a single coke user who tells me they haven't at least once opened their wallet only to watch, with a shudder of horror, their precious packet or baggy fall out and splash into the lavatory bowl below.* So, aside from the obvious advice to make sure you always close the seat before opening your pockets and getting down to business, consider the container. For a short time I favoured the highly fashionable, for sadly obvious reasons, condom holder. You could slip three well-packed wraps and a blade in this two-piece plastic container and then slide the two halves together. It was compact and safe. I would keep two straws in the other pocket. In later years I discovered Californian head shops, where simple grinders were on display in the window. Even smarter ones allowed you to grind out a dose and then quickly sniff it up, concealing the action behind a handkerchief. No visit to the loo, no waiting for said loo to empty so that the sounds of one's chopping and snorting went unnoticed, just a simple indiscernible action. Of course, buying such a thing and several spares too is an unspoken – even to oneself – concession of one's addiction.

Incidentally, using the phrase 'getting down to business' when describing a men's lavatory may seem a little

* As with smartphones, coke lore had it that storing the damp wrap in rice would eventually dry it out, but it never worked for me.

'ho ho', but during the 1980s the epidemic of cocaine fever sweeping through the mewses, squares and side-streets of Mayfair had reached such a pitch that I remember sitting one evening in the bar of the wildly successful nightclub Annabel's when a friend, a great wit, known by just about everyone in the world of London fashion and parties, a man one could genuinely call a play-boy, came up from the men's room with a look of outrage on his face.

'Do you know what just happened?' he asked, a frown of indignant disgust clouding his otherwise fair features.

'No.'

'Some arsehole just came into the coke-room while I was chopping out a line and, without so much as a by-your-leave, he took his cock out and had a piss in one of those porcelain bowl things ... I mean, should we get Mark to fling the man out and have him thrashed on the steps of the club?'

That really is how prevalent the white stuff was then and how utterly unremarkable the taking of it in public was. Inasmuch as the gentlemen's lavatories of Annabel's can ever be called public.

Incidentally, some of the paragraphs above look like I am writing out a template of instructions and encour-aging advice for the coke novice. It should go without saying and must be apparent if you read on and find out what damage I believe this noxious yet maddeningly be-guiling substance did to me that *I wouldn't recommend cocaine to my worst enemy*. Which won't, of course, stop someone taking it out of context and damning me. Goes with the turf. Chap gets used to it. Barely a day goes by without someone on Twitter favouring me with the information that 'I thought better of you than that' – the 'that' being anything from passing on the blandest of off-colour jokes, to employing a swear word that 'offends' them (don't get me started), to using a epithet that apparently slights a minority of some kind. Which I don't really get. 'God, there have been a lot of clever yids' doesn't seem in the least problematic. Nor does 'Amazing how many of the greatest ever American comedians have been kikes – must be something to do with their 2,000-year need to stay together and keep themselves amused', or whatever. Perfectly charming observations that don't need someone to say, 'Excuse me, those words are offensive. Kindly use the word "Jews" or better still the phrase "Jewish people",' (as if the latter takes the sting out of being a Jew, as if even that word is too strong). 'All Jewish people should be beaten up' and 'Fucking Jews run everything – you know they conspire to keep others out?' How is it better that whoever writes something so ghastly is using 'acceptable' words? It is the sentiment expressed that is repulsive or not repulsive, not the words. Hell, I'm turning into a foaming 'political correctness gone mad' animal. I shall shush on that topic. Paraphernalia then is described not for the purposes of an instruction manual, but as a warning: permanent sniffles, blood from the nose and other unwelcome parts, sleeplessness, diarrhoea, head-aches, itchy skin . . . and on top of these indignities, that of dealing with your dealer. We'll come to that interest-ing, intriguing and inscrutable being in a little while. Hold that thought.

Unexpected Diversion Ahead

Now this section isn't a diary (diary entries lie up ahead, waiting for you) but I do feel I have to insert here, by way of flavour, the unexpected nature of today, this day of my writing this sentence. A not untypical day in my life except for one rare but wild circumstance. In this inter-ruption itself, as throughout the book, there will be plenty of unexpected excursions, which I hope will not annoy.

I awoke early this morning, still tingling. Last night I experienced one of the strongest manic episodes of my life. It had been stealing up on me for some days, but last night I felt almost possessed. I texted everyone I knew furiously, knowing that safety with cyclothymia (my par-ticular variation of Bipolar Disorder) lies in the support of friends and family. They can tell from one's voice how over-sharp the edge of hysteria might be and talk one down or insist upon one accepting help. Hypomania (I know, one would have thought it should be called hyper-mania) often presents with a euphoric need to be in touch with people and a garrulity and excitable chattering manner that can make one barely comprehensible. It is, I am told, much harder to live with someone manic than someone depressed. The worst state for a family member, spouse or companion to deal with is the transitional mood that develops as one cycles between the two. I realized last night that this was what I had been going through the previous week, when I had felt angry and prickly about everything. I was energetic but in what you might call a negative manner.

But last night I was so charged, flying so high, feeling so positive and convinced of my worth that I suddenly understood historical figures like Joan of Arc and the wild prophetic ravings of Howard Beale, the radiant seer of broadcasting played so memorably by Peter Finch in his posthumous Oscar-winning last hurrah in *Network*. I'm sure you remember the scene where, raincoat over pyjamas, he comes dripping and possessed into the network building to take up his position in the newsroom as anchorman and, live on air, stands with arms outstretched exhorting all his viewers to go to their windows and shout, 'I'm mad as hell and I'm not going to take this any more!' God knows what drivel I might have come out with had I been in front of a camera last night.

If I didn't have a tiny core of sanity inside me I quite seriously would have believed myself imbued with some great spirit. Only those who have endured, or perhaps enjoyed, hypomania will understand quite what I mean. I am still today rattling away at top speed, though I dare say I will come back to revise this passage when I've either floated down (as I earnestly hope) or crashed to earth (as I worriedly fear).*

The nature of depression, mania's sinister twin, is that it is opposite in *every* regard. The one gives you hope and a vainglorious, grandiose belief in the future; the other convinces you of life's entire and eternal futility. The one gives an urge to communicate by text, letter, phone call, Twitter and personal visit. The other casts one alone into a darkened room, refusing visitors and rolling away to turn one's back on those poor concerned ones who love you and want to speak to you. Two poles.

So, I repeat. Yesterday was as high a day as can be. As a matter of fact I went to see my team, Norwich City, suffer a catastrophic and wholly undeserved defeat at Craven Cottage, the home ground of Fulham Football Club. How we will avoid the drop from Premiership to Championship I don't know.† But that is entirely another matter, and one that holds no interest for you. I mention it only because being in the directors' box in the company of Delia Smith and fellow board members and club staff allowed me to squawk and scream and jabber and joke and yell and yodel without it seeming the least odd. By the time I got home, undefeated even by the terrible loss of the match, I found myself in a state of unparalleled OCD busy-ness.

*I haven't . . . except to correct hasty typos.
†We didn't.

You will have the pleasure of learning more about my strange mind later as we go, but for the remainder of yesterday evening I polished shoes, tidied cupboards, reorganized stationery, cleared clutter and cooked a supper which took about half an hour to plate up, so fantastically symmetrical and exquisitely layered were its ingredients.

When I had finished this Adrian Monkish meal I began to feel my hands shaking, the blood singing in my head and a pressure pushing down on my chest. I was alone that evening so I set about sending long, long texts to those I knew best. I told them that I was manic, but that I was safe and had no feeling that I was going to do something mad, embarrassing or unsafe. Finally, I took the decision to text my psychiatrist, who was just returning from Marseilles, and he texted back with a suggested tweak to my medication and instructions to call him tomorrow, Sunday, by which time he would be home.

I slept well last night despite such an extraordinary and quite unexpected swing of the internal weather-vane. This morning I worked on a passage of this book, words tumbling furiously from me. I do hope, by the way, that this doesn't show. Marry in haste, repent at leisure, as Congreve wrote. Tweet in haste, repent at leisure, as I have learned. Sorely. Write in haste, revise at leisure, as experience has also taught me. 'I can write drunk, but must revise sober,' F. Scott Fitzgerald is said to have told his editor, Maxwell Perkins.

At two-thirty in the afternoon I slipped into a good shirt, knotted the silk salmon-pink and cucumber-green Garrick Club tie around my neck, selected some unassuming trousers and a pleasing jacket and trotted over to the Criterion Theatre, that little Thomas Verity jewel-box right by Eros* on Piccadilly Circus. The bar next to the theatre (the Cri, as it used to be known in its late-Victorian, early-Edwardian heyday, the age and locus of Wodehouse's Hon. Galahad Threepwood and his nemesis, Sir Gregory Parsloe-Parsloe) is where Doctor Watson met up with his old dresser from Barts Hospital, 'young Stamford', who was to go on that very afternoon to introduce him to Sherlock Holmes. So for me, despite the hordes of Chupa Chups-coloured tourists who clamber up to be photographed as they mime sucking the aluminium figure's elegantly veiled little dick while fingering his pert botty,† carelessly breaking the bowstring as they do so, despite their moronic, thoughtless littering of the surrounding area and despite at night drunks pissing into the trough at the base of the bronze fountain, despite all this, Piccadilly Circus – 'the hub of the Empire', as they used to call it – is sacred turf to me. Sacred paving, I should say.

---

*Technically Anteros, of course, but what the hey?

†The second best in central London. The best is, of course, that of the young man memorializing the Machine Gun Corps in Wellington Place. His matchlessly perfect buttocks present themselves to anyone travelling south along Park Lane towards Hyde Park Corner. One never minds a red light there.

I have the honour of being the chairman of the Criterion Theatre. It involves little more than a board meeting every now and then, but it is such a beautiful playhouse, and it does give me a little kick to see my name in the back of the programme, lost in the tiny print somewhere amongst the producers, investors and other board members. Our proprietor is the munificent Sally Greene, whose bountiful patronage (should that have been proprietress and matronage?) has also breathed life into the Old Vic and the great Soho jazz club, Ronnie Scott's.

So, I arrive at the theatre and descend to the stalls (the Criterion is one of the rare theatres where everything is underground: bars, dressing rooms, stage and auditorium) for an afternoon celebrating the life of the actor Richard Briers, who died some months ago. He was a fellow Garrickian, hence the choice of tie. Everyone who worked with him and is still breathing seems to be here. Pennies Wilton and Keith, Peters Egan and Bowles, Dickie's wife Annie, of course, his daughters and grandchildren and the great Sir Kenneth Branagh, a man as busy, if not busier, than I am, and whom I rarely get to see these days. Before the event begins I stand gabbling away with him, for once matching him in verbal pace and energy. I tell him of my current mental state. Like so many he responds with understanding and experience, recommending, of all things, meditation. The Kenneth Branagh I knew in the days of the film *Peter's Friends* would have sprayed out his tea derisively at the idea of meditation and embarked upon a hilarious, vituperative and brilliant extemporized monologue exposing the idiocy of staring at nothing and chanting, 'Om mani padme hum.' This is one of the many things I enjoy about ageing: I discover that I am so much less likely to find things twatty, pretentious and scorn-inducing, and I must assume KB feels the same.

Just as the houselights dim I approach the stalls seats from the wrong end and have to scuttle all the way round. I am rewarded with a hard glare from Penelope Keith, who is well known for . . . well. It is not my place to say.

She reads, however, the verse that Sir Henry Irving wrote as a farewell on his final stage appearance – a plea for the public to be charitable to lesser-known actors – very well. Everyone in fact is on top form as they summon up memories of a man who charmed all who knew him and swore more regularly and fantastically than anyone I ever met. Never having met myself, who would count as the one exception, I might boldly claim. Although the best swear I ever heard came from a close friend of both mine and Ken's, an actor who, forgetting his lines on a film set, reprimanded himself with the savage cry of 'Cunting Auschwitz!' Being Jewish, he could get away with it, I suppose. Just. But it's a curse one needs to keep for a serious moment of distress or fury, one can't but feel. For this person, forgetting his lines while filming was as serious and infuriating as anything could ever be. I am afraid I am more dilettante about such occasional lapses.

A remembrance of a much-loved man without a dud moment, although it is KB who, family aside, wins the afternoon by several lengths. Celebrations, memorials, funerals and charitable evenings are not competitive, you are thinking. To an actor, let me assure you, every single opportunity to open your mouth and perform to an audience alongside other actors is always a fierce and biting adversarial combat, and do not believe anyone who tells you otherwise.

Every story Ken tells about Briers (whose career direction he helped transform astoundingly to the extent of casting him, very successfully, as King Lear) I have heard many times before, yet I am reduced to an asthma attack strong enough to need a gulp or two on the inhaler I laugh so much and so uncontrollably. Branagh is always referred to as an exemplum of the self-regarding thespian lovie, or luvvie, or however you choose to spell it. This is rather unfortunate for me, since the Oxford English Dictionary cites *my* employment of the word (as it is commonly understood in reference to the acting trade) as the first known publicly printed usage. As a matter of fact, if he belongs to any class or subspecies of actor at all, I would say that Kenneth is blokey rather than luvvie. He is also – and for some reason people find this hard to believe – amongst the five funniest people I have ever met. We'll meet him again later in this unpredictably juggled narrative too.

I am sitting next to the legendary Frank Finlay, who

barks out the occasional laugh. I cannot say that he was entirely friendly to me when I breathlessly took my seat at the last minute, but then he is a devout Roman Catholic and perhaps he has heard of the debate in which I argued alongside Christopher Hitchens against the proposition that the Catholic Church is a force for good in the world. The number of people since who have accused me of being 'anti-Catholic' depresses and upsets me. Perhaps someone reported to him that I had rudely insulted the Mother of Churches and had harsh words for the pontiff (at that time Joseph Ratzinger, Benedict XVI, RC Ret'd).

I leave the event speedily to avoid being stuck with too many people. I am sure there is no one there whose company I am specifically avoiding, but I want to come back to this: the computer screen. My mind is still spinning, but I seem to need to share my afternoon with you, the uncomplaining reader.

The Richard Briers afternoon was typical in some ways of the kind of event that actors attend. Gossip and tales of thespian tradecraft and unspeakable theatrical disasters are told, retold and mistold. Academics, spies, doctors and lawyers are no different, give or take the dictates of their professional ethics. My life is so fragmented that I live the life of an actor and then the next day another life entirely. It may be the life of a writer or that of a sort of television presenter and host; I dine with classical musicians, with restaurateurs, playmates from the old drug days, plain downright socialites, chefs, fellow cricket lovers and new-found friends from the world of online networking. Unlike an envied and admirable few, I separate my friends and almost never dare mingle one group with another. When I do, it is usually a social disaster, like mixing drinks. I love good beer and I love good wine, but you cannot drink both on the same evening without suffering. I love the friends with whom I play or once daily played snooker and tooted quantities of high-grade pulverized Andean flake; I love the friends with whom I dine at preposterously expensive restaurants; I love the friends with whom I'm film-making or mincing on the stage. I love and value them all equally and don't think of them as stratified or in tiers, one group in some way higher or more important than the rest, but the thought of introducing them to each other makes me shiver and shudder with cringing embarrassment.

So today I walked away from the theatre, stopped off at a passing supermarket to buy some ice, turkey breast and tomatoes – an entirely random raid – and found myself, after I had escaped the usual struggle with the automated checkout (unexpected item in the bagging area *again*), trotting along the street in the company of the sartorially point-device Peter Bowles and the ever gentlemanly Moray* Watson†. For a hundred yards I was an actor, as I

* Pronounced like the mint you were a long time ago urged not to hurry and Andy the tennis champion.
† Moray played the definitive Colonel Bantry all those years ago with Joan Hickson's equally definitive Miss Marple.

tattled and swapped anecdotes with them before peeling off and making my way home and finding myself here. Still high on my own erratic and mercurial endorphins, I sit myself before you and think about what to write next.

We shall pick up the thread and theme of this chapter.

I mentioned in my list of shame that amongst the places I had taken cocaine was the House of Commons, and this is true. I was sitting in a low, satisfyingly old and comfortable leather armchair after a pleasant, but not too pleasant – it is a club after all – lunch with a Member – we needn't drag his name into it – and expressed a wish, as we swirled our brandies happily around, to betake myself for a young piddle. The MP pointed me to a door at the corner of the room and told me to take the second right in the corridor which would present itself. I swaggeringly entered until I saw to my alarm that this was a urinal only lavatory. And only one urinal at that. No single stall with a door. The shit, as William Morris predicted so accurately all those years ago in his utopian novel *News from Nowhere*, must be confined to the Chamber, I thought. So, heart beating like an engine, with the slightly trembling devil-may-care desperation of the true druggy, I wiped dry of condensation the rear section of the top of the urinal with the back of my tie, chopped a line there, drew out my straw and was just bringing it up to my nose when a merry, florid, well-lunched parliamentarian who would never see seventy again came in, humming happily.

'Sorry!' I said, in a rather muffled way, my shoulders shielding my shameful line. 'Thing is, silly I know. But I'm a little pee-shy. If there's someone waiting it just won't come.'

'Quite understand,' the man said cheerfully, backing out. 'You wait till you get to my age. Damned prostate won't let you get a drop out unless you curse and cajole it. Carry on.'

I took my courage in one hand and my straw in the other and with a sort of coughing House of Commons 'hear, hear!' roar, sucked in the line and straightened up. The old buster lurking outside was still tunefully and now tactfully humming. I swept away what little residue there was with my index finger, gummed it, contrived to achieve a genuine desultory wee and noticed in shame that I had left rather a puddle for this man's feet. I dived for the taps and the towels and made my escape back to the Smoking Room, as I seem to remember it was called in those days. It is probably known as the Herbal Tea Salon now.

Truss, Tweed and Intoxication

I may have mentioned before in book, blog or broadsheet that, as I grew to fame, I became more and more astonished at how even apparently observant and intelligent journalists would either tell blind lies, fail to notice the obvious or deviously ignore what was before them because it didn't fit with an image that they or their editor wished to project.

One sunny morning I was assigned to be 'profiled' by Lynne Truss, formerly my literary editor on the *Listener* magazine and soon to achieve fame in all English-speaking territories and beyond on account of her *Eats, Shoots and Leaves*, a declaration of war on what for linguists and those who love language are the ever-dancing, ever-dazzling, ever-changing particles, diacriticals, apostrophes and mutations that allow language to live, breathe, thrive and evolve. But that's another story. Lynne and I were to meet at the then very fashionable L'Escargot restaurant in Greek Street, run by Nick Lander. Lander's wife, Jancis Robinson, Master of Wine, caused L'Escargot to be, unless I am wildly mistaken, the first British restaurant whose wine menus were listed varietally.* You're very bored now, and I can see why. I am getting there.

So I arrive, and the delightfully frisky and beaming four-foot-nine-inch figure of Elina Salvoni, the maîtresse d', is there to welcome me. Lynne is already at the table. Now, a month or so earlier I had decided that it was about time to transform myself. I do this from time to time, rather like Doctor Who, only not like him at all. I had reinvented myself from nerdy bookworm to thief and

---

* In other words by grape variety – Sauvignon Blanc, Shiraz, Merlot, etc. – as opposed to the confusing traditional British manner of listing by estate without any mention of the grape. This once pioneering approach is now standard practice, of course.

convict, from thief and convict back to nerdy bookworm, from nerdy bookworm to tra-la-la acting and writing performer, from tra-la-la acting and writing performer to nerdy first-adopting computer user, and so on. And within those transmogrifications were so many more. My most recent mutation was from ponderous, tweedy, pipe-smoking paragon of pomposity resembling nothing so much as a Latin teacher at a school which was just going to be closed down in a blaze of scandal to leather-jacketed, jeans-wearing, trail-bike-riding, aftershave-slapping dude who knew which bands were going to be the Next Big Thing and could wear shades indoors without looking a prick. I know what you're thinking: every fibre of your being must be screaming that this must not be so, but for a year or so that is in truth how I was.

The fact is (I'm sure I shouldn't be so forward as to call it Fry's Law), such drastic and dramatic outward differences cut no ice at all. Any more than cosmetic surgery would have turned Heinrich Himmler into a pleasant companion for a spring walking tour of butterfly-filled alpine meadows.

Anyway, at the L'Escargot restaurant, I checked in my 'skid-lid', as we crazy two-wheeler sons of bitches called them, and joined Ms Truss at her table. We chatted amiably, old colleagues. I had a book to sell; perhaps it was my first novel, *The Liar*, I can't remember. She seemed very enthusiastic, the lunch and the Sémillon were well above par. Princess Diana shyly swept up to the first-floor dining room; security men dotted discreetly about down-stairs and upstairs tables, rendered conspicuous by their inconspicuousness. That was fashionable London in the 1980s for you. I had another appointment, and my Yamaha beast was growling for release in Soho Square, so I escaped the confining truss of Lynne and roared away, thinking little of the encounter.

Two weeks later the issue of the magazine Lynne had been writing for came out. The first words of her copy?

'Tweedy Stephen Fry . . .'

I had sat in front of her, radiating Guerlain *Eau de Verveine*, a goatskin US Airforce Golden Bear bomber jacket creaking and gleaming about my person before I took it off and hung it on the chair to reveal the pure white, captionless T-shirt beneath, a pack of Marlboro Red tucked, Brando-styley, into the sleeve. My legs were sheathed in Levi 501s and my feet shod in acid-resistant, heavy-duty Doc Marten working boots, the footjoy of choice for any Soho media fashionista (not a word yet in currency then) or fashionisto (not a word yet in currency now). The front upper of the left boot was already worn from gear-changing my hog, and the first word she can come up with is *tweedy*? Well, who am I to tell her that she is wrong? Webster was much possessed by death. He saw the skull beneath the skin. Or so claimed T. S. Eliot. Maybe Truss saw the tweed beneath the leather jacket and boots. Where others have cartilage and sinew, I have corduroy and cavalry twill, it seemed, and always will. We see in people what we want to see, and nothing can change that.

The first rule of being a rebel is that you can't *make* yourself a rebel. It is an action not an identity, a process not a title. You *rebel.* When I was a distressed, confused, manic, disruptive and disrupted schoolboy, rebellion did not come as a choice.

It is extraordinary how some single concentrated occasions seem to combine so many features of your life in one dreadful moment so as to stand as symbolic of your entire character and destiny at that point in time.

There came one such critical culmination of all that I was in the summer of 1989. I found myself in a restaurant in Soho's Dean Street, an establishment long since passed into memory. It was called Burt's, I think in honour of Burt Shevelove, the little-remembered (by most) lyricist and librettist – *No, No, Nanette* and *A Funny Thing Happened on the Way to the Forum*, those kinds of works. We had booked the whole of Burt's to give Kenneth Branagh some kind of stag party, for this was a Saturday night, and he was to wed Emma Thompson on Sunday at Cliveden, the country house hotel that once belonged to the Astor family and gave its name to a 'set' of supposedly appeasement and Germanophile aristocrats and politicians that flourished in the 1930s.*

---

* As in Ishiguro's *The Remains of the Day*, only more lively and convivial.

All the details are on the clapperboard.

Quiet, dignified downtime: Eilean Aigas, Inverness-shire, 1993.

Hugh, perfectionist as he is, always stays within his character: a drivelling poltroon from dawn to dusk while *Jeeves and Wooster* was being filmed . . .

Everyone always anxious to sit next to me on the *Jeeves and Wooster* set.

Official publicity still for *Jeeves and Wooster*. I remember it as if it were twenty-five years ago.

Filming *Jeeves and Wooster* at Farnham, 1989. Sister Jo visiting the set.

Giving Charlie Laurie his daily vodka and yogurt smoothie. Christmas, 1988.

It's that butch look. Christmas, 1988.

Newborn Charlie Laurie, adoring godparent, 1988.

My butch look,
1987.

Hysteria publicity shot, 1991.

Backstage at a *Hysteria* benefit show. Sadler's Wells, 1989.

Reading at, I think, a *Hysteria* show.

(*See over*) I know what you're thinking, and you're to stop it, January 1991.

All week Hugh, Rowan and my fellow Blackadderists had been rehearsing the final episode of *Blackadder Goes Forth*, so by the time we got down to Soho from Television Centre and the tech rehearsal we were rather tired. I had ridden in on my rearing, snarling trail-bike, which I parked dead opposite the restaurant in Bourchier Street, commonly known as piss alley. I worry to this day whether the lane's official name should be pronounced as spelled, 'Boor-she-A', or weirdly to rhyme with 'voucher'. The trouble is, I don't suppose there is anyone alive who can tell me the answer. I only fret over this question because a) I am a verbal nerd who does get in a tizzy about such things and b) I once judged a reading competition at Harrow School which was called the Lady Bourchier Reading Prize and was most definitely pronounced to rhyme with Sloucher and Croucher, solicitors at law and notaries public. I awarded one of the schoolboys, who went by the exotic name of Benedict Cumberbatch, second prize. *Second*. I cannot remember the name of the boy who won first, but I hope he will suddenly burst on to the acting scene, blow Benedict out of the water and finally vindicate my judgement. Something tells me that the contingency is a remote one, and I shall continue to look upon myself as the fisherman who let the big one go.

Whichever and however I parked my Yamaha, conveniently facing the entrance to Burt's restaurant, where Kenneth Branagh and friends were celebrating his last night as a bachelor.

I fully intended to be a good boy that night, for the following day we would be recording that last episode of the series *Blackadder Goes Forth*. I drank no more than a few vodka and tonics, my favoured drink back then, before turning to give Ken his obligatory farewell hug.

'Here,' said Ken, 'have this.' He passed me a large glass half full of whisky.

'I really . . .'

'Go on! Down in one.'

'Oh well, here goes.'

I swallowed it all down and weaved my way through to collect the skid-lid and gauntlets that, together with the previously described goatskin leather jacket, were all that might come between me and a skin-peeling 'moment', as two-wheel riders call anything from a slight loss of the back wheel to a somersault over the front on to the road.

This was a time when motorbikes swarmed over London streets. The *soi-disant* service industries were thriving in post-Big-Bang Thatcherite Britain, especially, of course, in London. The internet was in its hobbyist infancy, and fax machines were limited. I described the ubiquity of the motorcycle courier in the still in-print and still entirely fascinating *Fry Chronicles*. The noise and smell of them was all-pervasive (the motorbikes, not the chronicles, which are but lightly and pleasantly perfumed) and library footage of the era reminds one with a start how empty of them the metropolis now is. The delivery of scripts and documents could be achieved no other way, and many a student topped up his savings by haring about the city on delivery runs with scant regard to his or her or pedestrian safety.

I suppose we riders were easy meat for the busies.

I crossed Dean Street, pulling on the gauntlets and pushing the tightly fitting crash helmet down over my head with a smack on its crown, unjacked the beast and swung my leg over. I started the engine and was just easing forwards when a heavy hand descended on each shoulder. Fuck, I was going to be mugged. My adored motorcycle was going to be stolen. If I revved the engine and tried to escape, the bike would jerk forwards, and I would be left behind in Wile E. Coyote midair before thumping to earth with a coccyx-jarring thud.

I turned to face the aggressor.

Double fuck and twenty rotten arseholes. Uniformed police. What the hell?

Another constable stepped forwards from the shadows, signalling with a throat slit gesture for me to cut the engine. I complied, jacked the bike up, prepared a charming and conciliatory smile and pulled off the helmet.

The helmet, most unfortunately, almost airtight with the visor drawn down – which it had been – released right into the face of Second Constable a warm aromatic ball of something malty, peaty and Scottish.

'Oh dear. Oh dear, oh dear, oh dear,' said Second Constable to First. 'Whisky.'

First Constable had released his grip from my shoulders and allowed me to swing from the bike.

A van was parked opposite the Groucho Club.

'You seemed to be tottering a little unsteadily as you crossed the street to your motorcycle, sir,' First Constable explained.

I knew he was giving me his 'due cause' explanation. Since the repeal of the ancient sus laws, which had given the police the right to stop anyone 'on suspicion', a plausible reason had to be given. The police are very good at plausible reasons. *Not the Nine O'Clock News* had made merry fun with them on that very head some years earlier: 'walking in a built-up area in a loud shirt', and so forth. It was no good my protesting that I hadn't 'tottered' in the least. Crossing a street while donning a crash helmet is not a task easily undertaken, and while I may have wound and woven this way and that a little, it was certainly not in a manner that would cause a reasonable onlooker to suspect me of being inder the unfluence, ossifer. But none of this was of any use: they had me and doubtless they were going to invite me to blow down a tube of some kind.

Two vodka and tonics (doubles) and one very large whisky. Would that propel me over the limit? It was shock enough to think that a bike rider would be stopped at all. One of the reasons I had bought the damned thing, I reflected, was that I had had the idea that it would offer me a modicum of freedom from police interference.

A white tube was attached to a device, and I was invited to exhale.

'This reading indicates that your blood alcohol level is over the legal limit for the operation of a licensed motorized road vehicle, sir. We will now take you to the main station, where you will be asked to offer another breath sample to a Lionizer machine. This will be compared to the reading you have given us. The lower of the two readings will be used. If you do not wish to blow into the Lionizer, a blood or urine sample is acceptable. Failure, however, to provide any of these is a criminal offence. Do you understand this, sir?'

I nodded. Second Constable took my helmet and gloves, opened the rear doors of the van and hauled himself in. I was invited to sit on the bench opposite him. First Constable went round to the driver's seat, and we moved off. It was only as we turned right into Old Compton Street, which you could do in those days, that I realized my predicament. In my left-hand jacket pocket was a condom holder containing three grams of the best-quality cocaine, bought yesterday with a view to larks and fun at Cliveden. Surely I was certain to be searched or asked to empty my pockets when we got to the station?

I slowly moved my right hand to the jacket's right pocket, where I had some mints. This, I hoped, was where a decade of being obsessive about magic might pay off. I pulled out the mints and offered the bag to Second Constable, while at the same time putting my other hand into the left pocket and curling my fingers around the condom holder. A very simple act of misdirection which seemed to work.

'Thank you, sir. And if you don't mind, I'll keep these. Nothing is allowed in your mouth until you have completed the Lionizer test. I'm sure you understand.'

'Of course.' I spread both hands wide in a gesture of complete comprehension. The condom holder was now on my lap and I was leaning forwards, allowing the groin-crease of my trousers to conceal it in the half light of the police van. 'So which station are we going to, if I may ask, officer?'

'West End Central,' was the reply.

West End Central. How grand. I had heard of it. The name cropped up in news reports and police dramas. George Dixon (of Dock Green) would often say to his son-in-law, Detective Sergeant Crawford (played by the eyebrowy Peter Byrne), 'Now, now, Andy, we don't want to go treading on West End Central's corns,' and things like that. Famous as it might be, I had no idea where it was. Somewhere central in the West End would be a good guess. It was a pleasant surprise when we drew up in Savile Row.

As I had hoped, Second Constable rose to his feet before me. I stood up fractionally later, just as the brakes were applied. I slapped my hand to the metal roof of the van, and my right foot stamped forwards to give me balance.

'Oops,' I said cheerfully. My foot had kicked the condom holder deep into the shadows below the bench I had sat upon. Surely it would not be discovered for a few days, by which time dozens of malefactors would have had rides in the van?

I sprang down and allowed myself to be led into the station. Relief flooded me. Whatever punishment might be meted out for the infraction of driving a motorbike with a glass or so more alcohol in the blood than was permitted could not compare to the scandal, shame, possible imprisonment and career ruination that would follow the discovery of three whole grams of a Class A drug on my person.

It was generally understood in the druggy world that one or two grams would be taken to be 'personal use' but that much more might be construed by a bolshy or ill-disposed policeman to be 'intent to supply'. The first might result in confiscation and a warning; the second would certainly, if the judge was in accord, lead to a prison sentence. Three grams lay on the borderline, and although my poor, stupid, addicted mind was running through a plan to get hold of my dealer between now and tomorrow, I felt well rid of my stash.

The Lionizer gave a reading that was jeeeyust over the limit, and I hoped for clemency. They led me into a room where a female sergeant was sitting across a desk. She asked me to empty my pockets. I complied with scrupulous obedience, turning the pockets inside out. From my inside jacket pocket I drew a wallet and four tickets for the following day's audience recording of *Blackadder Goes Forth*.

'Oh,' said the sergeant, 'you're doing another series, are you?'

The problem with new series of *Blackadder* as they came along was that people were used to the one before. They were never broadcast until all had been recorded, so when the audience came into the studio expecting to see Queenie's throne-room and Blackadder's low-beamed chamber, they were puzzled by the Regency wallpaper of Prince George's suite. Our audiences over the last few weeks had come expecting Mrs Miggins's pie shop, and we had to hope they would get used to Captain Blackadder's trench and Melchett and Darling's Staff HQ.

I saw my opportunity. We were given four studio tickets every week as a matter of course, and I hadn't yet thought about whom I might invite.

'Would you like to come along to a recording? It's at BBC Television Centre tomorrow evening. As it says on the tickets . . .' I pushed them forwards.

The sergeant looked up, and First and Second Constables nodded enthusiastically. They came forwards to collect one each, and she kept the remaining two for herself.

'Right,' she said. 'Well. You were over the limit, Mr Fry, so we will be charging you with the offence of driving or attempting to drive while above the legal limit or unfit through drink. It says on your driving licence that you live in Islington?'

Well, so much for the corruptibility of the Metropolitan Police. I was scandalized. Was no one to be mistrusted?

And so much too for the slow turning of the mills of justice. I would be expected to make an appearance on Monday morning, complete with insurance documents and licence, at Clerkenwell magistrates court, which, as it happened, was situated at the end of Duncan Terrace, where I was house-sitting for Douglas Adams. I was not to drive home on the motorbike, but could collect it the following day – Sunday – morning.

I descended the station steps, crash helmet and gauntlets under my arm, thinking furiously. I wanted the next day to drive my Aston Martin V8 Vantage to the BBC, and then after the *Blackadder* recording to 'motor down to Cliveden', as one imagined Asquiths and Grenfells doing, back in the palmy days. At some point I would need to meet up with one of my three tame coke dealers, who might be induced to rendezvous either at the BBC (in that event I must remember to get another studio ticket, I told myself: funny if they end up next to the policemen and -woman) or somewhere in Soho early the next day as I collected my bike. Perhaps they could come to Islington that night? Damn! I realized that I should have brought my mobile phone with me. I rarely took it on the bike, as its bulk prevented me taking anything else in the limited storage area. Anyway, I would somehow get hold of a wrap or two of good gear, get happily wrecked at Cliveden and then up early next morning, that is if I went to bed at all, and gun the Aston – perhaps for the last time in a year – back to London in time for my court appearance, which was fixed for 11 a.m.

Then another, truly dreadful thought crashed into my mind. Suppose they found the condom holder under the bench in the police van, saw that it contained drugs and then brushed it for fingerprints? As I had a criminal record,* mine would be on file. But no, if they picked it up, they wouldn't do so with gloves. It was a van, not a crime scene. They would be lucky to find any 'latents' surely?

'Mr Fry? Mr Fry?'

It was the police sergeant. I turned to see her standing at the bottom of the steps waving her arm above her head.

'Yes?' I approached her nervously.

'I believe you left this in the van, sir.' She pushed the condom holder into my hand.

'Er . . . I . . . thank you . . . the . . .'

'Be careful, sir. And thank you for the tickets.'

I simply did not know what to say. It was already too late to disown it. She turned with an inscrutable look on her face, leaving me standing there, my mouth opening and closing like a landed fish.

* See *Moab is My Washpot*.

128

A taxi was rattling towards me from the Piccadilly end, so I hailed it and climbed in. En route to Islington I privily and gingerly slid apart the two halves of the condom holder. There, perky as a stripper's tits, lay the three wraps. I could have sworn they winked at me.

To this day I am at a loss as to the how and the why and the what-the-hell of it all. Did the sergeant think it rude to open a private condom holder in this, the age of AIDS? Did she open it and think, hell, I'm about to go off duty, I just can't be arsed to bust this man. We already had the paperwork on the drink driving, so we had to follow through, but this . . . not inclined to blight his chances. I shall never know. Unless she happens to read this, in which case she is very welcome to be in touch.

I do not watch myself in old films or television programmes, or even new ones, unless I am in the cutting room and a part of the process of putting them together, but if I do catch (it is repeated so often) the final episode of *Blackadder Goes Forth*, the one which ends with the Blackadder trenchful finally truly going over the top and the image of a field of poppies bleeding through to the sound of raking machine-gun fire and a final mournful version of the Howard Goodall theme tune, if I do catch it or a scene from it, I cannot but say to myself, 'That was the day after I was busted for drink driving. The day after the woman police sergeant handed my coke back to me in a condom holder, cool as you please. And that evening I took the Aston down to Cliveden, parked it and partied through the night in honour of Emma and Ken's union. And the following day was the day I lost my licence for a year.'

Waiting for My Man

I have always, since I can remember, been a – what word does one choose? A handful? No, that's a bit nannyish. A rebel? Too cool. A transgressor? The John Buchan generation would've called me a wrong'un. An outsider is the closest I can come to it. Perhaps it is just that, as those who had the pleasure of reading the opening chapter of *The Fry Chronicles* will know, I was a pre-teen crazed with a love of sweets and never felt I had enough money for them; this triggered an addictive path upwards, a desire for the illicit and the unattainable. Next came cigarettes. Being caged in prison took my mind off this, and I concentrated on getting out and getting into university. Once at Cambridge, I barely drank anything more than coffee and certainly didn't take drugs: I just threw myself into comedy, drama, smoking and writing.

So, two or three years later – already lucky enough to have a TV show in Manchester with Ben Elton, Robbie Coltrane, Hugh Laurie and Emma Thompson – Hugh and I were also starting on *Blackadder II*. Physically, I was, if it can be believed now, lean; socially, given to few nocturnal exploits: parties, as I have said, being abhorrent to me.

But those two toots of cocaine had awoken a long-sleeping giant. The same dragon that got me expelled from so many schools and that landed me on the flagstones of a prison cell was beginning to uncoil and rear up at me, snorting flame.

I cannot understand why, from the earliest days of my childhood, I had always been a problem. No uncle, godfather or family friend or (thank heavens) family member dandled me on his knee in a way which would prissily be called by my generation 'inappropriate' and more gracefully by the younger generation 'awkward'. It is true that I had, from the first, grandiose plans to be a scholar, a writer, an actor, a somebody. But I was never discouraged in these fields of endeavour. Only my own frantic wild behaviour got in the way until it seemed, lying on that previously evoked straw-strewn prison floor, something in my brain snapped, and I knew that I had one last chance, if I may mangle Tennyson, to rise on the stepping stones of my dead self to higher things.

And so we come round again to the unbelievably good fortune to have got that scholarship to Cambridge, to have been all-consumed by the acting and then writing bug and foolishly to have allowed myself to believe that every problem, propensity to bad behaviour and temptation to library book theft and wild destructive pranks was way behind me. I didn't really like alcohol so very much; I didn't like late nights, I liked work. My last book, *The Fry Chronicles* (I'm simply astonished and only slightly wounded that you haven't read it), had written on its title page a line of Noël Coward's: 'Work is more fun than fun,' something I am lucky enough still to find true. 'Young men sow wild oats, old men grow sage,' Churchill is reputed to have said. It almost never is Churchill. In fact collectors of quotations call such laziness in attribution 'Churchillian creep'. I made the mistake of thinking all my oats were sown and falling asleep on my watch over myself.

Unless you have been a user of illegal, street, or recreational drugs yourself at any time in your life, you probably have a clear view in your head of what a drug dealer is like. As younglings we were sat in front of terrifying films and taught to call them 'pushers'; they were rated on a moral scale somewhere between Fleet Street royal correspondents and dung beetles.

'I Blame the Evil Pushers,' parents and editorial articles would squeal, wringing their clean hands in despair, incapable of even imagining such unalloyed evil. 'Pushers' hung around the school gates, waiting for a chance to get a child addicted. At first they weaned them on legal solvents like glue, fast-drying wet cement, toluene, butane and propane. Once the dopamine and norepinephrine and noradrenaline – I am not an endocrinologist, but drug use is all about the body's pleasure/reward system, as I'm sure we all know – have introduced themselves, offered a handshake and a moment of bliss, usually followed by a wild arc of vomiting, the substances bind themselves to the young users' brains, who find their pleasure centres tickled and massaged and unconditionally adored as they roll on the grass of the local park and look up at the sky with new loving eyes that ice cream and family life won't give them. Next, according to this mythical and inevitable wicked process (cheap cider aside, the most dangerous and most overlooked of them), illegal weed is offered and before the defenceless infant has a chance their 'friendly', 'low-price' suppliers are introducing them to cocaine and heroin. And once those dependencies are formed, the price ratchets up, the threats for non-payment become very real and Little Jack is raiding his mother's purse, burgling gran's flat, snatching mobile phones from younger kids, and the monstrous social malaise that we call drug culture is upon us. Sink estates, gangs and random violence, Ladybird Book Britain transformed into a moral, civil and derelict wasteland in fewer years than my lifetime, which, dear reader, despite this being my third autobiography, is not really so very long after all. That is what drugs have done to blight Britain.

All the foregoing is, of course, horse-shit. No, it's worse than horse-shit; horse-shit is strawy and pleasant smelling. It is human shit, which is malodorous in the extreme. Successive government-employed 'Drug Czars' who knew what they were talking about physiologically, sociologically and neurologically have been fired for telling their masters of either political stripe the real truth. If drugs are not soon legalized and controlled, taxed and categorized, the situation will get worse and worse and worse. Coca bushes are now immune to the vile airborne pesticides sent over from America to Colombia in the 1990s; the drug wars in war-torn Mexican drug-gang cities like Juárez in the noughties and teens of the twenty-first century make 1980s Medellín in Colombia look more like Moreton-in-Marsh in the Cotswolds; the profit margins have become so colossal that at every stage of 'cutting' or diminishing through additives the purity of the original cocaine block, each player in the journey from peasant leaf-grower up to the nightclub dealer is going to make a pleasant living.

From what I believe are unimpeachable sources, the end purity level for the user who doles out £50 or £60 for a gram (twenty-eight and a third grams constitute one old-fashioned imperial ounce) usually comes out at between 20 and 30 per cent. The dealer is a tiny fish in all this. He or she (and yes there are plenty of shes) may have taken a career path that goes something like this: not having done so well at school, they drifted perhaps into the music business as a DJ or bouncer and found that they liked a gram or two of coke in the evenings. So they went into business with an existing dealer they knew, having a different circle of friends. They told some of their friends they could be relied on for whatever they wanted, and those friends were overjoyed. It's a sellers' market, they don't need to push drugs on people. They are more likely to need to push people *away*. They frequently don't have enough on them to supply a clubful of desperate potential clients (dealers often like to use the word client) keen to party away.

I cannot tell you much about what goes on further up the chain. Of course, there is violence, just as there was in America during the blockheaded days of Prohibition. A gap is left when a desired substance is banned; that gap will offer such profits that no amount of violence will be considered too great to get hold of a great share of the market. But I can tell you I have yet to meet a doctor, policeman or probation officer who does not believe that street drugs should be licensed, legalized and controlled. Only politicians who stick their fingers in their ears and go 'La, la, la, la!' until they think the people who actually understand the problem will shut up are obsessed with the unwinnable 'war on drugs'. That, of course, is because voters are misguided.

Aside from anything else, just think what coke is cut with in order to maximize profits at every stage. In my early days it used to be baby laxative, with an all-too predictable outcome. More recently sugars, creatine, benzocaine (to mimic the numbing effect on the lips that makes you think you are getting plenty of the real deal) were favoured and especially these days levasimole, a cow dewormer, is now found in anything from 50 to 90 per cent of street cocaine. Not only does it dilute, but it also uses its own properties to stimulate and set off our inbuilt happy drug, dopamine. Other additives include hydrochloric acid and potassium permanganate. Not nice.

If alcohol were banned today, you can be sure criminal gangs would do the same with their bathtub gins and moonshine whiskies. Ethyl and isopropyl alcohol, methylated spirits and all kinds of cheapening and dangerous additives would go into the illicit brews. We know this because history has shown us that it was so. Cocktails were invented to sweeten and diversify the rancid effects of chokingly foul speakeasy booze.

But let us return to the dealer – Mitch, Nando or Jacquie we'll call them. I have known dozens of Mitches, Nandos and Jacquies in my time. Not one of them violent, not one of them morally inferior to me or anyone else I know. In fact they have often stood out as incredibly decent friends, wonderful parents, kind, attentive, funny people, no more branded with the Mark of (Co) Cain than your mother is.

Business is straightforward. You, the user, have your wad of cash; you meet in a café, bar, the dealer's flat or (less likely) at your home. If it is a public place or space, you have already secreted the money in a newspaper, which you oh so casually slide across the table towards Nando, and he returns by pushing over a packet of cigarettes which contains the gear. This is followed by talk of football, music, fashion, gossip, friends, children and a hasty draining of the cappuccino mug before we go our separate ways. Most dealers follow the rule 'don't get high on your own supply', but a user will be slightly uneasy in the presence of a Mitch or Jacquie who *never* took a line. At their flat, say, when you pop by. On the other hand, one tends not to like a dealer to come to one's own house, especially dealers who really like the stuff. How do you converse with them in a personal way? When is it decent to ask them to leave? How much of the expensive powder that you have bought from them and are now sharing with them is she going to hoover up? All in all, it is a most strange unwritten contract. You are anxious not to treat them like servants and probably overdo the deliberately non-patronizing talk, just as one does in conversation with bin-men and builders, yet all the while one is slave to them and the service they provide.

There has only ever been one significant and maddening problem with dealers: it is almost unique to them as a class and it drives one *insane*. Punctuality. Hence the quotation from Lou Reed that heads this section. The poor, late-lamented rock god must have put together, as have I, hours on street corners, in cafés and bars wondering if ever the *hell* they'll come. Have they been arrested? With your phone number in their directory? Please God they use a code name for me . . .

I know you want to think of the dealer as the evil link in this chain, but the truth is dealers spend most of their time pushing clients away. Their phones are ever buzzing (pagers back in the day): 'I need four grams now, where can I meet you?' 'Be at the usual café at ten.' 'I'm having a party tonight, six of us want two grams each.' The dealer dashes from client to client, getting cash up front before they can then visit *their* suppliers (who are the big, scary, silent ones who don't take credit and you really don't want to mess with), pick up the gear, go back home to cut it to whatever degree they can get away with, fold it into wraps before haring round town, dropping off to each client as discreetly as possible. That is your average dealer, caught between gangsters and clients. It's a sellers' market, yes, but that doesn't make life easy. They never have enough to meet demand. Some bullying rock star, pockets stuffed with currency notes, will catch sight of them and buy all they've got: 'No, but I've promised Jack and Rosie and Bill and Tom . . .' the dealer will protest, but to no avail. Now he or she has to start the whole process again. *That* is why they are always late. No wonder Lou Reed wrote that song.

A dealer's five minutes is therefore, if you're lucky, an hour and a half. Well, you have to wait for the good things in life, I suppose. A pleasure deferred is a pleasure increased.

The good things in life? A pleasure? Stephen, have you run mad? Are you telling your readers that cocaine is one of the good things in life?

No, no I'm not. Do believe me. I'm treading that difficult balance here. When I started taking coke my life was more or less perfect. I had enjoyed preposterous success.

So let us just return one more time to that first evening, where our actor friend introduced our little group to two lines of coke. I think – if I remember it rightly, and you really must forgive me either if my memory is faulty *or* if it is correct – I think that I wanted from that moment to define myself as a coke user. What a ludicrous and incomprehensible ambition. Many of my 'life choices', looking back, have been incomprehensible from today's viewpoint, so this is just one more. Perhaps a little more sensational, but no less incapable of understanding.

A few days after my first encounter with the Devil's Dandruff, as Robin Williams so memorably dubbed South America's glittering granular gift to the global billions, I embarked upon the first of what were to become regular appearances on Ned Sherrin's Saturday-morning BBC Radio 4 programme *Loose Ends*, along with Emma Freud, Victoria Mather, Victor Lewis-Smith, Brian Sewell, Robert Elms and many others. I had invented for the show a character called Donald Trefusis, who claimed to be a fellow of St Matthew's College Cambridge and the Regius Professor of Philology there. I used him as a vehicle for what may as well be described as derision or querulous indignation about this Thatcherite thing or that dismal dumbing-down disaster that was beginning to infect the BBC. Being in my early twenties but satirizing in the voice of a piping old man somehow took a lot of the offence out of what I was writing. My natural speaking voice at the time, when I hear it now as it might

sionally survive on some scrap of old MP3 or You-
be material, shocks me with its fey public-school
youthfulness. You will be happy to know that a collection
of the Professor's thoughts is still available in the in-print
masterpiece *Paperweight*. The ideal lavatory book, and one
where you can decide for yourself how the voices of
Trefusis and other characters I made up should sound.
While in mercantile mood, I believe there is an audio
book on the market too, read by myself. All proceeds to
the cattery of your choice. That is negotiable. Actual offer
may vary. Terms and conditions apply.

I am not comfortable writing about the dead, or upsetting the public's preconceived view of them, but I noticed
in the Broadcasting House studio the Saturday following
my coke experiment that there was a little flake of white
in Someone Who Shall Remain Nameless's nostril and
the occasional telltale snuffle. At the George, the pub
round the corner from Broadcasting House we all flocked
to after a recording, I managed to get SWSRN aside and
shyly asked if he could recommend a dealer.

'Oh my dear,' SWSRN said, putting his hand on my leg
and shooting an almost pitying smile at my naïveté, 'you
couldn't do better than ask Mitch.' This particular Mitch
was well known to me, and it was a surprise that such a brilliantly educated and literate person dealt in a highly illegal
Class A substance. Never having bought it before, I was in
paroxysms of fear when I called her up and asked if she
might have some 'COFFEE' for me and that if I popped

round maybe a couple of jars of 'COFFEE' would be possible? Mitch giggled that this would be fine and that it was 'SIXTY PENCE A JAR' and very high quality. These codes used by dealers and users alike can be absurd. Jezzer is a common one, as a reference to Jeremy Clarkson, who I'm sure has never snorted except derisively, but the title of whose programme, *Top Gear*, suggests precisely what the client was seeking of the seller, material of the least-cut highest quality: absolute top gear . . .

So for my first drug deal, I called up Mitch from a phone-box to confirm the time, found a cash machine, took out £240, which was a matter of two credit cards in those days, and, after rapping lightly on Mitch's door (convinced there were police snipers on every rooftop), found myself shortly in possession of four grams of my very own supply of coke, in four tightly, neatly folded wraps. A part of me wants to show you what a wrap looks like, using an origami-style diagram with dotted lines, but I really do not think that necessary or desirable. The point of a wrap was that any square of reasonable-quality paper could contain the powder without there being any chance of it spilling from the corners. Some dealers, in an almost foolhardy manner you might think, had their signature wrap paper. Lottery tickets, for example, or squares cut from specialist magazines.

Mitch had, and has, a very successful broadcasting career, and I think in those days she and her boyfriend were having trouble making ends meet, and this little business on the side helped keep the wolf from the door. I always had too much respect for them to use them as regular dealers; it seemed like an insult. Soon enough they had introduced me to Nando, who worked in the Petticoat Lane market, a corner pub nearby being our regular meeting and dealing place. Nando introduced me to Midge, who passed me on to Nonny, until I had quite the network, and I don't think a day could go by without my being sure of a supply of a wrap or two in my pocket. Nonny was a great girl, and she had the best supply. The B-quality Charlie for her 'ordinary' customers and A-Charlie for actors, comics, musicians, loyal regulars, Euro-trash, wild childs (children seems wrong in that context), supermodels and aristos.

I didn't take coke because I was depressed or under pressure. I didn't take it because I was unhappy (at least I don't think so). I took it because I really, really *liked* it. Most of my friends screwed their face up at the thought of it, or at most had one or two lines at weekends. Over the years they began, I think, I *know*, to worry about me. But I had drug friends, very well-known artists and musicians and actors with whom I would regularly hang out and play snooker, smoking, drinking and snorting day after day after day. Amongst this crowd there was always a friend wilder by far than me, one who could pull two or three all-nighters in a row and then go filming on the third day bright as a button. I cannot tell you how much better that made me feel about my own growing dependency.

Underneath it all, I still valued my work above every-thing. Hugh and I had started *A Bit of Fry and Laurie* for the BBC, and it would no more occur to me to write, rehearse or perform in front of the cameras with coke up my nose and in my bloodstream than it would for me to drink all day and bumble into the studio tanked up. Coke was 'pudding', it was the reward that meant I could grant myself an extra three or four hours at a members' club somewhere, discreetly (but frankly back in those days, not so very discreetly) powdering my nose.

Snooker and poker played a large part: there was no appetite for food, but a gigantic one for alcohol. Cocaine, in sharp contradistinction to MDMA and cannabis, seems to increase one's threshold for pure liquor more than any-thing I've known.

I have tried to make this book as balanced as possible, by which I mean *true*. I am not going to squirt out a great list of famous names with whom I have shared lines – that simply is not my business. I don't want this book to be a snivelling apology, nor a boastful 'Coke, fuck-yeah!' So I have to be honest and say that the first ten years of my coke dependency seemed to cause me no trouble whatso-ever. Sometimes, very rarely, I had to postpone or cancel an early-morning appointment, but generally speaking I lived a high-functioning life. As my prosperity rose my ability to acquire higher-quality cocaine increased commensurately (hence Nonny), and that cannot have hurt either. Better purity meant less diarrhoea, nasal bleeding and nausea.

Was the presence of coke in the system noticeable to others? There is an old Greek saying: 'It is easier to hide two elephants under your arm than one pathic.' You may need to stop and do a little poking around and looking up to parse that, but what it is essentially saying is that if you walked through the Athenian marketplace with the boy you were sleeping with – your pathic or catamite – it was more conspicuous and obvious to all than walking with a pair of elephants. Much the same with coke, certainly with a chronic habit. Tooth grinding, the telltale running nose, the chattering, the lack of appetite. Much as I hate to disagree with Professor Freud, one line leads to another and another, certainly not to 'aversion'. Most coke users will acknowledge one particular rule of the stuff. There is either not enough or there is too much. Not enough, and you start to ring dealers at three in the morning. They will be far from best pleased. Too much, and you fill yourself up with it and won't be able to sleep till noon or later.

Another stroke of good fortune, which is something to do with my ambition or my constitution or some mixture of them both, is that I have always known when to stop, especially if I am working the next day. I am nearly always the first to leave the party, murmuring excuses about a film call the next morning or whatever it may be.

I was once standing at the bar of the Groucho Club with the painter Francis Bacon, the art dealer James Birch and those two inseparable art works in themselves, Gilbert and George. Everyone was in a very jolly mood when Bacon ordered a bottle.

'Oh, not for me,' I said, 'I'm up pretty early tomorrow morning.'

'Oh, don't be a cunt,' said a Gilbert or a George. 'Drink with us, ducky.'

'I'm really sorry . . .' I insisted.

Francis tapped me on the shoulder. 'Ah, you're like me, you've got a little man.'

'Well actually, I'm single,' I said.

'No, no, no,' he prodded the side of his temple. 'A little man in here. A little man who tells you when to stop and go home. Oh, the people I knew. So talented, but no little man to stop them. Minton, John Deakin, Dan Farson . . . no little men, you see? I understand. Off you go.'

I was profoundly touched (and flattered of course) by this fellow-feeling and thought myself lucky to have this little man and that such a legend as Bacon recognized it in me. For all I know, he thought I was a total arsehole and made the whole story up just to get rid of me. But it is certainly true that Francis himself would go on outrageous binges, drinking and drinking like a man who wanted to die and then *his* little man would intervene and say, 'No, Francis. Time for the studio.' And back he would go to work for another four or five weeks, producing some of the greatest paintings of his time. So far as I know, he was never much interested in drugs.

There is, however, a wonderful story that has done the rounds enough for me to believe it to be true. Skip if you know it. Lionel Bart, the endearing but woefully hapless songwriter and creator of the musical *Oliver!*, came round to dinner with Bacon and his boyfriend, John Edwards, some time during the late 1970s. They couldn't help noticing that every now and then Bart would disappear under the dining-room table, and a snorting, snuffling noise would ensue, accompanied by the unmistakeable rustle of a plastic bag. Bart would get up, apologize and then carry on with the merry conversation.

An hour or so later he left, with many hugs and thank yous. Francis and John (no staff, fantastically rich as Francis already was by then) started to clear the table.

'Oh, what's this?' said Bacon, who had found under Bart's seat a bag of white powder.

'Heavens, Francis, you're such an innocent. That's cocaine.'

'Ooh, ooh! What shall we do with it?'

'I know,' said John with a flash of inspiration. 'We'll go to Tramp.'

Tramp was a well-known nightclub in Jermyn Street run by the excellent Johnny Gold. It is almost always mistakenly called Tramps, with which Johnny would put up with sighing resignation. In the 1970s it hosted the wedding receptions of Liza Minnelli and Peter Sellers,* it was

---

* Not to each other. Two separate ceremonies.

the chosen watering-hole of sporting naughty boys like George Best, James Hunt and Vitas Gerulaitis, all kinds of models (before they were ever prefixed as super), various cashmere-cardiganned European playboys and film actors from both sides of the Atlantic. Nothing like as smart as Annabel's, but enduring and not without its own character and likeability. It is still going, but without the enlivening presence of Johnny Gold.

The pair arrived at the door to be met by a large doorman who had no more idea of who Francis Bacon was than Francis Bacon knew who Kenny Dalglish might have been.

'Sorry, mate, we're full. Queue over there,' he told Edwards.

Daringly, Edwards – who had an idea about club doormen that was more or less infallible in those days – let the man see a glimpse of the bag of white powder.

'Would you like a . . .?' he said.

'Just a sec, gents . . . follow me.'

The doorman beckoned to a second-in-command and pulled Edwards and Bacon into a little alcove next to the door. John tentatively proffered the bag, and the doorman took a healthy scoopful, which he transferred into a little bag he had ready in his waistcoat pocket. He next led them to an occupied table, which he swiftly de-occupied with a growl of 'reserved' and a sweep of his well-muscled arm.

'Juanito, the best champagne for my friends . . .'

Well, thought Bacon and Edwards. This is the life and no mistake.

A bucket of Dom Pérignon arrived and was poured out into glasses by the fawning and chattily verbose Juanito. All the while, John and Francis were impatiently planning their discreet visit to the gentlemen's lavatories, which they had noticed were being visited with great frequency by a steady line, as it were, of glamorous, well-known faces.

They had hardly taken one sip of the Dom Pérignon before the bouncer was clattering back down the stairs.

'You two, out! Out this fucking minute. If I ever see your fucking faces again, I'll fucking beat the living crap out of you. Got it, you fucking fuckers?'

Disconsolately they taxied their way back home, wondering what could have gone wrong.

'Did you notice,' said Francis, 'that his nostril was *frothing* slightly? And rather pinkly, as if blood had been drawn? Is that usual?'

They put the matter out of their minds, had some drinks – alcohol being a drug they well understood – and went to bed.

The next morning Lionel Bart called to thank them for the dinner party.

'Oh, by the way,' he said, 'did I leave my bag of denture fixative powder behind? Can't find it anywhere.'

The Groucho

Play by the Rules: The Groucho Club Rules

Upon arrival at The Club, Members shall approach the Reception desk to sign and print their names in the signing-in book – this Ancient Ceremony being a necessary preliminary to entry into all the Club Rooms.

The use within The Club of Mobile, Cellular, Portable or Microwave-controlled Telecommunication Instruments is an anathema, a curse, a horror, a dread and deep unpleasantness and shall be prohibited in all locations, save the Reception area and the Soho Bar, until 5 p.m. Please be alert to the acknowledged misery of Ring Tones and silence all such mechanisms before entry into the Club Rooms.

The ingestion into the bloodstream of powders, pastilles, potions, herbs, compounds, pills, tablets, capsules, tonics, cordials, tinctures, inhalations, or mixtures that have been scheduled by Her Majesty's Government to be illegal Substances of whatever class is firmly prohibited by Club Rules, whether they be internalized orally, rectally, intravenously, intranasally or by any means whatsoever. So let it be known.

A Member may invite into The Club up to four (4) Guests at any one time, for whose behaviour and respect of the rules the Member is responsible. Be it understood that a Guest will not be allowed into the Bar save that they be accompanied by a Member.

The wearing of String Vests is fully unacceptable and wholly proscribed by Club Rules. There is enough distress in the world already.

To step out into Dean Street owing money to The Club leaves a stain on a Member's character that cannot be pleasing to them. For this reason all bills and monies owing to The Club should be settled in full before a Member may leave The Club.

Upon settlement of aforesaid bills and levies, all Members are reminded that Soho is a neighbourhood containing many residents. Show dignity, consideration and kindness by leaving The Club quietly and with as little brouhaha as may be contrived.

The Club is a club. A place of sociability in which to relax and be affable and friendly. Respect the views of your fellow Members and ensure that your Guests do the same. Let amiability and charm be your watchwords.

It seemed to me from the late 1980s through the naughty 1990s and into the opening years of the twenty-first century inconceivable that there was anyone in London *not* doing coke. Every time I saw somebody in a restaurant rising from their table and moving towards the gents or the ladies I assumed they were off for an energizing sniff. It didn't stop me writing or performing or pursuing any other occupation that required hard work and concentration. It was only, as I have said, the reward for that hard work, the pudding or savoury that I had earned and that would give me five or six hours of convivial social immersion.

My usual port of call was the Groucho Club, from 1985 onwards the watering-hole of choice for almost all in publishing, music, comedy, drama and the arts in general. That section of society that the hero of my 1994 novel *The Hippopotamus*, Ted Wallace, cholerically called the mediahadeen* and was later scornfully to be assigned the sneering ascription 'the chattering classes' from another class of chatterers that chattered in other watering-holes.

As well as writing the official club rules (above) I also coined one evening in the late eighties the 'Groucho Rule', which states that any remark, apophthegm, epigram, aphorism or observation, be it never so wise, well intentioned, profound or true, is instantly rendered ridiculous and nonsensical by the addition of the phrase 'he said last night in the Groucho Club'.

*Feeble ref. to the Mujahadeen, who were one of the Afghan insurgency forces in the old Soviet–Afghan war.

Thus: 'Workers of the world unite! You have nothing to lose but your chains,' remarked Karl Marx in the Groucho Club last night.

Or: 'For evil to flourish, all it takes is for the good man to do nothing,' pointed out Edmund Burke in the Groucho Club brasserie late last night.

And so on. The Athenæum it is not and nor does it pretend to be.

Tony Mackintosh (of the Norfolk chocolate family which gave the world the Caramac and Quality Street amongst other memorable masterpieces) was a noted figure in the world of London hospitality, running for many years 192, a popular Notting Hill restaurant whose first chef, Alistair Little, was *the* premier metropolitan skillet-wielder of the mid-1980s. Mackintosh was also in charge of the Zanzibar, a very pleasant drinkery in Great Queen Street, Covent Garden. It was here that I learned to queue up for the single gentlemen's lavatory. Its seat had long disappeared, and there was no cistern lid. I assume this was an attempt by Tony to deter drug-taking. Although he was one of London's foremost and most fashionable restaurateurs (there is no *n* in 'restaurateur' despite the number of times you hear 'restauranteur') he resembled a kindly old-fashioned schoolaster (there is of course no *m* in 'schoolmaster', a little known fact), and to this day I am not sure that he knew what went on in his establishments. He was certainly present the night Keith Allen went crazy. Well, that is a preposterous thing to say. The night when

Keith Allen went *crazier*, I should have written. The wild Welsh whirlwind stood on the bar and hurled glassware at the mirror behind the bottles and optics. He was effectively Zanzibarred for the rest of that club's life, for it was only a few months later that the Groucho was born from its shards and ashes.

Originally the idea of publishers Carmen Callil, Caroline Michel and überagent Ed Victor, the club was conceived as a place where authors and their editors could meet for a mid-morning breakfast and talk in comfy chairs without the formal dignity of an old-fashioned West End club or the passing human traffic and distraction of a hotel lobby or dining room. This was the era of croissants, orange juice and newly enthralling Italian coffees. I cannot think of those days without the memory of buttery pastry flakes and marmalade. The evenings, however . . . the evenings were very, very different. More of them in a moment.

Tony, always a benign but hazily distant figure, had, as much more hands-on fellow managers, a radiant being called Mary Lou Sturridge, sister of Charles, the precocious director of Granada's barnstorming *Brideshead Revisited*, and Liam Carson, who was to become a very close friend. Mary Lou, Liam and their various colleagues, notably Gordana, a Serbian of magnificent charm and a voice like a factory foghorn, kept order and created the ambience of the club, which was an instant and stunning success. Indeed, such was the nature of the success that those who were not members made no secret of how much they despised the place and how posturing, pretentious and 'up themselves' the members were. As a matter of fact the only people I have ever seen behave revoltingly and unacceptably at the Groucho Club have been members' guests, who can become (or certainly could in those early, heady days) overheated by alcohol and the presence of well-known faces. Members and the staff know how to comport themselves in the club.

I cannot deny that for me such a place was something like an oasis. The better known I became, the more difficult I found it to go into a pub. This has become more and more the case over the years. Whenever I do, the chances are that someone will come up and offer to buy me a drink. This is charming and kind but places me in an unwinnable bind. If I refuse the drink I am considered top-lofty, lah-di-dah and hoity-toity; if I accept it I have been functionally purchased for half an hour. You can't take someone's drink and then make your way to the other side of the saloon and ignore them. It is often pleasant to speak to strangers, but there are times when one wants to spend time with one's friends, uninterfered with. So pubs, unless I am in my home county of Norfolk, where there seems to be an inbuilt understanding that people should be able to come and go unmolested, famous or not,* are off limits to me.

---

*After all, the royal family have a house not far from me, and Princes William and Harry have been known to pop into one of my favourite

It is unfortunate, then, that the well-known are excoriated for not being 'real' enough to go to ordinary places like pubs, whatever 'real' might be taken to mean. I do shop in supermarkets and high streets and often, absurdly, people say to me – sometimes almost in the most put-out fashion – 'What are *you* doing *here?*', to which I am tempted to reply, as I push my trolley along the aisle, 'Playing badminton / sitting my History A level exam / performing a tracheotomy on Jeremy Vine . . . What are *you* doing?'

I have mentioned before in blog or perhaps in interview that fame is wonderful, a picnic. Instant tables in fashionable restaurants that others have to wait weeks to book for, tickets to premieres, sporting occasions and gatherings of genuine interest and excitement and the opportunity to meet heroes in all walks of life. But, as at any picnic, there are wasps. Sometimes the wasps are no more than a nuisance and sometimes they cause you to pack up and run indoors yelping. It was Fellini in *La Dolce Vita* who called his 'society' photographer Paparazzo, a word that suggested to him an annoying buzzing insect. The Italian for wasp, *vespa*, was already taken of course . . .

Certainly paparazzi can be a nuisance, especially if you are with someone who is not in the public eye and would rather not have their features printed in a newspaper accompanied by speculation as to their identity. Then, of course, everyone is a paparazzo today, for everyone has a

pubs in the county: that being the case, some git off the TV is hardly going to cause excitement.

camera, one of higher and higher quality as year succeeds year.

To this day there are often amateur paparazzi every night waiting outside the Groucho Club, the Ivy Club, the Chiltern Firehouse, Annabel's, Hertford Street and sundry other 'haunts of the rich and famous'. They only need one photograph of a celebrity vomiting, or trying to punch a colleague, or snogging the wrong man or woman, and they have paid their rent for the week.

One Day in the Life of the Groucho Club

So, back to the Groucho. I will take you through a day. It is in fact an amalgam of many days, but it may suffice to give you a flavour of the club's high-water mark, or scumline if that is your point of view.

Let us say it is a sunny autumn afternoon in the early 1990s. I have had a late-morning meeting about a new book with my publisher, Sue Freestone, in the bar area of the Groucho and am due to lunch with my agent, Lorraine Hamilton, who tells me, over the navarin of lamb, that a producer called Marc Samuelson would like a meeting to sound me out about the possibility of playing Oscar Wilde in a new film.

Buoyed and excited by the very thought of such an idea, I take my post-luncheon brandy to the bar. A pair of adorably cute boys are sitting there, rhythmically drumming the bar-rail with their feet and looking nerv-ously about them. I estimate that they are in their mid-twenties.

I have always felt that the Groucho should be a club within the most sociable meaning of the act and that open friendliness ought to be a very part of its nature. People should be made to feel welcome and at home, not snubbed or avoided. Which is not to say that they should be interrupted or have their conversations crashed. It seems to me that these two young men are certainly in need of a solacing word or two.

'Hello,' I say, slipping on to a stool next to them.

They nod and smile.

'You look as if you are a little bewildered?'

'Well,' says one of them, who had charming mousy hair, 'it's the Groucho Club. You hear things . . .'

'Goodness,' say I. 'What sort of things?'

'That it's a bit, you know . . .' says the other, who has perfectly black hair and the deepest brown eyes, 'not for the likes of us.'

'Oh now, pish,' I reply. 'You look like just the kind of young bright people that the Groucho would most wel-come. Tell me, what do you do?'

'We're musicians,' says the mousy-haired one with just a hint of endearing mockney.

'Ah, well then. You're *exactly* the kind of members the club needs. I'll make sure your candidacies are fast-tracked. Don't you move a muscle. I'll be right back.'

I nip to the front desk and ask – Lily would it have been? – to give me a couple of membership forms. I return, brandishing them.

'Let's fill these in then,' I say. 'Hm. "Profession?" . . . Musicians. "Address?" . . . I'll leave you to fill those in, along with telephone numbers. "Proposer?" . . . I'll sign that. "Seconder?" . . .' I scan the bar area. 'Tim!' I call to an old friend and Groucho regular. 'Come and second these two splendid fellows. They're called . . . sorry, I'm afraid I don't know your names . . .'

'Alex,' says the one with the black hair and brown, brown eyes.

'Damon,' says the one with the mousy hair and, now that I look more closely, wonderfully blue, blue eyes.

'And they're musicians!' I tell Tim.

Tim takes the form and signs.

'Are you currently in work, or do you have a band or something?' I inquire of the pair.

'Stephen,' says Tim, 'this is Damon Albarn and Alex James. They are Blur.'

This is not very helpful to me.

'*Park Life?*'

'It's OK,' says the dark-haired one called Alex, extending his hand to be shaken. 'Big fan.'

Hands are shaken, and drinks ordered all round. I leave the filled-in proposal forms with the front desk and bump into Khaki Joe, another dealer. Currency notes are discreetly swapped for small, tight wraps. I am now, as

Americans say, loaded for bear. Ready for a full-on Groucho evening.

The afternoon takes shape. Damon has to leave, but meanwhile Keith Allen has arrived. Keith has entered in bonhomous mood. He already knows Alex James. In fact they are to go on and have a long and productive friendship. Aside from anything else, they give the world Fat Les and the hit single 'Vindaloo', for which the world will always be dizzy with gratitude.

Pages could be written about the strange and extraordinary Keith Allen: throughout the late 1980s (following his Zanzibarring) through the 1990s and up until the mid-2000s he was to be found in the Groucho Club most days and nights. He could be bruisingly rude. 'Some people are crap, some people are brilliant,' he once told a well-known TV comic loudly. 'You are mediocre, which is worse. So much fucking worse.' It's very hard to recover from this kind of assault. I sat with the poor recipient of this onslaught for two hours, trying to convince him that vitriol from Keith Allen was as healing balm from a seraph, a compliment of the highest order. Keith was an early figure in the alternative comedy world, and anyone who came after him or perhaps Malcolm Hardee* was a

---

*Famous in the wider world for his naked balloon dance. He drowned, aged fifty-five, much mourned by what was then the oxymoronic alternative establishment. His stand-up act was, I need hardly add, staggeringly unfunny in a way that must have taken enormous effort. He himself was astonishingly funny, however. Go figure.

sell-out in his eyes. For months in the Zanzibar and then the Groucho I tried to avoid him. One day he had come up with a drink, sat down and told me that I was great. This was most discomfiting. He had told almost everyone I liked and admired that they were complete wankers and that their work was shit and derivative. How should I take a compliment from this terror? Naturally, wuss that I am, I absorbed it gratefully, and we became friends, albeit warily on my side. Griff Rhys Jones, a man of exemplary forcefulness and courage, once confided in me that Keith scared him half to death. Long Groucho poker evenings drew them closer together. Griff is a non-drinker and good boy (unless you count poker as a vice), so Keith's acceptance of him could be counted as highly complimentary.

Why would one want to be liked or accepted by someone so loutish, rude, uncontrollable and horrific, you might wonder? Charisma, I suppose. Famed for his amatory adventures and now for the success of his children (Alfie the Greyjoy in *Game of Thrones*, and Lily the singer-songwriter), he has a quality of playfulness and boldness that naturally more cautious and bourgeois figures like myself cannot but be drawn to. And whatever your instincts may tell you, I can assure you that he is a very loyal and generous friend to those in need.

*

We decide to go upstairs to the snooker room. Oh, the hours and hours and hours and hours I spent there. I bought many of the accoutrements. A device for respotting a ball. Rests, spiders and extensions. Chalk. My own cue made from finest English ash. They rarely lasted more than a week before being broken or stolen. The room is only just big enough to fit a full-sized table. You almost have to open a window to play some shots. You certainly have to ask anyone sitting and kibitzing to lean to the left or right if you need to cue either side of the blue pocket. 'Lining up on the white' became a favourite, if obvious, joke. Coke, snooker, vodka, tobacco, chat.

There is a strange stumbling noise on the stairs. Up comes a round-faced, shaggy-eyebrowed young man.

'You're all fucking wankers,' he says. 'And you ...' he points at Alex. 'Where's that shithead All Bran?'

Alex smiles dozily.

'Fuck you all. You can't play for fucking toffee.' This strange interloper grabs my cue. 'And you,' he says to me, 'you are a poncey tosser.'

'Right,' I say. 'OK. Poncey tosser. I shall make a note of that.'

'Fuck off!' he shouts, stabbing the cue up in the air. The round end of the butt bangs violently into the low ceiling. Dust descends.

He drops the cue and throws himself back down the stairs.

'Well,' I say. 'Who on earth ... ?'

Keith is stepping on to a chair, magic marker in hand. 'Fuck's sake, Stephen. Don't you know *anything*? Liam Gallagher.'

He draws a ring round the circular dent left in the plasterwork and writes: 'The mark of a cunt.'

'Oasis,' Alex explains. 'There's this really dumb thing about which one of us bands is better.'

'Oh,' I say. 'Ah. Yes. Quite. I see.' Not seeing at all.

The afternoon folds itself into an evening. Other people, including many rather desperate known figures who never can or never will buy their own supply, drift in and look longingly at us as we now more unobtrusively flit from loo to table and back, sniffing up the residue from our nostrils as discreetly as we can. A coke addict's discreet sniff is like the trumpeting of an elephant and deceives no one but him- or herself. It is of a piece with the whisky drinker's mouth-freshening mint or the odorous farter's suspicious darting glances at other people. Futile fabrication, fooling none.

The pretty-please puppy-dog eyes of the liggers is distressing me. As usual, Keith ignores them. Liam Carson arrives up the stairs to join me as a partner in doubles.

Only the day before I had had an opportunity to watch Liam in action. The daily management of a club like the Groucho presents all kinds of unique problems. How to deal with the notorious Soho bohemian Dan Farson drunkenly pulling rough trade up the stairs to the bedrooms? Vomit in unexpected places. Indiscreet snorters ruining it for the rest of us by tapping out lines on the dining table. Out-of-control revellers who think the place is open to all trying to pile in after pub hours (the club is licensed to serve drinks until two in the morning). Liam calmly deals with all these issues. There is a steely Irish resolve inside what appears to be a placid, rather doughy exterior. He was taught by the legendary Peter Langan, father of all London's better restaurants. Peter begat Liam, Peter also begat Jeremy King and Chris Corbin of Le Caprice, the Ivy, J. Sheekey, the Wolseley, the Delaunay, Colbert's, Brasserie Zédel, Scott's, the Mark Hix group of restaurants, etc., etc. The better elements of London's hospitality industry can all be traced in a direct line back to Langan.

As we were: the previous night I was sitting in the back corner of the Groucho brasserie, chatting to Liam and sipping a vodka and slimline* tonic. He would have been on a glass of Chardonnay, this being the era before that grape and its wine were mocked into an unfashionable corner and a preposterous Essex girl Christian name to make way for Sauvignon Blanc. Liam was enough of an alcoholic to think that drinking wine by the bucketful didn't really mean anything. Only the hard stuff counted. We are interrupted by a flushed girl from the front desk.

'Liam, there's an awful tramp in reception. He's just standing there in a manky old coat with his hands into his pockets staring. What do we do?'

---

*Slimline it may have been called, but it imparted no such thing to my increasing bulk.

Liam slowly gets to his feet. 'Don't worry, darling. I'll deal with it.'

'Oh, do you mind if I come too?' I had never seen Liam handling street interlopers. I knew he would never be mean or threatening. He is a kindly man. Besides, part of his job is to avoid scenes.

In Soho, where the fashionable, successful and prosperous dine, drink and thrive in such close proximity to a parallel world of destitution, prostitution and misery, a bitter hiccup of liberal shame, embarrassment and guilt (which are of no use to anyone) rises in the breast of people like me, a kind of social acid reflux, which is the price we pay for too much good living. And useless, as I say, to the poor, who would rather have our money than our pink-faced, hand-wringing apologies.

I follow Liam as he opens the doors that lead from the bar area to the reception. The frightened girl from the front desk is next to me, just as anxious as I am to see how Liam will deal with this 'tramp', a word from childhood but what other does one use? Bum? Hobo? Panhandler? All rather American.

The tramp in question has his back to us, but I can see a thick overcoat a size too big for him into which his hands are thrust. As he turns, Liam quickly extends a cordial hand. 'Mr Pacino, welcome. How can we help you?'

The girl by my side quietly melts into a puddle on the floor. I can understand her mistake. The great actor has eyes, in the old phrase, like piss-holes in the snow. He is unshaven, and his 'affect' is ungiving. It is possible, probable even, that he is researching for some role. I think this was before his Richard III project, but maybe this was where his mind was at the time.

Back to this evening of evenings. Liam and I play Keith and Alex, our new best friend, at snooker. We are joined by Charles Fontaine, chef patron of the excellent Quality Chop House in the Farringdon Road, a 'working men's' restaurant more or less unchanged since 1869. As ever, he is anxious for poker, so we decide to go upstairs to the Club Room to play. Alex excuses himself from this and slides in a happy, lazy shuffling way downstairs. Something rather Bazooka Joe about him.

Charles, a French 'man of the mountains', as he likes to call himself, is passionate about poker. His skill is not in proportion to his enthusiasm, but he seems not to mind. We play Seven Card Stud, Texas Hold 'Em, Five Card Stud, Five Card Draw, Omaha, High Low, dealer's choice. A card-table to make modern purists shudder. We even allow the dealer to nominate wild cards. I have provided the packs and a neat wooden carousel of chips, plastic but serviceable enough.

'Oh, Stephen,' Charles says to me excitedly during a shuffle, 'you know the Peter Blake? I buy it.'

'I'm sorry?'

Charles has been in London for the best part of fifteen years, working in the kitchens of Le Caprice under Mark Hix, yet still his command of the English tongue is far from secure. I manage to grasp what he is trying to tell me. He has bought a découpage artwork representing me that the pop artist Peter Blake had been commissioned to make to accompany a profile for *Harpers & Queen* or *Vogue* or some such magazine the previous year. Somehow Charles had tracked the original down and hung it in the Chop House. As I look up from the computer this very minute I see it hanging on *my* wall now. Charles called me up a month or so back from Spain, where he has a restaurant these days. Spanish sovereign debt crisis, money tight, he wondered if I might be interested in buying the piece? A price was agreed, and now it is mine.

But back to that day in the early nineties.

Usually a poker game lasts from around midnight to four or five in the morning. Liam will be in charge of locking us in and letting us out. The greatest fear is his wife Gabby coming round and tearing a strip out of him. They have a daughter, Flossy, and how she would love him to settle down to something sensible and secure and unconnected to alcohol and druggy people like Fry and his fiendish friends.

Tonight, however, is a very special night. At round about midnight word reaches us that we should go downstairs. There is a palpable buzz at ground-floor level. The doors that lead from reception to the bar area are thrown open, and in charges Damien Hirst, accompanied by Jay Jopling, the gallery owner, followed by Sarah Lucas, Tracey Emin, Sam Taylor-Wood and Angus Fairhurst.

These are the leading YBAs, Young British Artists, graduates of Goldsmiths College, London. Collected by Charles Saatchi, reviled by bourgeois tabloids, they are all making a serious noise in the art world.

Damien, leader of them all for shock value and fame, is waving a piece of paper over his head like Neville Chamberlain on his return from Munich. It is not peace in our time, however, but a cheque.

'Here!' shouts Damien, pushing his way to the bar and handing it across. 'I've just gone and won the fucking Turner Prize. There's twenty grand there. Lock us all in and let me know when it's spent.'

A huge cheer. At round about six in the morning the barman wearily but cheerfully rings the cheque through the till. 'That's your twenty grand spent,' he says.

'Another twenty grand on me,' says Damien to another great cheer.

Six hours later I'm sipping a Bloody Mary. Somehow the club has been tidied, shifts have been relieved. Only we hardcore imbeciles are left.

Tracey and Damien vie with each other, trying to shock the shoulder-padded power-dressed publishers who are starting to come in for lunch.

'Oi,' shouts Tracey, sitting on the bar, 'are you calling my cunt a pussy?'

A knot of publishers scuttle away, baffled and alarmed.

'You,' says Damien to a couple as they enter, 'how do you make a queer fuck a woman?'

'Errrr . . . ?' They know who this terrifying man is and
don't for one minute want to look unsporting. 'I don't
know . . .'

'Shit in her cunt.'

Ah, les beaux jours . . .

Ach, die schöne Zeiten . . .

Those were the days . . .

I have almost certainly conflated several days into one.
I expect Keith Allen will call me up to say that he can't
have been playing poker with me the night Damien won
his Turner Prize because he was there at the Tate for the
ceremony. Alex will let me know that I proposed Damon
Albarn and him for Groucho membership in '93 and
Damon will say it was '94. Everyone's memory will be different, but none of them, I think, will dispute my
representation of the spirit of the age as we lived it, foul
as it may stink in your nostrils, self-indulgent as it certainly was: precious hours wantonly pissed away, good
money spunked, valuable brain cells massacred, execrable
shit talked. At the time I loved it. Lived for it and little
else. But I was fortunate, very fortunate, for I had a little
man. I know because that genius Francis Bacon told me
so, as related above.

The truly monumental Soho drinkers, carousers, wast-
rels and rakehells preferred the Colony Room to the
Groucho. In the era of its founder, the fabulous Muriel
Belcher, Francis Bacon was one of the first habitués. Dan
Farson, author of *Soho in the Fifties* and *Sacred Monsters*, drew

a splendid portrait of the early years of this tiny after-hours first-floor bar. When Muriel Belcher died, she was succeeded by Ian Board, the barman. Generally known as Ida, he had the most enormous spongy drinker's nose I've ever seen and was one of the few people I ever met who still used, well into the 1980s, in a cracked, camp sixties voice, the appellation 'ducky'. If he liked you more it was 'cunty'. Someone told me, I can't remember who – perhaps Michael, his assistant behind the bar – that when Ida died in the club, in harness naturally, everyone in the room, as he slumped to the ground, saw his great nose shrink down like a deflated balloon. The stopped heart no longer pumped blood to his scattered network of broken capillaries.

Jeffrey Bernard (whose drinking gave rise to the magnificent comedy *Jeffrey Bernard is Unwell*, for many the last chance to see the greatness of Peter O'Toole on stage) started to frequent the Groucho rather than the Colony Room or the French House the other side of Old Compton Street, another haunt of the old guard. He grudgingly grunted good mornings to me when I came in. Perhaps because his niece Kate Bernard was a school-friend of my sister's. I always felt that the pioneering generation regarded us as soft. Alcoholic dilettantes. And the coke they regarded as pretentious and pathetic. Which it is, of course. We were amateurs. Bernard was a warning to all, however. Stick-like, he was as withered and fragile as Tithonus, on whom Zeus finally took pity, turning him into a cicada. You felt you could snap him in half over your knee. In his later years he sat in a wheelchair in front of the bar, cigarette in mouth, vodka and soda in hand. First one leg was amputated, then the other. I saw him and Dan Farson at the bar together once. They each subsisted on almost identical diets of pure alcohol, yet one was as round, red and shiny as a balloon and the other dry and paper-thin.

Francis Bacon started to come into the Groucho too, overcoming whatever initial distrust of the place he may have had. Rather as email and then Twitter were to be met with howls of displeasure and sceptical derision when they arrived in the world, only to be embarrassedly embraced later, so it was amongst the founding fathers of SohoBoho degeneracy that the Groucho Club – sneered at and despised by right-thinking roués at first – came finally to be accepted and enjoyed in the evening of their years.

Heigh ho, twenty years have passed since those days. Jeffrey Bernard and Francis Bacon are dead. Charles Fontaine lives and works in the south of Spain. Alex James has moved from the Groucho Group to David Cameron's Chipping Norton set and makes award-winning cheeses in Gloucestershire. Damien Hirst lives and works in the West Country too, as does Keith Allen. Tracey Emin is one of the few YBAs, it seems, to have kept the bohemian candle alight. Not that she ever sucked things up through her nose to my knowledge. But she can drink. Yes, she can do that.

People, groups, movements, energies gather themselves into a ball sometimes and hurl themselves into
history. Then the time comes when the fire dies. The
great mass deflates like Ida's purple, spongy nose. Many
will regard the Britpop and YBA movements as shallow
and unimportant. But damn, it was fun to be caught up
inside as an amused, amazed observer.

Today and for many years the Groucho Club has been
as clean as clean can be. The surfaces in the bathrooms are
free of white powder, and no one sits on the bar telling
shocked arrivals frightful, yet appallingly funny, jokes.
There has been no lock-in for a Turner Prize-winning artist there since 1995. But it remains a good place to eat and
drink. It is ruled by Bernie Katz, the Prince of Soho. He
stands four foot ten in elevated shoes, but he can throw
out four unruly drunks without thinking. There is a yearly
quiz (for which I have from time to time set questions), a
staff party, at which favoured members serve the waiters,
kitchen, management and bar staff, and a Gang Show, at
which money is raised for the Soho homeless. The art on
the walls betrays the long connection with Hirst and Emin
and others. Securely screwed into the walls, they are worth
a king's ransom now. Some may regret the passing of the
old days and the inevitable deflation of that pumped-up,
alcoholic, coke-fuelled nose, but all things change. Another
time of energy and innovation will come and then go too.
A compensation of age is a realization of the cyclical
nature of fashion, politics and art.

Notes from a Showbusiness Career

From the mid-1980s onwards I was kept busy with a more or less huge writing workload and, after attending to new *Me and My Girl* openings on Broadway and in Australia, I found myself in the grip of a persistent, ankle-nipping producer called Dan Patterson. This, you should know, was before the coke days. We're looking at 1985 or '6, I think.

Dan and I met when he shadowed Paul Mayhew-Archer, a BBC radio comedy producer later to find more acclaim as the man in charge of most of the numerous series of *My Family* featuring *Me and My Girl*'s star Robert Lindsay. Paul was directing me in a series called *Delve Special*, in which I played a hapless investigative journalist. The series was written by Tony Sarchet and recorded, unusually for radio, 'on location'. Which is to say that, rather than using the standard sound effects gravel tray for walking and the three-textured staircase (wood, stone and carpet) and stand-alone car doors and front doors and bedroom doors with which studios were comically furnished, Paul decided for reasons of verisimilitude that we should take a Uher recording device up to the Broadcasting House roof, or on the street in Portland Place, or in some cupboard or busy *Woman's Hour* or *The World At One* production office.

Dan Patterson arrived as a work-experience observer and within seconds was bombarding me with questions. In Oxford, where his father David was a pioneering professor of Hebrew studies, Dan had seen our 1981 Cambridge Footlights revue and could quote huge chunks of it by heart. He was recently back from a trip to America, where the new world of improvisation had opened up before him like some beautiful flower. Now he was back and keen to get going as a producer himself. I have never met anything that wasn't a puppy so boisterously excitable, keen, persuasive and determined.

Before I knew what I was doing I had agreed to write six radio comedy programmes and to be in a new series featuring the kind of improvisation that Dan had seen and been so struck by in America. This latter was *Whose Line Is It Anyway?*, a jokey approximation of the title of the hit play and film *Whose Life Is It Anyway?* The show was hosted by Clive Anderson, who had been a coeval of Griff Rhys Jones and others at Cambridge, but taken a different course into law, where he had eaten his dinners, as their jargon has it, and been called to the Bar, or is it inducted? In other words, as any less magnificently potty country would put it, he had qualified as a legal advocate. He was a barrister.

The only other regular in the series was John Sessions, a phenomenally talented mimic (he had worked regularly

on *Spitting Image*) whose one-man shows combined imper-
sonation, deep learning and almost unbelievably vivid
and poetical writing.

The show suited his talents perfectly. He could instantly
tell the Red Riding Hood story in the style of Ernest
Hemingway or D. H. Lawrence or whichever author,
actor or indeed rock star was thrown at him by Clive or a
frenetic studio audience. Anyone from Anthony Burgess
to Keith Richards, by way of *EastEnders* stars and BBC
weather reporters, was grist to his remarkable mimetic
mill. From our Footlights days the ever-huggable Tony
Slattery forged ahead on the show too, as did Josie Lawrence, who specialized in improvising song lyrics and
tunes with astonishing rapidity and brilliance with the
help of pianist Richard Vranch, who had been with us at
Cambridge and whose remarkable ear and talent for
impromptu accompaniment to this day regularly supports performers in London's Comedy Store. As far as I
can recall, and nothing would induce me to listen to a
minute's worth of tape to confirm this, I just stood there
saying 'botty' or occasionally managing some kind of
actual joke or apt remark.

It was a remarkable success, and, as did a lot of radio
comedies (including *Delve Special*, which changed its name
to *This Is David Lander* for reasons that I cannot recall), it
soon transferred to television. I baulked, agreeing reluc-
tantly to appear twice. It made household names of John,
Tony, Clive and Josie – well, in the kinds of scrubbed-pine

households that marked out the middle-class viewer in those days. I only consented to do a second appearance because Peter Cook was going to be on. We were both a little the worse for drink, and both deeply uncomfortable. The funniest man alive, the most brilliant extempore wit that ever breathed in my lifetime, was not suited in any way to the ordeal of the programme. Nor was he. *Kidding*.

I think it was the upstage stools that I could not abide. Having to dismount from them, as if summoned down to the play-mat by Miss Spanky at some frightful kindergarten. Dan has continued his stool obsession (that sounds so wrong) with his highly successful *Mock the Week*.

But the other programme Dan pushed me into – well, it was hardly pushing – was one which would be of my own devising. It was called *Saturday Night Fry*, it is still available online, and, though I shouldn't say so, I really am very proud of it. I wrote all the episodes in one huge burst of energy over little more than a week and I think I was genuinely inspired. All my love of radio, a love that went back to my earliest memories, was poured into the construction of the scripts. I was helped knowing that Hugh and Emma and the matchless Jim Broadbent had already agreed to be a part of it.

At this time I was sharing a house in Dalston with Hugh, his girlfriend, Katie Kelly, and Nick Symonds, a mutual friend from Cambridge. I related in *The Fry Chronicles* how Paul Whitehouse and Charlie Higson, our painter decorators recommended by new friend Harry Enfield, seemed unusually gifted and amusing.

This was, looking back, a very productive time for me. Aside from *Saturday Night Fry*, I produced occasional pieces for *Arena* magazine and every week an article for the *Listener*. One of these, called 'Licking Thatcher' (a feeble title playing on the title of the David Hare theatre work* *Licking Hitler*), was a more than faintly impertinent call for Neil Kinnock to be more assured, confident and self-possessed when facing Margaret Thatcher across the dispatch boxes in the then twice-weekly verbal fencing matches of parliamentary Prime Minister's Question Time, popularly known as PMQs. 'He should give the impression that being Leader of the Opposition is the best job in the world under this régime,' I wrote, or some such twaddle. 'He should smile not snarl, shake his head with laughter at her crudeness, philistinism and asininity rather than shouting his head off in a lather of righteous indignation.'

I was very delighted to receive a letter a few days later with an embossed portcullis on the back of the envelope declaring in green heraldic splendour its House of Commons origin. Neil Kinnock was inviting me to join his team of speech-writers. I thought it rather classy of him to read a pissy critique of his manner from some Oxbridge upstart and, rather than dismiss it, invite him on board. I

---

*I once heard someone say they'd really enjoyed the new Hare piece at the National . . .

cannot claim for a second that I actually wrote an entire speech for him or for the two subsequent Labour leaders, John Smith, loved by all who knew him and sadly wrenched away from the world by a heart attack well before his time, and his successor Tony Blair, loved by . . . well . . . Once Tony had won in 1997 let's just say it stopped being fun. Writing for the underdog is infinitely more challenging and amusing.

Bit of gossip, though, which isn't too mean. I'm holding back on cruel revelations until I'm dead. A few weeks after he had been elected Prime Minister in 1997, Tony and Cherie Blair sent me an invitation to dinner at Chequers, the Prime Minister's *ex officio* country house. The invitation said 'informal', which in the strange British world of etiquette means, when referring to a dinner, 'not black tie'. Similarly, the phrase 'we don't dress for dinner' indicates that dark suits shall be worn, rather than dinner jackets. Well, so I understood, having grown up in this preposterous nobby British tradition. Yes, you are right: I secretly love it. Not so secretly.

As it fell out, I was the first to arrive at the grand Tudor mansion, ushered into the great hall by a pretty and slightly nervous blonde WAAF. Servicemen and -women customarily take turns to serve at such occasions. I sipped sherry and admired the furnishings and fitments for five minutes before Tony Blair, twenty days into his premiership, doe-eyed enough to have been nicknamed Bambi, pattered down the stairs before skidding to an abrupt halt at the sight of me. He was wearing a denim shirt and pale chinos.

'Oh,' he said, 'didn't the invitation say "informal"?'

'I took that to mean no dinner jacket,' I said.

He looked aghast. 'Do you think everyone else will think that?'

'There's a strong chance,' I told him.

By this time Cherie had arrived, and there was much confabulation before the PM hared upstairs to change.

Everyone else did indeed arrive in dark lounge suits, as they are revoltingly called. I thought Tony's (as one was always encouraged to call him) ignorance of these matters was rather touching. It is all absurd snobbery and unguessable usage after all.

I was impressed that the Blairs had invited Betty Boothroyd, the retired Speaker of the House, and Giles Wilson, mathematician son of Harold and Mary Wilson. Wilson Junior had never been back to the house he might have been said almost to have grown up in, and not once had Betty been asked to Chequers throughout her Speakership during the days of Thatcher and Major.

I recall getting rather drunk on a very fine cognac that was one of the gifts Jacques Chirac had brought the week before when he had been the first Chequers guest of the Blair premiership. Upstairs after dinner I found the red box that all government members are given by their civil servants at the end of the day. I knew they contained papers that our leaders had to work through. A scarlet leather case, stamped with the royal arms, the red box is one of the great mystical fetish objects in British politics. When no one was looking I committed the treasonable act of flicking the latches and lifting the lid. I was rather astonished, which I should not have been, to see that instead of papers, the box revealed the keyboard of a laptop computer. The astonishment came as much from my knowledge that Blair had no understanding of computers at all, despite his call of 'a laptop for every child' in the recent election. Still, it was a sign of the times.

My task for the Labour Party, from Neil Kinnock onwards, had been to write what I called 'bolt-on modules', paragraphs that addressed whatever it was that Jonathan Powell and others in Neil's/Tony's office thought needed addressing. I am pleased to say I had nothing to do with the disastrous Sheffield triumphalism that many believe dashed Kinnock's chances of defeating John Major in 1992, but I cannot claim that a single paragraph, sentence, phrase or word of mine made the slightest impact on British politics. It probably only served to annoy more people who found 'Labour luvvies' instinctively repellent than it attracted to the party. The idea that I would vote Conservative because Kenny Everett or, heaven help us, Jimmy Savile encouraged us to do so is clearly nonsensical and insulting. I always wanted to keep my name out of the list of prominent Labour supporters for just that reason.

*

While we're in gossipy mood, I suppose I might as well get His Royal Highness the Prince of Wales out of the way. It is fairly well known, amongst those who know these kinds of things fairly well, that I am an admirer of the PoW, and, I believe, vice versa. This puzzles, confuses, angers and distresses some who think that either I am blind to what they consider egregious faults in the Prince, or that I am sycophantic to, and glamourized by, an institution for which they have nothing but contempt. I don't mean in this book to defend the monarchy, which institution must of course appear like an oddity to many. My own view is that, since we have it and since it gives such pleasure to so many, especially around the world, it would be folly to get rid of it. The backside of whom are we going to lick when we send a letter in the Republic of Britain? William Hague? Harriet Harman? An elected British President will not glamourize the heads of state of other countries when they come on a state visit. Compared to carriages, crowns, orbs and ermine, an entry-level Jaguar and Marks & Spencer suit offer no edge over other nations when vying for trade advantages. By definition half the country will despise a Labour President or a Conservative one, and you can bet your bottom dollar that politicians will ensure that, if we do become a republic, there will be little other choice than the major parties. Which, at the time of writing, might include UKIP. Lovely.

I also admire the tradition of the Prime Minister having

to visit the monarch weekly and use him or her as an echo-chamber. I tell Americans that it is the equivalent of their President once a week being obliged to pay a call on Uncle Sam, assuming that that universally recognizable symbol of the nation were a real, bearded fellow in striped trousers and spangled coat. If a man as powerful as a President or a Prime Minister has to explain what he is doing, what he has enacted, how he has responded to this crisis or that, to someone who represents the nation in a way he or she cannot, I think it keeps them from going too power-crazy.

Many people, to return to the man in question, know more about military history than the Prince of Wales; many know more about architecture; many know more about agriculture; many know more about painting; many know more about flying; many know more about sailing; many know more about riding; many know more about horticulture, cheeses, geography, botany, environmental science and so on and so on and so on. You see where I am going. I can honestly say that I have never met anyone who knows more about all those things. This makes him, at least as far as I am concerned, good and interesting company. He was way ahead of the curve when it came to many environmental and agricultural issues, but there remain many things I fundamentally disagree with him about. Homoeopathy for one, and what seems to me his dangerous instinctive distrust of science and fondness for 'faith' for another. I am much more disposed to like some modern architecture than he seems to be. But if disagreements over such matters were causes for scourging and falling out, then who would 'scape whipping, as the man said?

I first got to know him quite well when I found myself at one of those line-ups after a comedy show of some kind in 1990 or thereabouts. He had heard, I think through Rowan Atkinson, that I had a house in the country not far from the royal residence at Sandringham in Norfolk.

'I believe we're neighbours,' he said.

'Indeed, sir,' I said. (Oh! Remind me to tell you a story about Penn Jillette. You'll love it.)

'We absolutely adore Norfolk,' the Prince said. Quite the right thing to say.

'You must come and visit me over Christmas,' I said, knowing that this was the season when the royal family spent most of their Sandringham time.

'Indeed, indeed,' he murmured as he moved on to the next bowing comic in the line.

I thought very little more about it. That Christmas in Norfolk I had a houseful. Something like fourteen people, I believe. I had somehow managed to provide stockings for them all on Christmas Eve (a fantastical effort of wrapping and Sellotaping on the snooker table, an ideal surface for Christmas) and made a chestnut soup, roasted a turkey and provided the approved pudding, bedight with Christmas holly on top, as Dickens phrases it. A week of game playing, film-watching, snoozing and light walking had followed. It was a period when I was off the powder and all the better for it.

One morning I was making hollandaise for Eggs Benedict, a breakfast dish I pride myself in having mastered to the point of professional excellence. Hollandaise, like mayonnaise or any emulsified sauce, takes concentration. The melted butter mustn't be poured too quickly into the egg yolk or the mixture will split. A thin, steady stream is called for. This I was achieving when the phone went.

'Someone answer it!'

Fourteen people slumbering, showering or shagging . . . not one of them, it seems, capable of answering the bloody telephone.

'Will someone just . . . oh never mind!' Abandoning that consignment of hollandaise to failure, I strode to the phone and yanked it from its bracket.

'Yes,' I barked testily.

'Um, can I speak to Stephen Fry, please?'

'This is he.'

'Ah, it's the Prince of Wales here.'

A moment. A heartbeat, no more. And in that short series of milliseconds my brain had instructed my mouth to say: 'Oh fuck off, Rory.'

But somehow one always knows when one is listening to the real thing, not to Rory Bremner or any another impressionist, no matter how skillful. That same brain sent an even faster order to overtake and countermand the first.

'Hello, sir!' I managed to choke. 'I'm afraid you caught me trying to make a hollandaise sauce . . .'

'Ah. I'm so sorry. I was wondering, um, wondering about taking you up on that offer and, um, coming for tea?'

'Of course. That would be marvellous. Absolutely splendid. When did you have in mind?'

'How about New Year's Day?'

'Fabulous. I look forward to it.'

I replaced the phone carefully in its cradle. Hmmm.

I stood in the hallway of the house and, like Rik or Mike in *The Young Ones*, called 'House meeting!' at the top of my voice. Slowly people appeared at the heads of stairways and grumblingly made their way down, like the guests in the fire-alarm scene in *Fawlty Towers*. It was probably about eight in the morning, and I am long used to the dislike and annoyance my being a cheerful morning lark engenders. Most people are owls and take a lot of getting up.

'Look, sorry everyone, but the day after tomorrow the Prince of Wales is coming for tea.'

'Yeah, right.'

'Ha fucking ha.'

'You woke me up for *this*?'

I held up a hand. 'Seriously. He really is.'

But I had lost my audience, who were already tightening their dressing-gown cords and trudging back up the stairs.

It was only when, on the following day, a dark green Range Rover appeared that I was finally truly believed. Two detectives and a dog got out, cordially welcomed a proffered tea and poked around . . . for what we were unable to ascertain. After this cursory security screening of the house and a multitude of chocolate Hobnobs they had gone. My house guests swarmed around me.

'Well!'

'Oh my lord!'

'What on earth am I going to wear?'

All of us adults were traditionally and pleasingly left-leaning without being rude, yet now we found ourselves to be as flushed and excited as a kennelful of beagle puppies hearing the clink of the leash.

We all arose early the next morning. Why I didn't photograph Hugh Laurie hoovering the drawing-room carpet I have no idea. It would be worth millions in blackmail money today. Ah well.*

Everything is polished, swept, cleaned, washed, waxed and prepared. Teapots are at the ready, kettles half on and half off the hottest ring of the Aga. Bread, crumpets and

---

* I was wise enough to run the manuscript of this book by Hugh to check for accuracy. I am sometimes accused of a good memory, but it is only good for useless things. Hugh's is both compendious and useful. I quote his response to the paragraph above: '. . . not that it matters, but it was definitely Rowan who did the hoovering. I also distinctly remember him driving to the petrol station – the only place open on New Year's Day – and coming back with fig rolls, for God's sake. They might have been there since the previous New Year.'

muffins piled up for toasting. Butter softened. Jars of homemade blackcurrant jam and lemon curd (two Christ-mases' worth of presents from my brother's sister-in-law). Sandwiches are cut. Honey! I know he likes honey in his tea! A pot of runny honey is found somewhere. Has it gone off? Honey can't go off, I am assured, a fact that is many years later confirmed for me by a *QI* elf. A wooden honey spoon is discovered in a drawer. The drawer also reveals a better tea-strainer, a proper silver one, not the rather naff Present From Hunstanton which was all I thought I had. Another teapot and a big Dundee cake for his police security men, who will be able to eat in the kitchen. Oh God, have we overdone it? Battenberg cake . . . hell, he might think we're taking the piss. Battenberg was his family name once.

We leave the kitchen and crowd into the drawing room, which has a view through the drawn curtains of the drive-way. It is dark, of course, and has been since early afternoon. It is only a week and a few days since the shortest day of the year. Hugh, who is diligent at this kind of duty, takes the log basket out to reload it. The fire is roaring splendidly, but you cannot have too many logs. Jon Canter, writer and friend, checks the candles that are artfully disposed around the room. I am still twitching one curtain and looking out into the night. Kim and Alastair are twitching another curtain and giggling like Japanese schoolgirls.

Headlamps, as in Dornford Yates novels, stab the air

and sweep the hedgerows. But they are bypassing the driveway. We all look at our watches. Was it after all some gigantic hoax?

Then, before we even seem to know what is upon us, the gravel is crunched alive with the sound of two cars skidding to a halt before the front door.

'Right,' I say, 'let's . . .'

They have all scrammed. Skedaddled. Vamoosed.

'Cowards!' I just have time to shout before gulping, breathing deeply and placing myself on the mat. The front doorbell is rung. If I open the door immediately it will look as if I have been waiting like an uncool cat, which I have been and am, but I count to fifteen to dispel the idea and, just as the second peal begins, swing open the door with a smile.

'Your Royal Highness . . .'

'Hullo. I hope you don't mind, but I've brought my wife.'

Out of the shadows steps Princess Diana. She lowers her head and looks up in that characteristic fashion, captured so many times by Mario Testino and a thousand other photographers, smiling from under her lashes. 'Hello, Stephen,' she sweetly murmurs.

I conduct them into the drawing room. They look around and say approving things about my house. It has six bedrooms and is by no means a cottage, but it would fit comfortably into a half of one Sandringham wing. Well, it is all mine, inasmuch as I earned it and didn't inherit it, so I can't be that ashamed. I am not sure 'earned' is the right word, but this isn't the time to go into that.

Slowly the house guests emerge like shy, hungry zoo animals at feeding time. Introductions are effected, the policemen shown into the kitchen by the back door. Is that rude and disrespectful? They don't show offence, but then they wouldn't. Of the Dundee cake not a crumb was left behind, so I must assume they felt at home.

Back in the drawing room. Hugh and Jo's first child, Charlie, is just at the toddling stage. He lurches zombie-like towards the television (yes, there is a television in my drawing room, which the Prince and you persons of tone and breeding must think grotesquely common, but there we are) and switches it on, a child entirely of his generation. Jo screams out 'Charlie!' and the Prince of Wales, one assumes unused to being addressed in this forceful, matronly manner, jumps sitting down, a clever trick. Meanwhile, to my mortification and that of his mother, *EastEnders* comes on to full blaring cockney life. She leaps to her feet to find the remote control. (That reminds me. Very funny Queen Mother story. Remind me to tell you.)

'No, leave it on,' says the Princess. 'It's the special New Year's edition. I want to find out what happens to Ange.'

The Prince is relaxed and cheerful, the Princess charming and beguiling. She wears cowboy boots that suit her very well. The Prince does not wear cowboy boots, which suits *him* very well.

The honeyed tea and the buttered crumpets and the toast and the cakes last out until it is time for the royal pair to depart.

At the front door the Prince thanks me and bids everyone else farewell. Princess Diana holds in the threshold for a second longer, checks over her shoulder that her Prince is out of earshot and whispers softly in my ear, 'Sorry to leave early, though secretly I'm quite glad. It's *Spitting Image* tonight, and I want to watch it in my room. *They* hate it of course. I absolutely adore it.'

And there you have her in a nutshell. By telling me this she was putting me in her power. It was a statement then worth tens of thousands of pounds. 'Princess Di Loves Anti-Royal Smut Puppets!' All I had to do was pick up the phone to any tabloid. But by confiding in me she had made me in some measure her slave: to be trusted with such intelligence was to be appointed one of her special courtiers. Even as intellectual, sharp, brilliant, knowledgeable and impossibly well-read and sensible a man as Clive James was utterly devoted to her.

I closed the door and leaned back against it in that afraid-it-will-soon-be-opened-again-but-I'll-defend-it-with-my-last-breath manner much noted in fast-paced Leonard Rossiter sitcoms.

'Well!' I said.

'Well!' said everyone else.

'Awfully nice couple,' said Jon Canter, 'awfully nice. I didn't get *her* name.'

For the post-mortem we opened a whisky bottle in the drawing room, caring nothing for clearing up the tea things.

'Unbelievable,' said one of the heterosexual male house guests, of which there were a more than ordinary percentage that Christmas. 'Did you see how she looked at me? I was in there . . . she was practically looking up at the ceiling as if to suggest we go upstairs. Jesus!'

'What are you talking about?' another man interrupted. 'That was me she was giving the eye to.'

'No *me!*'

In the PR war the Prince of Wales never had a chance. His tireless work, his initiatives, the Prince's Trust alone, none of these could compete with so perfect a piece of seductive nature.

For his fiftieth birthday (this is one of the stories I was going to tell you) I emceed an entertainment at the London Palladium. Afterwards I stood once more in the line-up. Next to me was Penn Jillette, one half of the brilliant Penn and Teller, American magicians, pro-science, sceptics of the highest rank.

Penn turned to me as he watched the Prince slowly coming down the line.

'Do I have to call him "Your Majesty" or any of that shit?'

'No, no. Not at all. If you were to use a title it would be "Your Royal Highness", and from then on "sir", but there's no need. After all, I haven't called you Penn once in this conversation until now, have I, Penn?'

'Oh, OK, just so long as he understands that we don't talk like that. And what about bowing? I have to bow? We don't bow in America.'

'No, no,' I reassure him, 'no bowing necessary.'

'Cuz I'm an American, and we don't bow.'

'Yes, he knows you're an American.'

'I won't get put in the Tower of London or anything?'

People always think that sojourns in the Tower of London, like knighthoods, are somehow in the gift of members of the royal family.

I reassured him on these points. No Highnessing, no kowtowing.

At last the Prince reaches Penn, who immediately falls almost prostrate to the floor. 'Your Majesty Highness. Your Royal Sir . . .' and so on and so forth, babbling like a gibbon on speed. The Prince passes on to me and whoever was the other side of me without turning a hair. Seen it all before.

After he had gone, I watched Penn, an enormous man, crouching on the floor, rolling about, beating the planks of the stage, sobbing, stuffing his fist into his mouth and moaning up to the fly-tower: 'Why did I *do* that? What came *over* me? What power do they have? I betrayed my country!'

During the course of the early 1990s, I got to know Sir Martin Gilliat quite well. An extraordinary man. If you didn't know him yourself I assure you you would have loved him. He was of a type that no longer exists and whose very background and manner would now, I suppose, be looked down upon very snootily. Ludgrove House, Eton and forty years Equerry and Private Secretary to Queen Elizabeth the Queen Mother. 'All Sir Martin's geese are swans,' was a popular saying in royal circles. Which, being interpreted, means that everyone was alike in splendour to him, low, high, of whatever background, breeding, race or gender. I never met a man of such natural charm, kindness and vivacity. He had had a 'good war', of which, naturally, he never spoke. He escaped the Nazis several times but was always recaptured. At last, like all serial escapers, he was sent to Colditz, the Eton of prison camps. I was told that he had never slept since. Not properly. Apparently doctors examined him until he got tired of it* and sent them packing. This made him ideal for the Queen Mother. She would dine festively, play amusing games and then go to bed round about one or two in the morning. He would sit up writing letters until she came down. They would walk the dogs together in the park. Ideal companions.

There is a story told in Hugo Vickers's biography of Queen Elizabeth, as she was known in the Household. She liked pranks at parties. One evening after dinner at the Castle of Mey, her favourite residence, right up in the very north of Scotland in Caithness, she and the ladies, having retired to leave the men to their port, decided it

* Not tired enough to sleep, obviously . . .

would be a lark if they all hid behind the curtains to surprise the men when they came out after their port and cigars.

Sir Martin led the men out and said in his very loud voice, 'Thank God for that, they've all fucked off to bed.'

I got to know him because he was an inveterate punter in the West End stage, what is known as an angel. He hit the motherlode with *Me and My Girl* and was forever grateful. He invited Rowan Atkinson (who also knew him) and me to Buck's, his club, for lunch. Over the gulls' eggs and asparagus he confessed that there was an ulterior motive for his invitation.

'Marvellous to have you chaps to luncheon of course, but I have to ask you. Do you know the Dowager Duchess of Abercorn?'

We both regretfully disavowed ever having had that pleasure.

'No? Well. She was a lady-in-waiting of Queen Elizabeth's for many years. It is her eightieth birthday in July, and we, which is to say Queen Elizabeth, are going to throw her a birthday party at Claridge's, and I thought perhaps you might provide a little light relief? We have a band, but comedy is always popular.'

Rowan and I digested this and exchanged speaking glances. The year before he and I had descended on the Middle East, a swoop known in Rowanese as a bank raid. Rowan and I performed in his amusingly entitled *One Man Show* in Bahrain, Abu Dhabi, Dubai and Oman, brightening the lives of expat oil executives with high-quality, high-priced comedic entertainment. So we did have a show.

Rowan expressed our reservations perfectly.

'Well now,' he said. 'We do indeed have material, b-but if most of the audience is the same age as the Duchess and the Queen Mo . . . Queen Elizabeth, then some of it might seem a bit . . .'

'A bit fast? A bit racy?' boomed Sir Martin, his resonant voice echoing off every surface of the dining room and rattling the glassware. 'Oh I wouldn't worry about that. The royal family loves the lavatory. I mean obviously not yer fucks or yer cunts.'

'Well quite,' said Rowan, swallowing and looking down at his plate. 'No indeed.'

Sir Martin, as a loyal servant, was not one prone to gossip but he could not help telling me this story of his employer. One morning in the upstairs drawing room of Clarence House she said to him, 'Martin, I think our television is on the blink. Do you think we might need a new one?'

'I shall have a look, ma'am.'

Sure enough the television – this was many years ago – was suffering from that annoying rolling horizontal bar affliction that was the bane of many an ageing cathode ray tube.

'Ma'am, I shall be straight on the telephone to those nice people at Harrods, and while you're at luncheon they will install a new one.'

'Lovely, Martin. You're an angel.'

This was, of course, before the days of the not-so-cold war between the royal households and Mohamed Al Fayed's Harrods.

After her luncheon the Queen Mother – Queen Elizabeth, I beg her pardon – tottered upstairs to watch the three o'clock from Chepstow or whatever it may have been, and there was Sir Martin, standing proudly by a brand-new, very large television set.

'Oh, how grand!' said Queen Elizabeth.

'Yes indeed, ma'am, and I'll tell you something rather special.'

'Oh do, do!'

'You might notice that it has no buttons for changing the channels.'

'Oh no,' she squealed, 'they've forgotten the buttons. How dreadful!'

'Ah, but no, ma'am. Do you see that grey box next to your gin and Dubonnet on the side table there?'

'Oh, now whatever can that be?'

'Well that is what they call a "remote control", ma'am. If you'll allow me . . . I press the button marked 1, so, and up comes BBC 1. I press button 2 and up comes BBC 2. And then button 3 for ITV. You see?'

'Oh, how clever!' Queen Elizabeth beamed approvingly and then added, 'I still think it's easier to ring.'

Living the Life

Over the decades I have been asked to deliver lectures, disquisitions and addresses on numerous subjects and for the most part I manage to excuse myself. Just occasionally, however, a subject is so appealing or a cause so close to my heart and my diary so surprisingly and unwontedly amenable that I find myself under an obligation to disgorge as requested. I offer you the opening of a lecture I gave in the Royal Geographical Society's lecture theatre some years ago: the first Spectator Lecture, or Speccie Leccie, as I called it. I have scavenged from it and present the exordium so as to make coherent some of my thoughts about America, a country I was becoming more and more fond of and anxious to visit more and more often.

Thank you. Thank you very much. Good lord. Well, well. Here we are. Gathered together in the very lecture theatre where Henry Morton Stanley once told an enraptured world of his momentous meeting with Dr Livingstone. Charles Darwin was a member and gave talks in this same hall. Sir Richard Burton lectured here, and John Hanning Speke . . . spoke. Shackleton and Hillary displayed their intimate frostbite scars to a spellbound RGS audience. Explorers, adventurers and navigators have been coming here for the best part of 180 years to tell of their discoveries. If only at school, geography teachers, surely the most scoffed and pilloried class of pedagogue there is, if only they had concentrated less on rift valleys, trig points and the major exports of Indonesia and more on the fact that geography could promise a classy royal society with the sexiest lecture theatre in the land. Actually, now that I think of it, one reason for me to be fond of the subject was the circumstance that in my prep-school geography room there were piles and piles of shiny yellow *National Geographic* magazines available for skimming through. These, with their glossy advertisements for Chesterfield cigarettes, Cadillac sedans and Dimple whisky, gave me my first view outside television of what America might be like. But there was another reason religiously to scan the magazines . . .

National Geographic, before it became best known for an imbecilic and embarrassing suite of digital TV channels, was – thanks to its anthropological coverage in a pre-internet, pre-Channel 4, pre-top shelf age – the only place where a curious boy could look at full colour pictures of naked people. For that alone it deserves the thanks of generations. One did get the false impression that many peoples of the world had protuberances shaped exactly like a gourd, but never mind.

National Geographic made films too, and at my school these would be run through an old Bell & Howell

Self, Ben Elton, Robbie Coltrane, Griff Rhys Jones, Mel Smith, Rowan Atkinson.

An idiot and an imbecile.

Ready to lay down their lives for my country.

A blithering idiot and a gibbering imbecile.

Radio Times 1988 Christmas
Edition: *Saturday-Night Fry* feature.

11.00 Saturday-Night Fry

A programme in the direct line
of comedy that runs like a
silken vase from Aristophanes
to the *Today* programme.
A show identical in spirit to
the great Mary Queen of Scots
tapestry that hangs in
Osterley House.
Starring **Stephen Fry**
Hugh Laurie and
Emma Thompson
A special guest appearance
by a special guest
Written by STEPHEN FRY
Additional material by IAN BROWN
and JAMES HENDRIE
Producer DAN PATTERSON. *Stereo*
(Re-broadcast Wednesday at 7.45pm)

Frying tonight

Saturday-Night Fry is, according to Stephen Fry (right), 'a radio comedy
that roams between E. M. Forster, Jimmy Savile and a small town in
Venezuela with the graceful ease of a mastodon migrating from grassy
uplands to a marshy swamp'. It's written by Stephen himself and co-stars
old chums Hugh Laurie (who also joins Stephen in a BBC2 special) and
Emma Thompson (of *Fortunes of War*).

'The show is Stephen's own peculiar brand of humour,' explains Emma
(currently writing her own comedy for BBCtv). 'It's got a sort of story
running through it, but basically it's a continuous stream of madness.'
Q. Who did Stephen play in *Blackadder II*?

Hugh, Jo and I.

With sister, Jo.

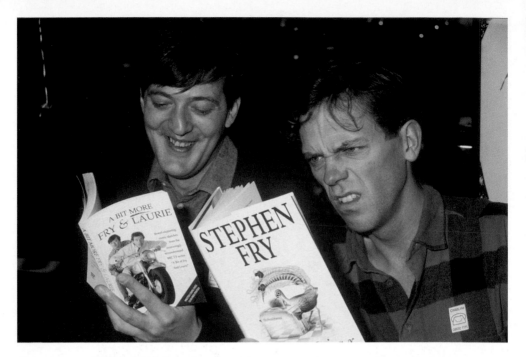

A signing at a Dillons bookshop. London, 1991.

Hugh's warmest, most approving look, 1991.

Despite his resemblance to a 15-year-old shuffling schoolboy, Stephen Fry has numerous television series, charity benefits and now a novel behind him. His sister Jo, *opposite page*, runs operations from his house in Islington

A profile of a liar for the publication of *The Liar*, 1991, with sister Jo.

TRUE CONFESSIONS OF A LIAR

Stephen Fry has confessed to everything: public school, prison, Cambridge, homosexuality, credit card theft and attempted suicide. But, strangely, his semi-autobiographical first novel is called The Liar. *Jessica Berens goes in search of the man behind the truth - and finds a mask.*

Photographs by Kim Knott

Tourrettes-sur-Loup
– my best audience.

Tourrettes-sur-Loup – picking
on someone my own size.

projector by the geography masters to keep us quiet and
to give them time to beetle off and pursue their amorous
liaisons with matron or the whisky bottle, depending on
which teacher it was. 'Fry, you're in charge,' they would
never say on their way out. But what strange films they
left us to watch. I seem to recall that the subjects were
usually logging in Oregon, the life cycle of the beaver or
the excitements to be found in the National Parks of
Montana and Wyoming. Very blue skies, lots of spruce,
larch and pine, and plenty of plaid shirtings. The unreli-
able speed of that hot and dusty old Bell & Howell
rendered the soundtrack and its music flat then sharp
then flat again in rolling waves of discord, but it was the
commentators that gave me raptures with their magis-
terially rich and rolling American rhetoric. What a peculiar
way with language they had, employing poetical tricks
that had been out of date a hundred years earlier. My
favourite was the 'be-' game. If a word usually began
with the prefix 'be-' it was taken off. Thus 'beneath'
became 'neath' and so on. But the 'be' of 'beneath'
wasn't simply thrown away. No, no. It was *recycled* by adding it to words it had no business being anywhere near.
Which would result in preposterous declamatory oro-
tundities of this nature: 'Neath the bedappled verdure
of the mighty sequoia sinks the bewestering sun,' and so
forth. And what is the proper name for *this* rhetorical
trope, also much deployed? It would start with the usual
'be-' nonsense: 'Neath becoppered skies bewends . . .'

199

but then this: 'the silver ribbon of time that *is* the Colorado River'. The weird and senseless maze of metonym and metaphor that *was* National Geographic Speak in all its besplendour was a great influence on me, for where others had rock and roll music, I had language . . .

And so I bewended and bewittered like the large slab of humanity that *was* Stephen Fry. Despite my passion for all things American and my obsession with its language, literature, history and culture, I didn't visit the country until I was well into my twenties. I had adapted and rewritten the book of the British musical *Me and My Girl* as alluded to *passim*, and it was decided that a Broadway production might be worth attempting. With Mike Ockrent, the director, and Robert Lindsay, the star, I took a PanAm flight from London to JFK. I had never been so excited in my life. My first view of the Manhattan skyline was like Dante's first view of Beatrice, Cortez's of the Pacific and, I dare say, Simon Cowell's of Susan Boyle. I fell for New York quite as much as Wodehouse, W. H. Auden, Oscar Wilde and my other literary heroes had before me. But we were only there for rehearsals. The musical was to try out and open in Los Angeles, California. My first visit, and I was to live for a while in both Manhattan and Beverly Hills. My cup ran over like a blocked gutter.

In Broadway's theatre district there is a famous eatery called the Carnegie Deli. It features in Woody Allen's

Broadway Danny Rose, you may remember. It was on my first full day in America that I went in there and ordered a pastrami sandwich. Big deal, you may say. Oh yes. Big deal. Huge deal. For those who have not had the pleasure, a proper New York deli pastrami sandwich is about the size and thickness of a rugby ball. Two thin layers of rye bread and in between slice after slice after slice of warm, fatty, delicious pastrami. On the side is served a pickle or so. Hold that image. Me facing off with a vast pastrami sandwich. Right. We now scuttle to LA. I blew all my per diems on a single weekend in the Bel Air Hotel, luxury on a scale I had never even imagined, let alone contemplated. Robert Redford winked at me from across the breakfast room. I nearly trod on a dog belonging to Shirley MacLaine. My over-running cup ran over even more till it was more like the Trevi Fountain than any sort of cup I know.

Then back to New York. I am happy to say the opening night of *Me and My Girl* was everything one could have hoped for. The *New York Times* raved; we were a hit. I won a Drama Desk award and a Tony nomination; Robert Lindsay went on to win a Tony and a hatful of other trophies for his brilliant performance. There and then I promised myself that one day I would live in New York, this city from whose sidewalks you drew electricity like a tube train from its tracks. At the time I had been staying in an apartment belonging to my friend Douglas Adams. On the flight back I garrulously chattered away to an

American lady sitting next to me about how I loved America and was planning to live in New York.

'But honey,' she said – she was rather in the Rosalind Russell Auntie Mame mould – 'honey, you told me you'd only ever been to New York City and Los Angeles.'

I confessed that this was true.

'Then you have never even *seen* America,' she said.

I suppose regarding a *part* of something as being congruent to its *whole* might be viewed as a kind of *pars pro toto* fallacy or lazy synecdoche, but I didn't truly understand what this woman meant until, as the *National Geographic* might say, I bethought me of the colossal continent of succulence that *was* a Carnegie Deli sandwich. How could anyone say they had eaten a Carnegie Deli pastrami sandwich if in fact they had only gnawed at the thin slices of rye at either end while the whole continent of meat lay untouched? How could anyone say they had experienced America who had only nibbled at New York and Los Angeles?

One of the tasks I was – er – tasked to do when in Los Angeles some time in 1990 or 1991 was to pick up a script in Las Vegas and transport it to London. To fax an entire 120-page script from Las Vegas to London might have been within the budget of a major studio, but not within the budget of Renaissance Films, Ken Branagh's production company, founded with a City gentleman turned producer called Stephen Evans. Email attachments were but a glint in the eye of the future. If you had a document to send you used a courier. Couriers came in the shape of DHL and FedEx or possibly in the shape of Stephen Fry.

I cannot remember what had taken me to Los Angeles in 1991, or even if I have the year right, but I do know that the previous winter I had invited Emma Thompson and her new husband, Ken Branagh, for a week at my Norfolk house. They had seen me chopping wood. We had talked of this and that and somehow, as is the way with Ken, a story idea had been born or confirmed in his head.

I think perhaps on reflection that I may have got this wrong. Maybe it was Martin Bergman* and his wife, the American comedian Rita Rudner,† who had been up to Norfolk, for it was certainly they who wrote the screen-play in question. Oh memory, what a ditzy queen you are.

Well, well. The facts of the matter are that Ken knew I was in Los Angeles and asked me to stop off in Las Vegas and pick up the latest version of the script. I had not read *any* version of it, but had agreed to be in it, such was my instinctive trust of Ken and such were his extraordinary powers of persuasion.

The film was to be called *Peter's Friends*, and I read it on

---

*Ex-President of the Cambridge Footlights. Before my time, but he co-produced our 1981 tour of Australia, magnificently described in *The Fry Chronicles*.

† Terrifically funny American stand-up comedian. 'I can't understand why cosmetics manufacturers make perfumes that smell of flowers. Men don't like flowers. If they want to attract men they should bring out a scent called New Car Interior . . .'

the plane back from Los Angeles with a mounting sense of horror. It was funny, I thought, but it was about *us*. About Hugh and me and Emma and Tony Slattery and our Footlights generation seven or eight years on. Ken had enjoyed great success with the film version of his triumphant Stratford *Henry V* and now he wanted to make a kind of British *Big Chill*.

Hugh and I, perhaps because of the permanent guilt derived from our perceived privileged upbringings, instinctively recited in our minds the likely response of critics whenever a new project arose. We had in mind some kind of antagonistic *Time Out* reviewer. The wrinkle in his nose, the snort of his derision, the slow downward curl of his lips – we were there before him, writing his copy as if inside his head and the heads of everyone else. This we will return to in a moment.

In the spring of '88 I played the part of the philosopher Humphry in Simon Gray's *The Common Pursuit* in Watford and at the Phoenix Theatre in the West End. During that time I had been making the television version of *Delve Special*, which had been retitled *This Is David Lander*. Filming all day and then just making it in time to the theatre and after *that* being naughty in the Limelight nightclub with rock stars, snooker players and other disparate low-life legends seemed to be something I could manage, although my doctor popped into the dressing room at the Phoenix twice a week to inject me with B12 to keep my

energy levels up. I don't remember asking for this, so I
assume it was the show's producer who probably worried, as producers do, that I might be running out of fuel.
The run of the play was followed by a period Hugh and I
had set aside to write all the material for a comedy sketch
show that we decided after much agonized debate to call
A Bit of Fry and Laurie.

In the early spring of 1989 we began taping the first
full series of this ('a lacklustre throwback trapped in an
irrelevant Oxbridge past', we imagined *Time Out* snarling
furiously). In the summer of that year we recorded *Blackadder Goes Forth* ('a sad dip in form after the delights of
Blackadder the Third', *Time Out* would be sure to mutter)
and immediately after that Hugh and I filmed the first
series of *Jeeves and Wooster*, again sharing throughout the
shoot what we imagined would be *Time Out*'s verdict:
'while the rest of the world leaps ahead in innovation and
edge, Fry and Laurie welter feebly in a snobbish and
puerile past'.* This had come about when a fellow called
Brian Eastman had asked for a meeting. Eastman had
previously worked in music for the Royal Philharmonic
Orchestra and the British Council and now had a company that produced most notably the series *Poirot* on ITV.

---

*For all I know this is deeply unfair, and *Time Out* welcomed us with
lavish praise. We were too scared to look. I remember years earlier Rik
Mayall opening a *Time Out* to see a review of the second series of *The
Young Ones*. '"Nothing like as good as the pioneering first series,"' he
read, then spluttered, Riklike, 'but they *hated* the first series. Bastards!'

It was his plan to bring Wodehouse's Bertie and Jeeves to the screen, and he felt that Hugh and I were good casting. Strangely, to us at least, he was quite open as to which roles we felt each should play. It seemed obvious to us that Hugh was a natural Bertie and I more suited to Jeeves. Hugh put it this way: Bertie's voice is a trumpet, Jeeves's a cello.

Actually, such was our insecurity and fear of failure we didn't really believe it could be done and might easily have turned Brian down, had it not been for a fear of any other two actors playing the parts. The pessimism in this case wasn't entirely our usual flabby lack of confidence, so much as an immense respect of, and devotion to, Wodehouse's work. His novels and stories, like any writer's, are composed of plot, character and language. What makes Wodehouse stand head and shoulders above any comic writer of the twentieth century (indeed almost any writer, regardless of genre) is his *language*. In the end we decided if we could get across character and plot and only a small amount of that peerless prose then we might turn enough people to reading the books, consigning them to a lifetime of endless pleasure. Clive Exton, who wrote the adaptation, was best known for his chilling screenplay *10 Rillington Place*, the grim, murky retelling of the Christie murders. But he had since moved to another world of Christie murders altogether as one of the lead writers on the *Poirot* series.

Fry and Laurie seemed sometimes to be a desperate affair,

writing and staring at the wall and not believing we were at all funny, performing dozens of sketches before a live audience on each recording evening and then worrying straight away about the next week. But I was working with Hugh, my best friend in the whole world, and while sketch delivery, like any kind of birth, involves pain and squealing, it was a period of fecundity, laughter, freedom and friendship that I would have been lucky to have experienced had I lived a hundred lives. Sometimes I will be sent a YouTube link on Twitter and out of curiosity follow it up only to discover that it is an old *Fry and Laurie* sketch that I have almost entirely forgotten. Forgive me if occasionally I find myself laughing and actually feeling proud. Naturally, as we all do, I wince and writhe in embarrassment at this mannerism or that, but I do really believe that some of our writing and performing was . . . well . . . top hole . . .

Straight after *Fry and Laurie* we made *Blackadder Goes Forth*. The audience that came into the BBC studios, as I have mentioned, had almost certainly seen *Blackadder II* and *Blackadder the Third* on their televisions at home and were somewhat alienated by new characters and settings. In rehearsal there was a lot of pacing, smoking, coffee-drinking and throwing out ideas, not to mention having ideas thrown out. We were young, we were buzzy and we were also, although we had no idea of it at all, making a comedy series that for whatever reason appears to have stood the test of time. The character drawing and imagination of writers Richard Curtis and Ben Elton, our own additions, I would modestly suggest, the extraordinary talent of Rowan, Hugh, (Sir) Tony Robinson, Tim McInnerny and the late and hugely lamented Rik Mayall all seemed to combine in a way that simply clicked. John Lloyd, the producer, kept us all on point, as Americans like to say, but on a couple of occasions we made such drastic changes to the storyline that whole new sets had to be ordered from the production designer just two days before recording, and it was John who manfully took the blame each time. My own proudest achievement is perhaps not the playing of the insane General Melchett, but the suggestion after the first read-through that Tim McInnerny's character's name be changed from the proffered 'Perkins' or 'Cartwright' to something that might explain his animosity, suspicion and hostility to all around him. I wondered if 'Darling' might not work, and Rowan and Tim ran with the ball as only actors of their quality could.

Jeeves and Wooster, which started more or less straight after *Blackadder* finished, was unalloyed pleasure. Hugh and I both took to single-camera filming (as opposed to the multi-camera TV studio set-up then customary in which sitcoms were recorded on tape) like ducks to bread crusts. We had wonderful fellow actors to work with and lively, funny crews full of banter and inventiveness. Between them they had been involved in many of the best films ever to have come out of Britain, from *Dr No* to *Dr Strangelove*.

Somehow during this period as well as my involvement in those three television series I had also written four or five twenty-minute films for John Cleese's company Video Arts. Video Arts specialized in training films for business and industry. These films had been constructed around psychological ideas all vetted by John Cleese's pet psychologist, Robin Skynner, with whom he'd written the book *Families and How to Survive Them*. They had thrilling titles like *How to Schedule a Meeting*, *How to Run an Interview*, *How to Succeed in a Job Application*. I secretly called the whole project 'How to Make Money by Stating the So Fucking Obvious It Makes Your Nose Bleed'. If businesses needed to be told in firm language:

- make a list
- stick to it

then no wonder the British economy was swirling round the lavatory pan. They were fun films to make, however, and to be around John Cleese, a towering hero from my early teens, still made me rub my eyes with disbelief. I had written roles for myself, John, Hugh and Dawn French. Other parts were played by Ronnie Corbett and Julian Holloway.

It was during this period, post *Fry and Laurie*, *Blackadder* and *Jeeves and Wooster*, that I made simply the best decision in my entire life. It saved my health, my career and (for a time at least) my sanity.

While I had been deep in this absolutely brutal schedule (although it seemed natural to me), my sister Jo had completed a TV and film make-up course in London, and one evening we had dinner in Orso, the popular Covent Garden restaurant.

I had been turning something over in my mind and finally, over the *panna cotta alla fragole*, I ventilated it.

'Jo, I know there's always the possibility of your going off to do make-up work on a film or something. And I know Richard might get stationed abroad,* but do you think you might like . . . ?'

'Yes?'

'Well, if this is out of order just spray wine at me, but how would you feel about . . . ?'

'Go on.'

'Well, over the last few years I've started to get more and more fan mail, more and more requests for appearances and after-dinner speaking and the lord knows what else. It's kind of out of control . . .'

'Right . . .'

'My diary is so packed that I can hardly keep up with what I'm doing, and I need, well I need a . . .'

'A secretary?'

'Well, the term for it is Personal Assistant. PA. But in your case, being a personal sister, you'd be a Personal Assister.'

'Oh God, that is so exactly what I hoped you'd ask me. I was going to suggest the same thing. I'd love it. I'd love it more than anything.'

---

* Her husband, Richard, was an RAF pilot.

For the past twenty-six years, then, Jo has been my PA. She is the best PA anyone ever had. Naturally I would say that out of family loyalty, but a story illustrates the point.

During filming with John Cleese somewhere in West London for a Video Arts project, Jo visited the set with her Filofax to go over the next week's diary business. This was before you could electronically sync diaries over the air, well before PDAs and smartphones. She stayed for lunch, joined John in watching me film a scene with Ronnie Corbett and then biffed off.

About ten minutes later John stalked over.

'Well, don't I feel a total dick.'

'What's happened?'

'All my working life I've looked for the perfect assistant, and you, you bastard, have found her. So naturally I said to her while you were on camera, "Whatever he's paying you, I'll double it."'

'Ah. What did she say?'

'She smiled very sweetly and said, "That's very kind, Mr Cleese, but he is actually my brother." I don't know when I last felt such a complete tit.'

'Well, you weren't to know . . .'

I was, of course, very pleased to hear such praise. It was entirely typical that Jo herself never mentioned this story to me. I finally raised it a week or so later.

'You do know John told me about trying to poach you?'

'Oh that! That was funny . . .'

'You could have told me, and I'd've had to double your pay . . .'

Which I think, I *hope*, I did.

It is no exaggeration to say that I would not be alive now were it not for Jo's gentle but firm control of my life. I tease her by calling her Martina Bormann, my diary Nazi, but it would have been impossible to have done a tenth of the things I have done without her understanding of how diaries, film schedules, call sheets, production companies, television executives, airports, drivers and above all her capricious, weird and impossible boss/ brother operate. Or fail to.

I was called one week the following year, which was probably 1990 but don't quote me, to visit a certain Roger Peters, who was installed in splendour in Suite 512 of the Savoy Hotel. The man turned out to be an American of middle years. He gave me to understand that he was the heir and last lover of the American composer Samuel Barber. I had always believed that Barber had died of a broken heart after his long-time partner and fellow musician Gian Carlo Menotti traded him in for a younger model, but it seems he found Roger Peters at the end.

Roger, it seemed, had the film rights to Noël Coward's *Hayfever* and wondered if I was interested in writing the adaptation. I politely demurred, knowing that: a) *Hayfever* was Coward's favourite play and he had specifically given orders that 'no cunt ever be allowed to fuck about with it';

and b) it was all set in one place and just about one time, adhering as closely as possible to the Aristotelian unities, making it a bugger to adapt for the screen. Not that Reginald Rose and Sidney Lumet didn't do a bang-up job with *12 Angry Men* . . .

He didn't seem too offended, and we drank and chatted and gossiped. I guessed that he had asked just about everyone who had ever held a pen or tapped at a keyboard to take on this job, starting, as one did, with Stoppard, Bennett and Pinter and then reaching after exhausting weeks of refusals the bottom of the barrel. Not false modesty, just realism.

The suite was magnificent, with spectacular views that gave out on to the Thames. The idea of living permanently in such splendour filled me with a perfectly unforgivable mixture of envy and ambition. One day, I thought to myself, one day . . .

The calendar pages peeled and blew away, as Vivian Stanshall phrased it, and it is now early 1992, and I find myself window-shopping along Piccadilly.

'Hello, Stephen!'

I have a mild case of prosopagnosia, absolutely maddening. Nothing like the severe face-blindness that afflicts some. I have a friend who cannot distinguish his own family members until they say their name. My level of this disorder may not be severe, but it does mean I frequently appear rude. So if you know me and I cut you in the street, it doesn't mean that I don't like you and wish to blank you out of my life, it just means I haven't the faintest idea who you are. Tell me your name, and I'll be absolutely fine. Most people are the other way about and remember faces but not names.

This fellow, fortunately, was happy to supply the name without prompting.

'Roger Peters!'

'Of course,' I said. 'How's tricks?'

'Well, you know,' he said, falling into step. 'You're just the fellow. Do you know of anyone, *anyone* . . .'

Oh God, he's going to harp on about the bloody *Hayfever* script again, I moaned inwardly.

'. . . *anyone* who'd be willing to live in my Savoy suite for four or five weeks. I have to go to America for family business and I don't want to move all my stuff out. I have a deal with the hotel whereby I pay by the year anyway, so it's just a question of someone suite-sitting. Anybody come to mind?'

'We-e-ll . . .' I said doubtfully, 'there is one person it might suit. He's about this high . . .' I raised my hand to the level of my head. 'About this wide . . .' I parted my hands to the width of my body. 'He has a bent nose and he's talking to you right this minute.'

'Oh, that's fantastic! I'm leaving Wednesday. Why don't you come round tomorrow afternoon, and I'll introduce you to the floor butler and show you where everything is.'

And so it came to pass that the Savoy Hotel became my home for just over a month. For eleven days of that time we filmed *Peter's Friends*. The script that I couriered over to London the year before had been polished and burnished and buffed to a light sheen, but Hugh and I were still, to our eternal discredit, deeply embarrassed about the whole thing. Occasionally in the hallways, corridors and drawing rooms of Wrotham Park (the grand house outside Barnet where we had already shot some scenes in *Jeeves and Wooster* and where I was many years later to shoot scenes in Robert Altman's *Gosford Park*), occasionally, Ken would see Hugh and me looking hangdog and licked to a splinter between set-ups.

'Everything all right, darlings?'

'They're going to hate us,' I moaned.

'Who? What do you mean?'

'"This incestuous, up-itself tale of Oxbridge wankers who reveal their feeble, wimpy and effete so-called 'problems' over a weekend of excess in a country house ..." Can you imagine how *Time Out* are going to react?' (I've no idea why *Time Out* was still the symbol and focus of all our insecurities.)

'*Time Out*? Who gives a fuck? It's read by about twelve people. Seriously, loves, why would you worry about what they think?'

We admired Ken Branagh, and still do, for many reasons, but his magnificent ability not to be downcast or diverted by concerning himself with how some reviewer was going to react to his work was near the top of the list of his accomplishments. Daring and courage are half the battle with acting, directing and film-making. If you have a newspaper reviewer or even the ghost of a generalized and antagonistic public over your shoulder tutting and hissing in through their teeth as you try to concentrate then you are doomed to failure.

Ken, of course, does not associate his place in the world with guilt. He grew up in Northern Ireland in no position of prosperity. His love of theatre was in-born and absolute; any money he managed to earn he would spend on the ferry to the mainland and the bus to Stratford-upon-Avon, where he would watch every season from his early teenage years onwards. It is no accident that he arrived for the first full day of shooting for *Peter's Friends* already filled with knowledge, courage and self-belief. It is also, I would argue, no accident that Hugh and I arrived almost sick with apprehension, shame and foreboding. The very good fortune that took us from our public schools (by way of other schools and prison in my case) via Cambridge, the Footlights and into *Blackadder, Jeeves and Wooster* and our own sketch show, far from filling us with confidence, made us feel utterly unworthy. Please do not think we are asking for sympathy and certainly not for admiration. I speak as it was in our befuddled minds, and you may take it as you will. Perhaps if you have imagination you can see yourself feeling the same way under the same circumstances. Perhaps we were just peculiarly weird.

That a whole feature film could be shot in eleven days

was testament to the work ethic of Ken and his crew, the tight unity of time and place within Martin and Rita's script and, of course, the sparsity of the budget.

Meanwhile, the pleasure of having a car coming to pick me up from the Savoy and dropping me there in the evening was almost more thrilling than anything I had ever experienced. The top-hatted 'linkmen', often incorrectly referred to as doormen, were unfailingly polite to me, and I soon got to know the rest of the staff. If you want to know anything about the depths of degradation of the human being, make the acquaintance of the executive housekeeper of any large hotel. You will never be the same again. Discretion prohibits me from going any further, this is a journey you must undertake yourself. It is a bit like telling someone to look up the word 'munting' in urbandictionary.com. I take no further responsibility.

Otherwise the joys of suite-sitting were altogether delicious. No bathrobes were ever softer and fluffier, no shower-rose wider and more generous in its precipitation. One small and entirely preposterous annoyance however, a something that got under my skin, was the daily *sameness* of it all. That ashtray on that table in the drawing room was always placed *exactly* there. That chair always angled *exactly* that way. One day I mentioned this to the floor butler.

'Whenever I come back from filming or from a walk,' I said, 'the suite has been wonderfully cleaned and tidied, but – and I really don't mean this as a criticism – everything is always in exactly the same place. The ornaments on the mantelpiece, the . . .'

'Sir, say no more. From tomorrow we will surprise you in small ways each day.'

Which they did. It made me, and I like to think the chambermaid and other staff members, giggle, each time they made a small alteration. Playing Hunt the Ashtray kept me on my toes and freshened the experience of hotel living.

One spare evening I had gone to see a production of *Tartuffe* in which my good friend Johnny Sessions played a role. Also in the production was Dulcie Gray, whose husband, Michael Denison, had played Algernon in Anthony Asquith's *The Importance of Being Earnest*, delivering the line: 'I hope, Cecily, I shall not offend you if I state quite frankly and openly that you seem to me to be in every way the visible personification of absolute perfection?', that very joyous progression of words that had so made me wriggle and writhe and squirm with delight when a young boy.

Michael and Dulcie, a grand and much-loved theatrical couple, made a tradition of having a summer party at Shardeloes, a marvellous eighteenth-century house in Old Amersham with noble Robert Adam interiors and a 1796 landscaped garden by Humphry Repton. The house had been saved, restored and divided up in the 1970s after falling into the customary nursing-home use and further slow decline. Dulcie and Michael had the best ground-floor rooms, giving out over the great lawn; their party, when I arrived, was already crammed with figures from the British film and theatre world. I found myself falling into conversation with Doreen, widow of the great Jack Hawkins, one of my favourite British film stars. Then who should I see across the room? Did my eyes believe it? My favourite of them all, John Mills. A certain amount of excited hopping on one leg, a little light coughing and I found myself sitting on a sofa next to him. He twinkled, just as I expected him to, this nimble, unutterably charming and deeply gifted man. His wife, Mary Hayley Bell, author of *Whistle Down the Wind*, barked and laughed just as I expected her to.

John Mills was the man Noël Coward wrote 'Mad Dogs and Englishmen' for. In the mid-1930s he had been a singer, hoofer and all-round entertainer for a company with the unfortunate name of 'The Quaints'. Coward, on a journey back from Australia, stopped off in Singapore and saw a poster offering the unlikely double bill (surely not in one night?) of *Hamlet* and *Mr Cinders*. It was in the latter that the lithe, lissom and perky Mills impressed. Coward went round afterwards and told him to visit him in London, where he would find a part for him.

Johnny Mills had a genius for friendship. Coward (whom Mills was the first to dub 'the Master'), Laurence Olivier, Rex Harrison, Richard Attenborough, Bryan Forbes and many others benefited from his selfless and sweetly unegotistical charm.

As we sat on the sofa at Shardeloes I must have bombarded him with dozens of questions about his films and career. *The October Man, In Which We Serve, Ryan's Daughter, Hobson's Choice, Tiger Bay, Swiss Family Robinson* and above all *Ice Cold in Alex, Great Expectations* and *Tunes of Glory* had affected me profoundly.

When I paused to draw breath, Johnny asked me what I was up to. I explained that I was in the middle of making a picture with Kenneth Branagh.

'Oh, no, really?' said Johnny. 'I wonder, would you do me a favour?'

'Anything.'

'Could you tell Kenneth that, as a friend of Larry Olivier's, I just know how much Larry would have loved Kenneth's *Henry V* and how much he would have loathed the vile comparisons the critics have made. Can you tell him that?' Johnny was referring to the fact that, while Ken's *Henry V* had been an undoubted success, many snarky responses along the lines of 'Who does he think he is? He's no Laurence Olivier' had greeted its release.

'I'm afraid I can't pass that message on,' I told Johnny.

'Oh.' He looked rather nonplussed.

'I'd much prefer you to pass it on yourself. If I gave a dinner party, would you and Lady Mills come along?'

He beamed assent, telephone numbers were swapped, and the thing was fixed.

There is nothing quite like hosting a dinner party in a five-star hotel suite. Yes, of course, I'm aware of how utterly appalling that sounds, but I might as well get the story out.

Here's how it goes. You tell Alfonso and Ernesto on your floor that you plan to have six guests for dinner next Friday, and they bow with pleasure.

When the day dawns, Ernesto comes in with a menu card and the suggestions from the executive chef and his team toiling in the hypocausts six floors below. You select what you hope is an agreeable dinner* and then, at round about six o'clock, Alfonso, who doesn't want you under his feet while he sees to the flowers and place settings, comes in and commands that you go on a walk. When you arrive back at the suite everything is simply perfect. The armchairs have been moved back to the window, in a semi-circle looking out over the Thames at dusk. In the centre of the room the main table has had an extra leaf inserted to accommodate seven people: I have invited Hugh and Jo Laurie, Emma Thompson and Ken and of course Sir John and Lady Mills.

Starched white napery, crystal glassware and silver

---

*I bore in mind the fact (told to me years ago by my mother, who knows these things, when watching a Mills film) that Sir John had been for fifty years on the Hay Diet. When he was a young man he had developed a stomach ulcer, then the most common cause of death of men under forty in Britain. Today, of course, suicide is the most common. Someone recommended to him the Hay Diet, in which protein and carbohydrates are never combined. Vegetables are 'neutral'. You can have steak and salad or pasta and salad. You can have cucumber sandwiches, but not cheese rolls. Ham and eggs for breakfast or just pancakes. You get the idea. His ulcer was allayed, and for the rest of his life he remained trim.

cutlery gleam in the candlelight. Two low bowls of perfect peonies on the table, vases of roses and exquisite flowers I cannot identify distributed about the room. On occasional tables occasional nuts, olives and cornichons. Fortunately this is the age before the uneatable Bombay Mix or palate-destroying pretzel assortment. A bottle of champagne in a silver bucket shifts slightly in the ice. I pour a solacing vodka and tonic, light a cigarette and pretend to myself that I am not a little nervous. When out on my walk I withdrew enough cash to tip Ernesto, Alfonso, Gilberto, Alonso and Pierre as lavishly as might be appropriate.

I have arranged with Alonso that as soon as the first guest has arrived he will come in to serve cocktails and the fizz. If he has not been alerted by reception I will press the bell by the fireplace.

A thought strikes me: perhaps the front desk won't know who John Mills is! It would be dreadful if so august a figure should slip anonymously in without being treated with the respect he deserves. I call down.

'Good evening, Mr Fry.'

This was a time when I still got a little disconcerted by the hotel staff being able instantly to identify me as soon as I called.

'Hello, yes it's me. Stephen here in 512. I just wanted to say that I'm having a dinner party, and the thing is, the guests of honour are Sir John and Lady Mills, and I hope you will –'

'. . . Oh, sir, we know Sir John very well indeed. Rest assured we shall welcome him most enthusiastically. Most enthusiastically!'

Hugh, Jo, Ken and Emma arrived together. We were still young enough to be excited by such a preposterously grown-up business as holding a dinner party in a place like the Savoy.

Alonso made cocktails and stood discreetly by the drinks trolley as we giggled and shrieked.

The buzzer sounded, and we all straightened up and put on serious but welcoming faces.

I opened the door, and there stood Sir John and Mary. He stepped in and looked blinking about him.

'Oh . . . oh! It's . . .'

I noticed with alarm that he had started to weep.

'Sir John, is everything all right?'

He took my arm and squeezed it tight. 'This is *Noël's* suite!'

He let go and walked about. 'Every first night, this was the suite Noël took. Oh gracious!'

It was a perfect evening. Johnny and Ken quickly made friends. Anecdotes rained down, and many beans were spilled. The front desk had already made a great fuss of Johnny and Mary, lining up to greet him at the famous porte-cochère as soon as his splendid old Rolls-Royce had arrived with his faithful driver, factotum and friend John Novelli at the wheel.

It was the beginning of a long friendship between

John, the Mills family and me. Not long enough as far as Johnny was concerned of course; he died in 2005 at the age of ninety-three, and Lady Mary, who had lost herself to dementia many years earlier, joined him in death later that year.

Their sixty-four-year marriage was an extraordinary achievement. I bumped into Johnny in 1996 in an artist's green room at the Sitges Film Festival. He peered up at me.*

'Oh, Stephen. Do you know something? This is the first time Mary and I have spent a night apart since we were married.'

Astonishing. I once asked him what the secret of so strong a marriage might be.

'Oh, it's very simple,' he said. 'We behave like naughty teenagers who've only just met. I'll give you an example. We were at a very grand dinner a couple of years ago, and I scribbled a note saying, "Cor, I don't half fancy you. Are you doing anything afterwards? We could go to my place for some naughty fun . . .", something like that. I summoned a waiter. "You see that ravishing blonde at the table over there?" I said, pointing towards Mary. "I wonder if you'd be good enough to hand her this note?" I was then rather horrified to realize – my sight was just going at this stage, you have to understand – that he was hand-

* He had been unable to see properly for at least five years by this time and spent much charitable energy helping the Royal London Society for the Blind.

ing the note to Princess Diana. She opened it, read it and with her eyes followed the waiter's pointing hand back to me, squirming in my seat. She smiled, waved and blew a kiss. Oh dear, I did feel a fool.'

Two events gave me especial delight during my years of friendship with Johnny. One was the good fortune I had in spotting that Christie's were selling an old dressing gown of Noël Coward's. I won the auction and gave it to Johnny on his eightieth birthday. He remembered Coward wearing it, and owning it gave him a remarkable amount of pleasure, which in turn, of course, gave me a remarkable amount of pleasure.

The second event took place on a freezing winter's day in the grand old house Luton Hoo, former seat of the Marquesses of Bute and latterly the diamond magnate Julius Wernher, much of whose famous Fabergé collection was stolen from the house in a daring motorcycle raid. I was using it (some time after this burglary) as a location for scenes for the film *Bright Young Things*, an adaptation of Evelyn Waugh's second novel, *Vile Bodies*. I tentatively asked Johnny one day whether he would consider playing the part of Old Gentleman at a Ball. He immediately consented. I explained that what I wanted him to do in his scene was to spot Miles, a fey young man played by Michael Sheen, apparently taking a pinch of snuff from a small silver box. Miles would offer the old gentleman a pinch of this 'snuff', which was peculiarly white for milled tobacco, and then resignedly allow him to take more and more in odd moments when we returned to them as the ball progressed. Johnny was very excited to be playing his first drug scene so late in his life and took it, as he did all his work, very seriously. Though just about stone blind and in a large chilly house, he asked for nothing extra. We had made up a small interior tent for him, however, which we furnished with a day bed and five-barred electric heater.

A few years later Johnny lay dying in a new house in Denham Village (The Gables I think it was called), up the road from Hills House, where they had spent so many years. I went to visit him. He had a chest infection and couldn't really speak, but I sat and held his hand. I had brought with me an iPod, on which I had uploaded as many Noël Coward numbers as I could find. He was dressed, as he liked to be, in a velvet jacket, his KBE and CBE medals proudly attached to his chest. I put the iPod down by his side and gently pushed the earbuds in. As I heard Coward's voice crooning 'I'll See You Again', I saw his mouth form a smile and tears leak from the corners of his eyes.

Back at the Savoy Hotel a few days after the Mills–Branagh dinner party I am waiting at six in the morning for my car to take me to Wrotham Park for the day's filming on *Peter's Friends*. I find myself chatting to Arturo, one of the linkmen.

'You a fan of Frank Sinatra, Mr Fry?'

'Am I? You bet I am.'

'Ah, well. He's coming to stay with us today.'

'You're kidding!'

On the ride up to Hertfordshire I rehearsed what I'd say if I bumped into the great man. Ol' Blue Eyes. The Chairman of the Board. The Voice.

The filming, as it does, went on and on and on and on and on. It must have been past midnight before I drew up again at the Savoy. Arturo opened the door for me.

'That was a long day, Mr Fry.'

'Looks like it was for you too.'

'Just started my shift, sir. Now, why don't you follow me? Something I'd like you to see.'

Baffled and faintly irked – all I could think of was bed – I trailed after Arturo along the passageway that led, and still does, to the American Bar. We went down the steps, and Arturo pointed towards a man sitting in a pool of light, head bowed over a crystal lowball glass, backlit cigarette smoke ribboning up. A living album cover.

'Mr Sinatra, I'd like you to meet Mr Fry, a long-term guest.'

The man looked up and there he was. He pointed to the chair opposite him.

'Siddown, kid.'

'Kid'. Francis Albert Sinatra had called me 'kid'. It reminded me of the moment in Richard Lester's *The Three Musketeers* when Spike Milligan says in a stunned, reverent voice, after Charlton Heston has grasped his wrist and whispered him into conspiracy against his wife (Raquel

Welch), 'The Cardinal has taken me by the hand and called me friend!'

I think I had about three minutes alone with Frank before the room was filled with old friends and I found myself pushed to the edge of the party. But it was enough, and I wound my way back to 512 as one in a holy dream.

A few days later I saw Arturo on duty again. I pumped him by the hand and pushed a fiver on him.

'As long as I live I will never forget that moment, Arturo. What a favour you did me. I can never thank you enough.'

'It was my pleasure, Mr Fry.'

'Is he still here?'

'Left this morning. Quite funny actually.'

'Oh yes?'

'Well, just before he got into his car for the airport he gave me a roll of cash. Great thick roll it was. "Thanks for a terrific stay, Arturo," he says. "Well, thank you very much, Mr Sinatra. Always a pleasure for us to have you at the Savoy." "Tell me," he says, "is that the biggest tip you've ever had?" I look down at the money. Huge roll of twenties and fifties it was. "Well, as a matter of fact, sir, no it isn't," I says. He looks most put out. Most put out. "Well tell me," he says, "who gave you a bigger one?" "You did, sir, last time you stayed," I says. He got into the car, laughing his head off.'

'And next time he stays you'll get an even better tip,' I said.

'Ooh, the thought never crossed my mind,' said Arturo.

Dear Diary

By 1993 *Peter's Friends* had come out, *Fry and Laurie* had had a second series, and I had written my first novel, *The Liar*, and a collection of journalism, essays and other scraps called *Paperweight*.

I am an irregular diarist, but the months leading up to the completion of my second (and favourite) novel, *The Hippopotamus*, and the delivery to my flat of its galley proofs were well covered by me. I offer them to you because I think they recapture better than my memory ever can the hectic, intensely busy and fractured nature of my life back then. That it was leading to a catastrophic explosion I did not realize. Perhaps it will be apparent to you as you read. I have remained loyal to the intentions laid out in the first entry and have not altered or added, except for the sake of respect for those who would rather be kept out or have their identities masked. From time to time footnotes have been added for the sake of clarity.

Monday, 23 August 1993 – London

I'm going to be 36 tomorrow: three dozen, a quarter of a gross. A very factorable number, but otherwise nothing special. Nonetheless it seems a good time to restart my diary. (*First resolution*: no going back and altering this chronicle. No reading back, no emendations, no retrospective editorials. It must come out of me absolutely in one. Otherwise, what's the point?) Ha! 'Oh, what's the point?' ... the last words in Kenneth Williams's diary, just published and just skimmed through by me. I'm mentioned once in the index, a reference to an appearance on a *Wogan* that KW guest-presented. 'Stephen Fry OK', that's my reference. An epitaph. Listening to Strauss's Alpine Symph. while writing this. It's on Radio 3 as a prom. Rather wonderful version by some Russian conductor I've not heard of.* Introduced in traditionally hushed tones by James Naughtie. Naughty James sat next to me at the John Birt Cup Final lunch earlier in the year. Nice chap.

Lazy day today. Very lazy: like all the days I've spent recently. Having such a reputation for hard work is satisfactory and bolsters my *amour propre* but it is *such* a lie. Spent most of the day polishing off the seating-plan for tomorrow's birthday dinner. How can it take that long? Well, I've decided to do anagrams for the guests' names. Here's a list, with explanations:

- Henry F. Pest – Me
- Lacey Easy-Fleece – Alyce Faye Cleese (wife of John Cleese, Okie psychotherapist)

---

* Almost certainly Valery Gerghiev, who has since become a kind of friend.

- Irma Shirk – Kim Harris (darling friend from Cambridge)
- Lady Orlash – Sarah Lloyd (wife of John)
- Mercie H. Twat – Matthew Rice (sweetie designer and splendour)
- Sonia Wanktorn – Rowan Atkinson
- Katie Labial-Scar – Alastair Blackie (friend of Kim, agent, and my gardener)
- Martie Badgermew – Emma Bridgewater (wife of Matthew Rice, designs crockery)
- Jones Leech – John Cleese
- Maria Sillwash – Sarah Williams (producer, currently back with Nick Symons)
- Harold Clit-Shine – Christian Hodell (assistant of Lorraine)
- Julie Oar – Jo Laurie (wife of J. H. C. Laurie)
- Coke Toper – Peter Cook
- Reg Gowns – Greg Snow (friend from Cambridge)
- Slim Noble – Simon Bell (Oxonian layabout and charmer)
- Nik Cool – Lin Cook (wife of Peter)
- Dolly John – John Lloyd (producer of *Blackadder* etc.)
- Mario Nolan–Hitler – Lorraine Hamilton (my agent)
- Miss Nancy L. Soho – Nicholas Symons (old Cambridge chum producer of *Bit of F&L*)

- Antonius Stanker – Sunetra Atkinson (wife of Rowan)
- Eli Cider – Eric Idle
- Uriah H. Glue – Hugh Laurie

Anyway – spent all fucking day working out those anagrams (Alyce Faye Cleese way the hardest – all those bloody E's and Y's)* while I should have been working on the nov. Satisfactory in its way. In the background Radio 3 (not music this time but the Test Match – England *won* can you believe it? Never doubted them. Atherton clearly good captain; he'll have his hellish moments in the years to come, but a sound fellow) while I strained my verbal skills on this useless anagrammery which will probably annoy the guests tomorrow anyway. No bloody *fun* in the world any more: no one doing mad silly things, no one playing practical jokes or organizing stupid parties with games and tricks like they did in the 20s. Even melancholy Virginia Woolf (heard Dame Edna on *Kaleidoscope*† a year or so back: 'Darling Virginia, a woman with whom I have so much in common, except of course that I can swim.') even she and her set used to love practical jokes. Everyone's so sodding *serious* and ordinary now.

God knows whether the seating plan will work. If

---

* Some might think the anagram rather appropriate given the astounding settlement awarded her when JC and she divorced. I couldn't possibly comment.

† A BBC Radio 4 arts programme, forerunner of *Front Row*.

Simon Bell is sober it'll help. Well I'll report the day after tomorrow.

Talking of the morrow, although my birthday, I seem to have filled it up with interviews to publicize *Stalag Luft*,* endless TV magazines and similar.

Bottle of wine at my elbow, Kanonkop, a S. African claret mimic, not enough tannin. Strauss's storm is brewing up, all those flutey interjections seem borrowed from Rossini's Wm. Tell overture or I'm a Flying Dutchman.

Tuesday, 24 August 1993 – London

Well – thirty-six then. Usual cliché of searching for grey hairs in the mirror. Some individual white flecks around the temples, but it's hard to tell whether they're real or a trick of the light.

The whole morning given over to publicity interviews for *Stalag Luft* at the Groucho. Endless stream of women from *TV Quick*, *TV First*, *TV Super* and *TV Cunty* all wanting to talk about my celibacy. 'Surely you must fantasize? Surely you must meet people and . . . *fancy* them?'

Basically, they want to know what pictures go on in my mind when I masturbate. Had the same thing a few weeks ago when I went to dinner at Ken and Em's. Ken got a bit in his cups (it doesn't take more than a glass with him)

---

*Comedy POW drama written by David 'Reggie Perrin' Nobbs. I had filmed it with Hugh Bonneville, Nicholas Lyndhurst and others earlier in the year.

and he was all, 'Come on, *darling*, what do you think about when you wank?' Em tried to slap him, but I bet she was too intrigued really to mean it.

Very pleased that my dreams and fantasies aren't too out there. I mean, only today the papers are full of this Michael Jackson thing. Some woman apparently reporting him for abusing her son. Let's face it, whoever doubted that Jacko was a boylover? My God, there's going to be a fall there if they find anything at his ranch. Porn, film, whatever . . . poor deranged sod, I don't think his own childhood fell far short of abuse in its way.

Then – the party. Everyone turned up. Everyone got me presents though I told them not to. The anagrams seemed to tickle them all too. Most people in a good mood and seeming to enjoy it, even Rowan managed to last to the end.* I sat next to Jo Laurie and Alyce Faye Cleese, I put Hugh down the other end near Eric and John C. Peter Cook in great form, talking about *Derek and Clive* which is about to be re-released, most people lightly drunk by the end. The bill came to almost exactly £1,000, which is reasonable, I would say. Damn good tuck. Did I mention earlier that it was at 190 Queensgate, run by Antony Worrall Thompson, who was there and joined for a drink earlier on? Turns out he was at school with John Lloyd. Home with Simon Bell, whom I gave a whisky before he eventually left.

* Usually notorious for bowing out of parties with a gentle yawn at about 9 p.m.

Wednesday, 25 August 1993 – London

Voice-over with Hugh this morning, for Energizer batteries. Hugh in good form, which is always a treat. A fun one and a half hours. Bumped into Norman Beaton before going into the sound studio. Mad old duck, rather a fan. Wants us to write a sketch for him to be in. Hum.

Afterwards a lot of leisurely shopping down Cecil Court. Bought an original *Vanity Fair* print of Gillette as Holmes and a signed photograph of Basil Rathbone. Don't ask me why. Might make a good present. Also got hold of a copy of Ricky Jay's book *Learned Pigs and Fireproof Women* which I have been after for ages.*

Eventually got home in time to read a little before popping out to the Institute of Directors in Pall Mall just around the corner. This was to meet a man by the name of Robin Hardy who is producing a film called *Bachelors Anonymous* (nothing to do with the Wodehouse story of the same name). He wants me to play the second lead and to DIRECT it. Flattering and pleasing that he can be confident enough to give such a relatively big movie to a first-time director, but there is a problem. Firstly, is the script good enough? He has written it himself from a novel called *Foxprints* by Patrick McGinley. Really rather fascinating, but needs improvement so as not to look misogynistic or just plain silly. The major problem

---

*Wasn't so easy to 'source' a book in the days before the World Wide Web and Amazon and so on . . .

though, is WHEN. I have *got* to try and finish the novel soon. Then I spend from October to January writing with Hugh for *A Bit of F&L* series 4. Then we make the thing, six weeks of studio, rehearse/record. That takes us to the end of March. John Reid will, I assume, want to go with the Elton musical next and the BBC will make noises about filming the adaptation of *The Liar*. There is no chance I could start pre-production prep on *Bachelors* until end of June, which would mean shooting it in September, over a year from now. Mad to think my life is that booked up. And where does that leave a second script for Paramount and Hugh's film *Galahad*? WHY is my life always like this, and why am I complaining about it?

He seems a reasonable fellow, this Hardy. Strange place to meet, the IoD. He fits it well, having a rather box-wallah version of an upper class accent. He did, on the other hand, write and direct *The Wicker Man*, a great classic. I feel it odd that I've never heard of him. Lorraine (Hamilton) is running a background check to see what she can see. Perhaps it will be a good thing to do, direct a film. I feel I can. I lack a lot of common sense, always have done, but I think I'll keep my head above water with a good operator, a good First and someone like Dougie Slocombe to light the film. Lor . . . what to do, what to do. Just aren't enough hours in the frigging day, are there, Stephen old love?

Thursday, 26 August 1993 – London

Parents are going to arrive at any minute. Father's birthday. I'm taking them to the premiere of Ken's *Much Ado* tonight at the Empire, Leicester Square and then to a party at Planet Hollywood of all places. So I'll do this entry now, rather than tonight when they'll be hanging around the flat.

Actually spent most of the day doing no more than preparing for their arrival. Hiding all the Euroboy videos, tidying up, trotting over the road to Fortnum's to buy fruit, flowers, tea things and so forth. Spent a merry hour in Hatchard's buying books. Got Alan Clark's diaries (signed) for Father, as well as the new Bill Bryson, as he likes him and a biography of Einstein (*not* the salacious one). For myself I rounded up a lot of books on theology . . . mostly beginner's stuff. All this reading of Susan Howatch recently has got me interested in knowing more about the subject. I don't believe in God of course, but I sometimes think I *want* to believe. And then there's that foolish vision of myself as a bishop, sermonizing and saving the poor old C of E from itself. So fond of the C of E. The 'broad backed hippopotamus' as T. S. Eliot called her. So much better a liturgy . . . and the music! Russell Harty* once confidingly said to me, while playing hymns at the piano (he had a perfect ear and could play anything you named that he knew), 'I don't think I could

---

*TV chat-show host: a simply adorable man who died from Hepatitis B in 1988.

ever love anyone who didn't love English hymns.' Mind you being a roamin' cat-lick his last lover the sweet Jamie O'Neill can't have known much Anglican church music.*

Appalling arrogance of me to think that I would be a good church leader without a concomitant shred of faith. Very Henry Crawford.† Mind you, probably a better life than my other footling fantasy, Fry the politician, Fry the scourge of the Right and the hero of the Chamber.

Also, bought a first novel called *In the Place of Fallen Leaves*, simply ghastly title but Roger, the sweet old queen at Hatchard's, recommended it.‡

Still haven't been able to face my own novel. I'm banking on being able to work when I get to Grayshott on Saturday, but how is one to tell? I'm always assuming that words will come and that I'll be able to get down that tunnel of concentration when I put my mind to it, but there's so much to do and I do desperately want it to work. If I don't finish it this year it'll spill over into next and then what happens to the idea of directing, or the TV version

---

*Jamie struggled after Russell's untimely death in 1988 but then wrote the wonderful *At Swim, Two Boys*, one of the best Irish novels of the past however many years.

†The wicked cad in Jane Austen's *Mansfield Park*, whose casual allusion to how good a parson he would have made had he minded to become one so shocks Fanny, the heroine, who is shocked by everything, to be honest.

‡And rightly. It went on to win the Hawthornden Prize (which had been recently resurrected by the munificent Dru Heinz, widow of the 57 Varieties chap), and the author, Tim Pears, went on to write the hugely successful *In a Land of Plenty*.

of *The Liar*, or the Elton John thing, or *Galahad* or God knows what else besides.

I'll report on *Much Ado* tomorrow. I've seen it already, at a preview cinema months ago. Really enjoyed it then, but perhaps it'll be less fun in front of a bigger audience and now that I have expectations. Hugh made a good point about how Ken on film sometimes does this thing of laughing and throwing his head back and slapping people on the back when wit is being offered. He did it in *Peter's Friends* and he does it in *Much Ado*, clearly encouraging his cast to do the same. Especially of course, the blissful Brian Blessed who roars like a speared ox through most of his scenes. Hugh's theory is that actors laughing prevents audiences from laughing and that this is perhaps true of screen or stage tears as well. Rather a convincing idea. And no doubt the Branagh haters and Ben Elton* haters will be out in force anyway. I'm so lucky that I don't seem to be quite so despised as they do. Mind you, not as admired either, which is only right. I suppose people think of me as some kind of reliable old thing, rather than as a threat. Ken and Ben are certainly threatening, those who dislike them regard them as the kind of yappy Jack Russells who leap up and spunk all over your trouser crease. The snobbery in Britons makes them believe that I, on the other hand, however rude or leftie I may seem, am fundamentally sound and reasonable, like a trusty labrador.

*Ben played Verges.

Frankly, I'm too lucky. Filled in a *Guardian* question-naire the other day. In answer to the question 'When and where were you happiest?' I answered, 'At the risk of tempting providence, I'm pretty chipper at the moment, as it happens.' Tempting prov. is right. Even now, in Plum's immortal phrase, Fate must be lurking around the corner quietly slipping the horseshoe into the boxing-glove. Shit, there goes the doorbell, here are the parents.

Friday, 27 August 1993 – London

Well, they arrived yesterday, admired the flat and seemed in good order and spirits despite a visit to their account-ant. Impossible to imagine how things are with them. They just carry on as always, the business continuing in its gentle way, Mother doing the VAT, Father exercising his extraordinary mind. I am more certain that that man could have been absolutely anything he wanted to be in the world than I am of almost anything else. The gloss of complete admiration may well have worn off in some regards. There's no question that he seems curiously unsophisticated to me now, but his mind is still a remark-able thing.

Anyway, after tea-ing them and cocktailing them we sal-lied forth on foot for the Empire Leicester Square. *Unbelievable* crowds ... a greater number, according to today's papers, than turned out for the opening of *Jurassic Park*, which says something for Ken and Em. We approached, naturally, from the West, only to discover that the crash barriers were arranged such that we had to walk all the way round and enter from the Charing X Road end. Highly embarrassing. Many cries of 'Steve!' and applause as I trotted the gauntlet, parents in tow. I suppose it must have been strange for them, really, to walk with me and know that everyone there was cheering their son and knew who he was. Lot of posing for the paparazzi outside the doors and then I managed to get inside. Naturally, the really smart ones were indoors, including Richard Young, who really is extraordinary. He instantly sidled up and said, out of the side of his mouth, 'Those your parents, then?' I said, amused, 'Yup' and he asked for a shot with them. I reckon that man could tell, instantly, if two people enter a party, whether or not they are sleeping together. Remember that Greek saying? 'It is easier to hide two elephants under your arm than one pathic.'

After Richard there were endless TV crews. God knows how many showbiz and local news programmes there are these days.* All wanting pre and post screening comment. (Oh, dear me, on TV as I type this there's a documentary about a man with cystic fibrosis going on in the background. Sounds of a great quantity of mucus expression going on.) Up at the party there was a sprinkling of theatrical knightage, Sir John Mills and Mary, who both kissed me sweetly. Johnny kissed my mother, which

* A lot fewer than there are now, Stephen young sausage.

was divine of him. Dickie, now Lord, Attenborough was there and Sir Peter Hall. A couple of *Peter's Friends* stalwarts, Alphonsia and Tony S.,* and of course Ken and Em, the latter looking divine, the former surprisingly like Noel Edmunds. Kim Harris turned up with Hugh. Kim looks absolutely zonked. A few months ago, Ken rang up and asked me to rewrite *Frankenstein*. It was exactly when I was shooting off to Texas to make an episode of *Ned Blessing*, a new Western series for CBS. (I played Oscar Wilde, directed by David Hemmings of all people). I told Ken I couldn't do it, but suggested that he try Kim. Well, it seems Kim has turned out well, but is being driven like a dray-horse by Sir Kenward. Just as well I said no, I suppose, though it would have been fun to meet Robert de Niro. I hope Kim is alright. One worries when he gets so tired.

Eventually the reception broke up to go into the cinema and we watched the movie. Speeches by Stephen Evans the Renaissance Films supremo and Ken. The film was even more moving the second time around. Still thought that Michael Keaton and Ben were a little out of their depth, but Em was staggeringly good (of course) and Ken fabulously likeable and witty. I hate the way I've been influenced by the critics: as I watched I started to

---

*Alphonsia Emmanuel and Tony Slattery, who were also in *Peter's Friends*. Richard Curtis of *Four Weddings* fame unkindly remarked that surely Alphonsia Emmanuel is a drag name . . . you might think that, but I c. p. c.

notice flaws in the lighting and background action. Brian Blessed's heartiness and the general laughing and merriment now grated a little. Nonetheless a wonderful movie and what a reaction! The whole place stood and cheered for ages. A genuine spontaneous standing ovation. It made me cry, I'm afraid to say. Ken really is a mensch and a half.

The party afterwards was at Planet Hollywood, which I hadn't visited since that bizarre opening party with Bruce Willis, Schwarzenegger et al. Parents still excited and merry. Richard Briers, who is about the kindest man in the universe, stopped and chatted to them for ages. They were the only people in the room for him. I do hope I'm not a starer-over-the-shoulder type person, but give whomever I'm talking to my full attention as Dickie B does. Mother and Father are the same. The only difference was that Dickie toned his language down a bit: normally he starts every sentence with 'Fucking hell love,' no matter whether he's bumming a cigarette or admiring a building. After next standing about with Richard Curtis and Emma Freud for a bit we were invited over to the area where Ken and Em had booked a table. Chatted a lot to Paul Boateng the MP, who was in merry form and wearing rather startling clothes. Cozed a bit with Slatbum* and his boyfriend Mark, who's just won a Drama Desk award in New York. They met on *Me and My Girl*

* Tony S.

years ago.† Rather touching. Dan Patterson turned up, despite a recent operation. Anthony Andrews has absurdly petite hands and feet (sounds like a clerihew) and ludicrous Prince Charles mannerisms, but otherwise seems a very charming cove. There was an unbelievably choice young man with blond hair with whom I exchanged smiles.

At half past one or so I managed to tear the parentals away and we sloped off back home. *Still* an enormous crowd outside the place when we left. Lots of photography and signing before we could get away.

Now we're back to today. Arose at nine-ish, said goodbye to M and P and joined Hugh for a VO. Alliance and Leicester radio commersh. In Tottenham Court Road bought a load of jockstraps, trainers and so forth ready for Grayshott. Watched a video when I got home: a film called *The Living End*, billed as 'an irresponsible movie'. It's about a couple of guys, both HIV+, who decide to let the world go hang and jag about the States, fucking and shooting. Sort of *Henry: Portrait of a Serial Killer* for the smart gay set. Witty, neatly done, despite abominable sound-recording. At three I wandered about Soho, fetched up at the Groucho where Simon Bell (surprise, surprise) was propping up the bar, had a couple of glasses of wine and biffed off to Magmasters for another VO.

I rang Johnny Sessions to see if he felt like hitting the

---

†Still together *sentimental gulp*.

West End this evening, but he was having another of his old chums to dinner, plus wife, so I've decided to stay in with a bottle of Fleurie and some videos. Just watched the original episode of *The Sweeney* and must now decide on another. But tomorrow, ha! *tomorrow* sees a new Stephen. A hardworking, concentrating, novelizing, non-drinking Stephen.

Jo Laurie rang to say goodbye. Her new baby will be hitting the straw while I'm away. She told me Kim was okay, just healthily tired. But one day, one day, I am going to hear that he is ill and I am going to know what that 'ill' means. It's impossible to believe. Fuck it, he's 35 and there's a time-bomb inside him. It's all just happening too, the *Frankenstein*, the relationship with Alastair which seems so good. Makes you vomit, doesn't it. God blast AIDS.

Spent a merry hour writing notes for my brother Roger, who's going to be borrowing the flat with his wife and my two nephews Ben and William. Arranged with the manager of Planet Hollywood that they could barge the queue with my special celebrity card (eugh!) which I left for their use.

Showed on the map where it was and where the nearest shops were. Hope they have a good time.

Saturday, 28 August 1993 – Grayshott Hall, Surrey

Well, for heaven's sake.

Grayshott Hall, once, apparently, the home of Alfred Lord Tennyson, is now a 'Health Retreat', featuring spas, hydros, gyms, golf, tennis, badminton (it's beginning to sound like that speech of Lucky's from *Waiting for Godot*), swimming, snooker, scrabble, bridge and the lord knows what else besides.

I arrived for lunch and found myself in what I subsequently discovered to be the 'Light Diet Room', where salads and a gently cooked poussin seemed not unconscionable. At 1.30 I had an appointment with 'Liz' who checked my blood pressure, weighed me (16 stone and a lot, yuk) and asked me what sort of 'treatments' I required. Everything here is a treatment. If you had sex with one of the waiters it would be called an erotic treatment. Drink (alcohol treatment) is not offered here, no bad thing, there is a smoking room, complete with card tables and so forth, which hasn't been made impertinently uninhabitable, which is something. I haven't volunteered for any particular treatments, though reflexology is something I've had before and is rather relaxing and splendid. I might, for the hell of it, try smoking hypnotherapy too. And there's some kind of men's 'facial' which teaches you how to shave. Come to think no one has *ever* taught me to scrape the face and for all I know I've been doing it wrong all my life. Included in the price, £150 p.d.* there is a 'heat treatment' (steam room, hot box or sauna) and a Swedish massage. Reminds me of Shrublands, the health resort you see in *Never Say Never Again*† but

---

*Now between £300 and £700 p.d.

†Sean Connery's 1983 remake of *Thunderball*. Rowan Atkinson made a brief appearance in it.

not quite so grand. I book myself a 'deep tissue massage' which sounds potentially painful for 10.00 am tomorrow.

Actually the place is quite pleasant. Mostly women here. Everyone is encouraged to go round the place in dressing gowns and tracksuits all day, so no formality, which is a blessing. I suppose the fellow guests are what you would expect, rich Totteridge Jewry, executive wives and thin girls who certainly have no need of this kind of regime. My room is pretty spartan actually. I applied this afternoon for a suite should it become available. Started work on the novel anyway, which, let's face it, is the point of being here. I don't know . . . I really don't know. I am going to have to plan it out, and that's a fact. I know how bad I am at planning. Never did any with articles, with essays at Cambridge or school, but in this instance it's got to be done. There are so many threads. The novel has to be about the redemption, if that isn't too ghastly a word, not of the hero, Ted Wallace (that's his current name, anyhow, though I'm getting annoyed with having to avoid the inelegant 'said Ted') which everyone will think it's about, but rather of those around him. He's a poet and knows that poetry is chthonic not ethereal. Of earth and water not fire and air. It's also seemingly about Purity and the Operation of Grace and horrifically dull and off-putting Bridesheady things. But that isn't my problem, my problem is structural. I have to find a way of pulling together the past and present and getting the characters introduced properly.

At the current pace, the novel won't get to the half way stage till I've written 100,000 words. I'm quarter of the way to 80,000 which is an acceptable novel length, but it looks as if this is going to be longer, which is the last thing I want. And there's nothing worse than reading a novel where you sense the writer has speeded up towards the end. I've got to remain true to the idea of it. One of the problems with *The Liar* was my lack of confidence that people would be interested enough in Healey and Cartwright and so I shoved in all the spying crap, which, in fact, most people found less interesting than Adrian in love. I mustn't make the same mistake again.

Anyway, I wrote for a few hours, then dined on plaice and vegetables, washed down with plain water and followed by fruit. Came back to the room, couldn't work any more, watched some dreadful Brian Dennehy film called *The Revenge of the Father*. Tomorrow, massage and a quick nine holes before breakfast excepted, must see me At Work.

Sunday, 29 August 1993 – Grayshott

Not much to report. Up at 7.30, breakfast was a mess of cottage cheese, All Bran and coffee. Whether or not the coffee here is decaffeinated I can't really tell, which I suppose means that it doesn't matter. Played 9 holes on the golf course. No hole is longer, which suits me, than 150 yds. Tried out for the first time the 'Killer Whale' which

John Lloyd* gave me as a thank you for doing his *South Bank Show* comedy spesh. Sliced it, which is a first for me as I usually slice.†

Had my massage after that. I didn't realize you were supposed to arrive half an hour earlier for the 'heat treatment' so I missed that. Kept my swimming trunks on all the time under my towel. All the fat men with hairy backs (who all resemble Ari Onassis and Picasso) waddled around slapping their bellies and showing their acorns, but I was damned if I was going to. I'm not having some *For Women* magazine telling the world about my cock length.

Had the Swedish massage, which was nothing special and went back to the room to work. Making *some* progress, but I need a breakthrough, there's no question about that. The chances of my finishing this novel for publication in the spring are remote in the extreme.

Spoke to the front desk about changing the room, I'll be moving into more luxurious quarters tomorrow.

Monday, 30 August 1993 – Grayshott

Yup. I'm in Room 5, now. It has coffee-making equipment, a mini-bar containing mineral water and skimmed milk, complimentary flowers and fruit basket and all the

---

* Producer of *Not the Nine O'Clock News*, *Spitting Image*, *Blackadder* and – in 2003 – *QI*.
† I meant that I usually hook.

things one has come to expect in one's life these days, tee-hee.

They sent me a letter telling me about the new room rate, this suite is £298 per night as opposed to the old rate of £195, but what the fuck. In this letter they said, and I quote 'We are now requesting all guests to refrain from smoking in the bedrooms however, the functions of the Billiard and Smoking Rooms have not changed.' What a fucking nerve. Some slatternly skivvy has gone and squealed, by which I mean some plump, curranty sweetness of a chambermaid has informed the management of my 'in-room self-administered tobacco treatment' . . . thing is I'm turning into that character Ted Wallace in my frigging novel, it's not like me to call chambermaids slatternly.

Another nine holes this morning and then waddled off in my dressing-gown to experience the steam-room effect. Horrific place. Some old boy sweating it out next to me said it was newly installed. He's a regular, must be rich as Croesus. It's like a sauna, but to be frank, not quite as unpleasant, as the humidity is exceptionally high. A minute takes a quarter of an hour to pass. Horrifying. Still contrived to keep my bathers on, though. Everyone must be beginning to talk about my strange modesty . . . much better massage, however. Chap called Pete, I'll try and stick with him.

Midway through the afternoon I genuinely despaired with the novel. I've changed its working title to *The Thaumaturge* as much to annoy the critics as anything. I came within an ace of packing up and moving either back to London or to some country house hotel where I could drown my sorrows in lonely jugs of claret. Then, two things happened. Firstly a man came in with an ashtray and said I was welcome to smoke in the room, they must have seen me nipping down to the smoking room and billiard room every half an hour and taken pity. And then I had an idea. A whole chapter that I've written should be in the form of a letter from Ted to his goddaughter Jane. It may not work out fully, but it's driving me along a little. Wrote a couple of thousand words after that. Still not enough, but let's hope it's a good sign. Have to go to London tomorrow, chiz. A VO for Compaq computers. I'll drive to Haslemere, get on a train and hope to be back by two-ish. Wonder if I'll be a naughty boy and guzzle sandwiches on the train. Nothing but chicken and fish and fruit and veg. so far. Night, night.

Tuesday, 31 August 1993 – Grayshott

Well, frankly. Rose with the lark, lark rise under candlewick you might say. Drove like stink to Haslemere, parked the car and discovered that I'd left my wallet back in the room at Grayshott. Fortunately, God knows how or why, I'd got my cheque-book with me. Avoided the queue for the tickets and jumped straight on the 08:06 to London. Sat all of a quiver in a second class smoker wondering what the issue would be. A ticket conductor arrived some time after Woking (Lord, Home Counties place names have such negative evocations, don't they) and I explained the posish. Thank God for fame, he recognized me and seemed tickled pink (as did my fellow passengers, regular commuters to a man, and I mean man), said something about it being a good way of making his quota (there's a surcharge, natch) and waddled off.

Fetched up at Waterloo at 0900 precisely and, having not a bean to my name (well 40 odd pence) I walked all the way over the bridge, along the Strand and to St James's. Halfway up the Strand I remembered that Roger, Ruthie, Ben and William were all staying in the flat. Thought they may have left for Norfolk but arrived to find plenty of traces. Assuming they were out for brekker at Fortnum's or somewhere I left them a note and hared off to Lexington Street where the Voice Over was. The sweet girl at the Tape Gallery, the studio, cashed a cheque for fifty quid, thank God. The VO for Compaq Computers (yah, boo) was booked as a two hour session, but I finished it to their satisfaction in twenty-five minutes. My internal clock going great guns. They wanted each of the VO's to last 18 seconds and I duly obliged first crack out of the box with each of the seven scripts. Scuttled back to the flat, Breda the cleaner was there, but no sign of R & R. Hung around for an hour in case they showed and then got a cab back to Waterloo.

Car at Haslemere amazingly not towed away, so I was back at Grayshott in time for a nutritious lunch. A chappie told me that Imelda Staunton was staying, so I arranged to meet her at the cocktail hour, 6.00.

Heat treatment and massage at 3.00. Actually took my clothes off this time! Mustn't do exclamation marks, it's so Adrian Mole. That's all Mummy's fault, she does them in letters to the milkman, everything 'Thank you!' and so on.

The less efficient masseur, Steve, did the business, must remember to ask for Peter next time. Got back to the room, worked on *The Thaumaturge*, which seems to be coming along okay and dipped down for revivifying cocktails with Imelda and her mother, Bridie, an Irish poppet the spit of Imelda. Cocktails, you should understand, comprise either cucumber or tomato juice, but actually that's fine. Imelda, who's eight months pregnant, was telling me all about Jim Carter, her man,* and his nightmare shooting on a film of *Black Beauty* for Warners. All the horses misbehaving and that kind of thing. Peter Cook's in it too.

Anyway, then dinner and now, before I hit the mattress (not like a Mafioso fortunately), a video. I collected an armful from the flat. Time I think to enjoy Jeremy Brett once more, this time in 'The Dancing Men', one of the best Holmes stories. Sleep tight.

Wednesday, 1 September 1993 – Grayshott

And a pinch and a punch to you.

Doing this diary must be good for me, I had an inspiration last night after writing yesterday's entry. I suddenly saw that of course the thaumaturge is not David, but

---

*Now known the world over for his portrayal of the Downton butler.

Simon. I had thought all along that David, the pure poetical son of the Logan family would be the miracle worker, but of course it must be the apparently dull, ordinary, less intelligent or sensitive boy. That's the poetic truth as opposed to the poetical one. There's a sense in which I'm saying my brother Roger is the miracle worker of *our* family, not me and I think that's true. He's decent, no, more than decent, he's *good*, decent in the way Tom Wolfe means it in *Bonfire of the Vanities*, he's hard-working, he's loyal, he's true, he's . . . well he's what makes man great. Sounds sententious put like that, I suppose. The key to it in the novel though means that at least some kind of twist or surprise can be guaranteed. Everyone was fooled by Davey (who deliberately allows Jane and Ted to believe that *he's* the one).

Talking of the diary, this being the first of the month, I've decided I will print out an entry at the end of each month. This will guarantee that I can't go back and change things. That's the devil of a computer-kept diary, it looks impersonal and there's no assurance that it hasn't been tarted up. When I get back to London, I will print out all of August, it only started late in the month, of course.

Usual nine holes. Got a birdie! Yippee! My first. I was playing the six iron as Brendel plays a Bösendorfer today. Usual steam business followed by a massage from Peter, who is infinitely better than Steve. I have asked the desk if I can always have him, there should be no problem. Then I had a consultation with the Sister. I have lost 8 pounds in the time I've been here. Eight pounds. Unbelievable. I only arrived halfway through Saturday (hogged a load of sandwiches on the road on Saturday morning anyway), three and a half days, over two pounds a day. I won't be able to keep it up at this rate, but still. Not bad, eh?

In the afternoon (Sister's advice) I had a holistic massage. All kinds of bollocks from Janice the masseuse about energy and channelling and healing and so forth, but I have to say it was a wonderful feeling. An hour and a half of intensely gentle, yet intensely deep massage. Felt very woozy afterwards, but then keyed up and raring to go.

Imelda and Bridie joined me in the Light Diet Room for dinner and we chatted about this and that. Since then I've been working at the nov. Spent most of this evening trying to write a poem that David Logan (who's aged 15) could have written. Tricky. Can't be too sophisticated, but no point if it's too childish. Takes bloody ages, poetry. Can't wait to get back to dialogue and description. I need words by the thousands!! Oh no! More Adrian Moling!!!

Nighty night.

Thursday, 2 September 1993 – Grayshott

Well, usual thing really. Nothing too outrageous to report. Nine holes in the morning. Started badly, but really began to hit the ball well (yawn, yawn, yawn) and felt good about the game. Came back, steam room and massage as per usual. Lots of work, then lunch. Some work after lunch then decided to take half an hour off to play another 9 holes. Really genuinely actually frankly properly hitting the ball. Very exciting. On the ninth, the pro was walking past as I hit the ball from the tee, spang on line with pin, right onto the green. 'Good shot,' he said. From a pro!

Back to the novel, it continueth. I've done an exhaustive word count. 30,034 words so far. That means I've written 9,174 since I've been here. That's an average of 1,529 per day, which isn't frankly enough to get the thing finished when I want it finished. But, and it's a but the size of Hyde Park, I am sure I am writing more each day. It started slowly, after all, so perhaps things aren't going too badly. Do wish I was in Norfolk, though. I'd've had the thing finished a fortnight ago if I could have been in Norfolk. And I'd've saved myself the three or four thousand pound bill I'm going to get for this little lot (let alone the gigantic cost of the building work that's being done): by fuckery it'd better be worth it.

Heigh ho. *Fry and Laurie* on in half an hour. Might as well catch it. Sleepums wellums.

Friday, 3 September 1993 – Grayshott

Well, watched *F&L* all right. Not bad, actually. Laughed in places, but Christ I wish I didn't always wear such a smug expression. My face in repose always looks as if it's smirking which is peculiarly repellent.

Usual thing this morning: nine holes (a step back in competence this am, but made up for by a screamer at the ninth again), steam, massage, lots of writing and then, as a treat, a Flotation and Facial in the afternoon. The Float is a strange bath, barely long enough for me to lie in, filled with salts so that the water takes on the buoyancy (and viscous consistency) of the Dead Sea. You go into an ante-room, shower, smear Vaseline over any abraded skin, bung wax in your ears like Odysseus and then lie down and float. There is an open intercom with a floozy at the desk in case you panic or something. Music (well, I say music, whale song in fact, as you might have guessed) is then played which, on account of the earplugs and something else besides, Boyle's Law* possibly, you can hear best with your ears below the level of the water. You have control over the light switches too. The idea is that you bob there, completely buoyant, utterly blind, listening to bull whales telling cow whales to get their knickers down. I sort of enjoyed it while it happened and did feel good afterwards. Next treat(ment) was a facial, actually just a big plug for Aramis products (scalp revitalizer, cucumber face mask, that sort of tosh). Lovely feeling to have your face woman-handled, though. Like being made-up for film or TV without the silly gossip and drivelling on about horoscopes. The popsy also shaved me, which is always pleasurable.

*Not even *vaguely* like Boyle's Law, Stephen, which is to do with gases.

257

Then, basically, back to the nov. I've now decided to call it *Other People's Poetry*, which the publishers will hate, if anything, more than *The Thaumaturge*. I stupidly gave Sue Freestone, my editor, the working title *What Next?* a few months ago and she loved it. I think it's too junky or possibly Joseph Heller-y (not that JH is junky). Sounds like the kind of title people give books that they are desperate to become best-sellers. Not that I am desperate for anything else, naturally, but it's also a hostage to fortune as far as critics are concerned. 'What next indeed, Mr Fry? A proper novel we hope, snicker, snicker . . .'

I wrote over 3,000 words, anyway, which is an improvement. Mind you, I've written 7,061 words in this diary so far, which is an average of (as you can surely work out for yourself) 588.416666 per diem; time which you might believe would be better spent novelizing. Actually though, I feel this diary, if nothing else helps prime the pump (that *must* be drivel because I always write it *after* I've been working, well, you know what I mean).

Well, bed time. Cricket tomorrow and my first real food for ages. Lost nine pounds so far, don't want to put any on. Must be careful not to drink too much.

Bedly beddington now.

Sunday, 5 September 1993 – Grayshott

Went up to London for to see the cricket. *Bloody* good match. Sussex v. Warks. Nat West final, Lord's. Settled by the last ball. Warks needed 2 runs from the final delivery to score a winning 322. Actually, one run would have done, as they'd lost fewer wickets, but in any case a humdinger. Was so dark by the end I'm amazed the batsmen could see the ball. Just shows what gamesmanship there is when they appeal for bad light when things are going against them. Went because Will Wyatt invited me to a BBC box. Mostly full of corporation figures, Roger Laughton, Michael Checkland* etc. But spent most of the match as the ham in a playwright sandwich. David Hare to the left, Simon Gray to the right (in every sense). David turns out to be a manic Sussex fan. Poor man: for the first time I really warmed to him as he sat gnawing his knuckles and turning into a closer and closer simulacrum of Munch's *The Scream*. His tonsure was purpling with passion. All this seemed to matter far more to him than the opening next week of his new play, *Murmuring Judges*. Turns out he is also working for Scott Rudin. We compared notes on the impossibility of getting in touch with him. Scott's office has been ringing my London number daily as usual, as if they know I'm away in Grayshott. Scott himself is in Venice for the film festival, so it's rather pointless my ringing back anyway.

Simon, whom I haven't seen in a pig's age looks frankly bloody awful. Rheumy, weeping eyes and squashed pug's

* Last three named all BBC high-ups of the time. Checkland (known as 'Chequebook' as he came up through the ranks of admin and business rather than programme-making) was Director-General.

face in no way enhanced by a deep tan. The thick hair with its characteristic flick looks no longer boyish, simply the-portrait-in-the-schoolroom-ish.* He's been in Greece, the island of Spetses, writing a novel of all things for Mark McCrum's brother Robert at Faber's. Still drinking clearly: Simon not Robert McCrum. Confessed to some guilt about leaving Beryl and gave me the lowdown on how Eddie Fox trampled on the possibility of taking the revival of *Quartermaine's Terms*† into the West End. The best ever prod of *QT* Simon thinks, but Fox scared of being compared to his original performance, despite his mother's firm statement that the revival outshines it. Amazing thing is that Simon is still very very prolific: as well as the novel there's a new play waiting, a couple of radio plays just written and two films for Verity Lambert's 'Cinema Verity' (ho, ho) outfit.

David Frost turned up a little late: he'd just got in from Moscow where he'd been interviewing Mikhail and Raisa Gorbachev. I swear that man still talks and acts as if he's just left Cambridge and is desperate to make a name for himself in television. Wonderful really. Can't help adoring him. It's been a week of Frost on TV lately, as it happens, coinciding with the issue of a fat First Volume of autobiography and at least five TV programmes about him. He

---

* In *The Picture of Dorian Gray* it's a schoolroom in which the eponym hides his portrait, not – as everyone says – an attic. But only I would be so pedantic in a diary.

† Subsequently re-revived by Rowan Atkinson.

tells me that the one being shown this very night, 'Frost-bites' (ho, ho), which is a compilation of interviews over the 30 years, includes a section of one he did with me earlier this year. He leaves early to edit the Gorbachev material.

John Sullivan, author of *Citizen Smith*, *Only Fools & Horses* etc. is also amongst those present. We swap stories about Nick Lyndhurst and David Jason. I've just been filming with Nick all June doing the *Stalag Luft* film for Yorkshire TV. Bill Cotton is here too. He tells a story of how he is in a train compartment with Peter Sellers, Tommy Cooper, Barry Cryer and Dennis Main Wilson.* Dennis is telling one of his stories when Tommy gets up to go to the loo. After about ten minutes they start wondering where Cooper has got to. Sellers and Cryer get up and go down the corridor to the lav., which is locked. They bang on the door. No reply. Worried, knowing that TC is well-sauced, they search for the ticket conductor. 'Mr Cooper's in there,' they say. 'Can you open the door somehow?' The conductor does so. Tommy is sitting on the bog, lid down, trousers up. He gives them his signature creased eyebrow look of worry and asks 'Has Dennis stopped talking yet?' No good unless you know D.M.W. of course, but we did.

The match takes up most of our attention from then on. I've been a good boy, combining food like Hay him-

---

* The splendidly mad old producer of *The Goon Show*, *Till Death Us Do Part* and, in 1982, Cambridge Footlights for the BBC with me, Hugh, Emma and Tony S.

self and sticking only to one sipped glass of red and a small vodka and tonic. As the ante-penultimate over is about to be bowled I ring up the cab company and order a taxi to be waiting outside the Grace Gate so that I can go on to Hugh and Jo's for dinner, where Ben Elton will be, having just returned from Oz. Simon asks if he can borrow my phone to do likewise.

Leave as soon as the result is clear, having thanked Will and commiserated with David H. Taxi not there, hang around feeling a fool. People approach, but are not too pesky or autograph hungry. Then, amazingly, *Nigel Short* bounds up! He's spent the whole day watching the match. He's about to sit down and face Garry Kasparov for the World title on Tuesday and there he is . . . I'd be covered in a wet blanket forcing coffee down myself while I sweated over variations of the Maroczy Bind and the Winawer. I suppose he knows what he's doing. He begged me to come along to the match and say hi. May do. We'll see. So far I have resisted the blandishments of Channel 4 and BBC2, who are both covering the match. What can I actually say on air? I can't keep up with Ray Keene as an analyser and I'll be reduced to a sort of media hack who says clever things about the psychology and witty non-sense about the body language. Pyeuch. There's a programme on as I write this: Dominic Lawson, Bill Hartston, David Norwood GM and Florencio Campomanes, the President of FIDE. It does begin to look as if Nigel has blown it before it's started.

Hugh and I revealing our weekend recreational identities.

Mandela Birthday Concert, Wembley Stadium, 1988. About to perform in front of 80,000 people. Not in the least nervous. Oh no.

I felt comfortable and ALIVE.

Incredibly, I still have that shirt. Haven't burnt it or anything . . .

Self and Hugh wining,
dining and pointing at
Sunetra Atkinson.

A bit more Fry and Laurie.

Cap Ferrat with Mrs Laurie.

Cap Ferrat, 1991 – Charlie Laurie, by this time, rightly, bored of my attempts to amuse.

Stripey me.

Self and self at
the National
Portrait Gallery.
Maggi Hambling's
completed work.

Next to Maggi
Hambling charcoal
portrait of me
commissioned by the
National Portrait
Gallery. Do NOT
mention the hair.

Maggi Hambling's National Portrait Gallery picture of me.

Taking pleasure in red wellies: life gets no better, 1990.

Simon totters out and his cab is waiting. Bugger those Computer Cab sods. But Simon, sweetly, suggests I hop into his, so we go first to Tufnell Park before it takes him on to Notting Hill . . . a long distance out of his way. Blimey . . . they'd just finished the chess programme and started *Blow-Up* . . . I think David* looks better now than he did then. No that's not true. It's just that in *Blow-Up*, as an actor he doesn't communicate a tenth of his amazing *energy*.

At the Lauries' everything hunky-dory. Jo desperate to drop now. She had told me a couple of days ago that Ben and Sophie were going to get married *and I completely forgot*. Christ I'm hopeless with gossip. Not that that was gossip, but you know what I mean. Other people's news. Other people's poetry. (I'm surer than ever that this is the right title and that Sue will hate it.) Sophie is going to come and live in England. Ben thinks April or May for the wedding.

I told him May was traditionally looked upon as unlucky for weddings. Like the colour green. Don't know what I was thinking. I'm not in the least superstitious and I could see it rather rattled the happy pair. Was I subconsciously being malicious? I'm sure not.

We talked a little about our respective novels. Hugh's writing a thriller: I've read about a third of it and it's *very* funny.

Next day: ie today, got up early, trained to Haslemere

* Hemmings.

263

and had played my 9 holes at Grayshott by half past ten. Toyed with the nov. a bit, but just that one day away has lost me a lot and I couldn't concentrate properly enough to write anything new, so spent time rewriting and rejigging here and there. Had a massage at 3.00. Steve's away so it was Willy Blake, well named. He's a Norfolk friend of my sister Jo and a rather endearingly nonsensical New Age freak. Gibbered on, while rubbing away, about channelling and auras. I asked him if he'd ever seen anyone's aura himself. 'No,' he said. 'Not a proper aura, but I once saw a very clear etheric sheath.' Well I mean frankly.

Mostly watched TV after that, the Muse having taken a powder. Then dinner, bit more telly and this diary, really.

Monday, 6 September 1993 – Grayshott

Very little to report today. An absolutely bog standard Grayshott kind of a day. Nine holes, slightly disappointing, heat treatment, massage, work, bed. Another nine holes in the afternoon, adequate play. Not much more to it than that I'm afraid.

Tuesday, 7 September 1993 – Grayshott

Much the bleeding same. Sister Jo is back today and I spoke to her on the phone. She and Richard and the baby* seemed to have a good time in France. No vital

---

*My beloved nephew George. All three of my nephews are equally beloved of course. No nieces sadly; sister and sister-in-law just weren't

messages: Greg Snow's present of a Lesbian Cunt Coloring Book from Florida is being despatched, to which I look forward eagerly. I've been invited to the first night of *La Bohème* at the Coliseum next week, which might be a lark.

Sue Freestone, my publisher, sent a fax saying she is insanely excited that I am getting on with the novel. She seems to think it will be finished as a matter of course. Gulp. Wants to know what ideas I've got for the cover. I'm not half way through and she wants a cover. Oh shit.

Spoke to Maggi Hambling† on the phone. She wants two more sittings for her portraits. I have arranged to go over on Tuesday and Wednesday next week.

In the afternoon I watched some of the opening game in the Kasparov v Short match. Both Channel 4 and BBC2 are giving it plenty of air. Channel 4's coverage is taking populism to new depths. The presenter can't even let Daniel King or Jonathan Speelman use the phrase 'queen-side' without jumping down their throats. 'So that's the left-hand side of the board is it?' 'Yes, that's right.' Well it isn't the left-hand side to Nigel, playing black, is it? She is trying desperately to find dramatic phrases culled from

---

concentrating. Actually, it's the sperm that determines gender come to think, no pun intended. Help, I've become infected. Writing footnotes in diary style now. It'll be exclamation marks next!! Oh merciful heavens!! No!!!

†The painter and sculptor. She had been commissioned by the National Portrait Gallery to paint a picture of me, which she had long wanted to do anyway.

any other arena than chess, to describe what is an intellectual battle utterly beyond her grasp. Or mine for that
matter. Granted, it's a good idea to widen the audience,
but treating it like a benzedrine-driven joust between two
wild-eyed exponents of gamesmanship is hardly helping.

Sadly Nigel lost *on time*. He had weathered a storm, a
battering in fact, from Garry K, but as he was preparing to
make his *very last* move in time control, his flag fell. Disaster. He must be sick to his soul. It was good that he ended
in a position that was at least drawn, but calamitous that
he should have lost the game so stupidly. Went to bed in a
thunderstorm. Lovely feeling. It wasn't attacking my king.

Wednesday, 8 September 1993 – Grayshott

No golf this morning: wind blowing hard, grass sodden.
Lots of work, now definitely half way through. I've written over twenty thousand words in 9 days, which isn't
bad. Unfortunately I won't get another stretch of time
like this. I spoke to Sue Freestone on the phone. She's
coming round next Thursday to look at what I've got. My
novel, which she still insists on calling *What Next?* is going
to be 'the biggest publishing event of Spring '94.' Great.

Ian McKellen rang too. He wants me to present some
bloody Age of Consent* benefit at the London Palladium

---

*The sainted Edwina Curry was bringing a Private Members Bill before
 the House of Commons to make the age of homosexual consent equal
 to the heterosexual age. At the time the gay age of consent was twenty-

for Stonewall. Well, not present, just introduce. I've also agreed to do a debate at the Cambridge Union on the same issue. All these things are going to take up time I cannot spare. After all, there's the Sam Wanamaker Globe bash at the Albert Hall too.

Talking of the Albert Hall, I'm going to the Last Night of the Proms on Saturday, after Charles and Carla Powell's wedding. Well not *their* wedding, their son's.

Played golf in the afternoon, during a lull in the weather and a lull in my inspiration. *Played like a fucking genius.* As I was addressing the ball I just *knew* that it was going to go long and straight. For the first time in my life I consistently hit overlong and had to go down a club at almost every hole. Birdies and pars and virtually nothing else. Ridiculous because I am the most uncoordinated, least able striker of a ball who ever pulled a club from a bag. But every dog has his day, I suppose. I will probably never play another round like it, so it is as well to be pleased.

The novel steaming along too. Not that it's anything other than balderdash, but at least I feel as if I'm achieving things. Elements are coming together. So far, however, it is lacking in any passion. I want people to cry at parts of it, and those stages haven't yet been reached. Gonna be tricky. Ner-night.

---

one, the original Wolfenden Report recommendation, passed into law thirty-odd years earlier. Final equality had to wait until 2000, three years into the Blair administration.

Thursday, 9 September 1993 – Grayshott

Reasonable day. Fair old quantity of work done, over 4,000 words. The post contained Greg Snow's present from Florida: *The Cunt Coloring Book* by Tee Corinne. I quote from the introduction. 'The *Cunt Coloring Book* published in 1975, was immediately and wildly popular, although many people complained about the "awful" title. Three printings later, in 1981, the title was changed to *Labiaflowers* and the book virtually died. So much for euphemisms. Welcome once again to the *Original Cunt Coloring Book* (with a few additions). May you color it with pleasure. The drawings in this book are of real women's cunts. My love and thanks to the many women who participated with me in this project and to those who encouraged and counseled me. These pages are a celebration of your energy.'

That was from the foreword by Tee herself. There is also a little prefacing essay entitled 'In The Beginning' by one Martha Shelley.

In the beginning we come from the cunt, not from some man's side; and we are washed in the water and blood of birth, not the spear-pierced side of some dying god. In the beginning women made pots and jars shaped like wombs and breasts, and decorated them with triangles, which were symbols of the cunt.

So the first art was Cunt Art. The bones of the dead

were laid in jars – perhaps to speed the soul to its next
womb? Did the ancient women sing, how delicate,
sensitive, delicious, how strong the ring of muscle between one life and the next? There are tribal women
today who sing praises of their cunts, how pretty and
long and full their lips are, how the hair curls and glis-
tens with moisture.

Well, I mean dah-ling . . .

Naturally the pages themselves contain hideous warped
oysterish things that look like the result of an explosion
in an organ-donor depot. I hope that doesn't sound
misogynistic – a Cock Coloring Book would be just as
beastly.

The book even has an ISBN no.* can you credit it? For
the rest, there is sadly, no text, just these line-drawn quims.

Otherwise, the only other post was a card from Rory
Bremner, asking me to be a 'guest-writer' on one of his
new Channel 4 shows. Kindly offer but I think I'll pass.

Rang Kim during the second Short/Kasparov game.
He seems to think, with me, that Nigel's blown it again.†
Invited K to accompany me to the opening of *La Bohème*
and *Oleanna*, the new David Mamet. Still no news from
Hugh and Jo L. They *must* be dropping even now, surely?

---

*0-86719-371-9.

†Kim was seven thousand times more likely to know. He was a chess
master and had been at school with Nigel Short. Taught him the French
Defence and its many variations, Kim's favourite for black.

Had a reflexology and aromatherapy massage. Not bad. Still feel pretty energized. All my masseuses now seem to be in agreement that I am 'balanced and relaxed', which is pleasant.

Spoke to Scott Rudin. He's pleased I had the session with Terry Gilliam about T's new film *The Defective Detective*, but wishes I was harder on Terry about the script. Hyuh! What's it to do with me? I'll try and liaise with Scott about my next script for him when I've done with the novel.

Sue F. faxed me with a suggestion for the jacket. 'How about Michelangelo's David wearing Y-fronts?' Well, I mean really! A tad homo-erotic, for a novel that is primarily non whoopsy. Thought of a scene today in which Davey will fuck a horse to heal it from some mysterious illness like ragwort poisoning. Could be good.

News just in. Nigel drew the game. Phew. Ho-hum.

Friday, 10 September 1993 – Grayshott

Last full day here. Arose in time to do some work, biffed off for the massage and heat treatment and returned to the room to find a message under the door: 'Please ring Rebecca Laurie, 071 580 4400, Room 101.' Just for a moment I thought I'd gone mad and then . . . of course! Jo decided to have a Caesarian today. The child had been up there for too damned long, putting on too much bloody weight. 8lb 13oz. Jo was barely able to walk or breathe. The doctors thought it would probably stay up there for another two weeks, just liked it too much. University College Hospital said they wouldn't do a section for another fortnight, so Jo and Hugh took the reluctant decision to go private at the Portland. A big bonny baby girl. I shall see her on Sunday.

Plenty of work, then a holistic massage, pleasure as always, followed by a swift nine holes. Some great shooting, some average (as if you care).

Then more work: reached three hundred words shy of the fifty thousand. That means I've written just about 30,000 words in the last eleven days. Not bad. I've just finished writing the scene in which Davey fucks the horse. My lord I'm going to get some stick for that. 'So, did you try it out, Stephen? . . . in the interests of research naturally . . . hyerk, hyerk . . .'

It might be dreadful I suppose, we shall see. Wonder what Sue Freestone will think. Final treatment tomorrow will be a facial with which to present a smooth and glossy countenance to the wedding and the Proms. All in all, this has been a truly splendid stay, I've lost over a stone in weight. I've enjoyed the work once it's started flowing and I've been more relaxed and happier than for years. And I've kept off the booze, plenty tomorrow though . . .

It's past 11.00 now and I shall hope to be asleep by twelve. Nightly-nightington.

Sunday, 12 September 1993 – London

Back in town, one stone two pounds lighter and thirty thousand words to the good. Finished off with a facial yesterday and hit the A3 looking shiny, fit and relaxed. Those fine dryness lines the commercials love so much didn't have a chance. I challenged the visible signs of ageing.

Arrived in time to zip over to Lipman's in the lower Charing X Road where I hired a morning suit, my own being stuck up in Norfolk. Then I bought a print at the Chris Beetles Gallery for the happy pair, quick change in the flat before high-tailing it by taxi to the Old Church, Chelsea. Charles and Carla Powell looked in great nick. Well Sir Charles has aged a spot, but that's hardly surprising as he regularly jets to Hong Kong for half hour meetings with Chris Patten* before jetting back again the same day. Takes a toll. Carla, on the other hand in supreme shape. Spending most of her days in Italy looking after her father. Their son Hugh was marrying one Catherine Young, daughter of Sir William and Lady Young, whoever they might be. He is a director of Coutt's the bankers but chaps of his background are directors of banks much in the way they might be members of a squash club. Dennis Thatcher was there on the groom's side, as were poor

---

*The last Governor of Hong Kong, who oversaw the rain-sodden handing over of the Crown Colony to China in 1997. At time of writing Chairman of BBC trustees and may well be the last of those too, given the corporation's plight.

old Rosemary and Norman Lamont.* Ha! That'll teach him to be a loyal Tory.

Good service: Schubert's *Ave Maria* and Mozart's *Ave Verum*, beautifully sung. Good trumpeter in evidence for inevitable Jeremiah Clarke† and Grand March from *Aida*.

Soon as the service was over I cabbed back to the flat to change for the Albert Hall. Arrived good and early so I could track down Patrick Deuchars who runs the place. He had invited me for the Prom's Last Night and I had initially turned him down, thinking I'd stay for the wedding reception. It occurred to me last week that this was silly as I really wouldn't know that many people at the wedding and the L. N. of the P's would be larkier. So I rang John Birt's‡ office and said I could come after all. That's right. John Birt's office. Like an arse I had thought it was *he* who had invited me, not Deuchars. John is always inviting me to *something* after all . . . Wimbledon, Cup Final etc. His office had said 'fine, help yourself . . . no problem. You'll be squiring Lady Parkinson (wife of Cecil).' Only then did I realize my bloomer. At the RAH therefore I found Patrick who was highly amused and said not to worry. John Birt when he arrived was similarly tickled,

---

* Norman Lamont had been sacked a few months earlier as Chancellor of the Exchequer by Prime Minister John Major. He made a snidely neat resignation speech in the House: 'This government gives the impression of being in office but not in power.'
† Supposedly the composer of Purcell's 'Trumpet Voluntary', although I have heard a theory that it was by someone called Mud.
‡ Then Deputy Director of the BBC.

so was able to play the self-lacerating idiot and make them feel good.

Who was there? Well, a load of old Tories really. Michael Heseltine and his wife. They turned out to be enormous fans of *J&W*. 'We've got a butler who absolutely bases himself on your Jeeves,' trilled Mrs H. 'Lah-di-fucking-da, darling,' as I stridently didn't say. Peregrine Worsthorne and his wife Lucinda Lambton, who came in the most extraordinary Union Jack frock, Alan Coren and his wife Anne, Terry Burns of HM Treasury, Debbie and David Owen, the latter hot-foot from his notable failures in Switzerland.* Jane Birt and self made up the numbers. I like Jane I must say – American, as is Debbie Owen.

Pretty good time had by all, though the event is significantly less moving in the flesh than on TV. Secretly I felt it all rather anticlimactic, as if I had been expecting some other element that actually wasn't present. We dined afterwards at Launceston Place, the Owens giving me a lift in their brand new Volvo. Rather comical actually. They argued about absolutely everything. The way to the car, how to get to the restaurant, how to park once there. I said, 'Well, if you can't decide how to walk to a parked car, no wonder there's such hell in Bosnia,' a bit obvious, but really ... U.N. negotiator and he can't negotiate a one-way system.

Sat at one end of the table flanked by Lucinda and

* Trying by diplomatic means to stop the slaughter in the wreckage of the former Yugoslavia.

Lady P. She's all right is our Lucinda I think, in a batty aristo way. A professional enthusiast, and therefore slightly overdone, but I think not a fraud. Home to bed at two-ish, my latest night for a fortnight.

Today I went to the Portland to inspect young Rebecca Laurie, who is stout and sweet. Jo, poor thing is absolutely knocked out, pneumonia, the works. She's got either a nebulizer or an oxygen mask on at all times. Hugh showed up and seems, for him, rather confident about the novel he's writing. I bet it's blissfully funny.

Strange things, private hospitals. You ring a number on the phone and get the answer 'Room Service . . .' I had noticed a TVR parked out the front which had the number plate A1 OB ST, which turned out to belong to Mr Armstrong, the consultant who did Jo's Caesarian. He turned up too, all jeans, Kickers, navy blue Guernsey sweater, your casual Home Counties weekend uniform.

Then back home and a bit more work on the nov. I *think* I may be able to do things here. I damned well hope so. Only a thousand words today. A lot of fucking about with the formatting of a couple of faxes that are contained in the novel.

Well, it's past midnight and I'm for sleepies.

Monday, 13 September 1993

A quiet day. Barely stepped out of the flat. A lot of letters to get out of the way, which I managed. The world has

gone wild today on account of the PLO Israeli agreement being signed in Washington. Henry Kissinger and
other so-called wise old birds are being very cautious.
Not surprising, really. A lot of work to do yet, if right
wing Israelis and nationalist Palestinians are to be quiet-
ened.

Worked on a different kind of chapter of the novel.
The third person narrative of Michael Logan's upbringing, vaguely based on my grandfather's life. Where else
would I get the idea of a Hungarian grower of sugar
beet?

Not much else to report. Still trying to eat well, but it's
so hard not to raid the fridge. Must buy a set of scales,
that would help.

Tuesday, 14 September 1993

Up early to sit for Maggi Hambling again. It started badly,
both of us a little nervous. She grew in confidence however, drawing with a stick of charcoal that was roughly the
size of a milk-bottle. Amazing implement. Christ it's a
chore standing stock still for so long. Towards the end she
played some Ink Spots on the cassette player and wanted
to draw me as I danced, a procedure she finds endlessly
amusing, as does anyone fortunate enough to witness so
rare and unwilling an occurrence. A car came to pick me
up at 12.45 to take me to a studio in Islington for photographs for the *Radio Times*. All to do with *Stalag Luft* whose

screening date they really can't decide upon. I think it's back to late October again now, having been the 8th at one point. The photoshoot, by Brian Moody, absolutely sweet guy as a lot of good photographers are I've noticed, was followed by an interview. Reasonable outcome I hope. Must say I felt good all through, despite longing to be at the keyboard novelizing. The Grayshott effect still keeping me relaxed and cheerful.

More work in the evening, hours of it. Continuing the chapter in which we go back to Europe to see Michael Logan's father as a Hungarian Jew.

Wednesday, 15 September 1993

Another sitting with Maggi. She wanted me to bring a DJ this time, more consonant with whatever image she has of me. As we progressed I realized these sessions weren't enough for her. She has a large black canvas she wants to paint in oils, and we clearly didn't have time to get near it. I suggested another couple of sessions and she was clearly relieved. Next week then.

Back home for more work before Kim could arrive to accompany me to the Coliseum for the opening of *La Bohème*. Helen Atkinson-Wood* rang to ask if I would talk into a cassette for a boy who is a friend of her family. He had a cycling accident and is now in a coma. Turns out to be a huge *Blackadder* fan. Said I'd do what I can.

* *Blackadder the Third*'s Mrs Miggins.

Naturally I have now discovered that I have no recording facilities here.

Kim arrived looking well and smart and we shogged off to St Martin's Lane. What a disappointment! Dreadful production, simply dreadful. The work of Steven Pimlott. Chorus abominably handled, no interval, which enraged Kim who thought it made the thing stink structurally. He knows it better than me, so I took his word for it: very short evening even without interval. I would otherwise have assumed that the opera itself was a structural mess. The Rodolfo was ghastly, barely audible above the band, and the whole thing sounds so foul in English. Mind you, I wept like a baby at the end, who couldn't? Saw Melvyn Bragg there: he's lost a ton of weight and looks twenty years older for it. His chubbiness was what gave him the boyish, almost cherubic look for which he is famed. Jeremy Isaacs* present also, and Anna Ford and Frank Johnson and assorted Mediahadeen. Kim and I went to The Ivy afterwards. Saw Harold and Antonia, Mike Ockrent (also looking older for weight-loss)† and Tim Rice, mercifully at full weight.

Back in time for bed.

---

*Then running the Royal Opera House, Covent Garden, formally head of Channel 4.

†He was sadly to be wrenched away from the world by leukaemia six years later, while working on the musical version of *The Producers* with Mel Brooks.

Thursday, 16 September 1993

Sue Freestone today! Great nerves. Final checks, then a print out. She read half before we went to Green's for a quick oyster or two. Then back to finish. She seemed immensely pleased. Great relief. No real criticism. I worked on her as regards the title *Other People's Poetry* and she seems to be warming to it.

At 5.00 I trotted off to the Lauries' to inspect Rebecca again and deliver my nebulizer, which Jo and Hugh feel they ought to have on hand, given Jo's recent pneumonic state. Stayed for supper and *Die Hard 2*.

Friday, 17 September 1993

Frustrating morning wandering up and down Regent Street and Mayfair looking for a tape-recorder. Maddened by being ignored by the five or six staff at Wallace Heaton in Bond Street. Can't kick up a fuss or they'd think I was annoyed because of 'who I am'. Eventually had to go all the way to 76 Oxford Street, where I got a Sony Professional Walkman. Wrote and delivered a monologue as Melchett for the boy in the coma, printed out the novel thus far for Anthony Goff my lit. agent and got a taxi to deliver the tape and the manuscript. Anthony said on the phone that Sue sounded frankly ecstatic about the work so far. I MUST NOT LET THIS DIVERT ME FROM CONCENTRATING.

Then, down to work. It all seems to be coalescing in

my head, and as always when things are apparently going well, elements I had put in the novel frankly on spec early on in the writing, when I had no idea what the plot was doing or what the outcome would be, suddenly make absolute sense and look natural and right, as if I had always known they should be there. What does that mean though?

Heigh ho.

Saturday, 18 September 1993

Mostly work, as usual. Had an idea that each chapter should be headed with a verse from Eliot's poem 'The Hippopotamus'. It seems so appropriate. I know the poem is really supposed to be about the C. of E., but it fits the character of Ted to see him as an apparently mud-baked hippo who is in fact more likely to rise and be washed by the angels and martyrs than anyone else. Should the novel itself be called *The Hippopotamus*? Is that over-egging the pudding?

Skipped around St James's and the Burlington Arcade, trying to find a present for Alastair's b'day. Ended up getting a rather splendid dressing-gown at Turnbull & Asser. £390 odd but worth it. Kim and he held a party at their place in Dalston. Nick and Sarah were there, but Hugh never showed. Trevor Newton back from his year's sabbatical in Australia, teaching at Rochester again. He seemed good, if a tad subdued and self-conscious.

Strange: at Cambridge he was infinitely more urbane and polished than any of us, but since he's become a dominie he's grown away from London; it must be hard for him now that Kim is doing well writing for Ken B. and Greg Snow (also present) is getting on with things as a writer. Why a schoolmaster should feel inferior . . . yet we know they do. We are the ones who should feel inferior.

Kim and I talked a bit about Oscar. K is getting on with the screenplay for Ken. They showed the Peter Finch film this afternoon, I was writing, so I've recorded it to watch tomorrow. Bet he's unsurpassably good: it'll only depress me to see him.

I had some lines of coke for the first time in months and months. Weird having that old feeling coursing in the blood again. A large hammer of guilt was banging away in time to the accelerated beating of my heart. All that health and weight loss at Grayshott and now I was guzzling pink champagne* like a beast. That's the trouble with the old nose-candy: it may suppress your appetite but it sure as hell increases your intake of alcohol. Still, one night in five hundred can't be fatal. Fuck me, it's appealing stuff though. Simply too gorgeous and delicious to be trusted. I could fall back into my old ways oh so easily.

Stayed and chatted for much longer than I otherwise

---

*Allergic to standard champagne, but not pink. Go figure. A pink champagne socialist.

would as a result of the Charlie. Ian, Ceri and other of Alastair's Oxford friends made up the majority of the guestage. Quite fun. Got back at two-ish. Not an excessive amount of leg-thrashing, skin-twitching insomnia. Probably clocked out at three.

Sunday, 19 September 1993

Awoke at 11.00-ish feeling worse than I have for ages. But not a massive hangover. Knew I'd be able to work when it came to it. Took things easily and wrote two and half thousand words . . . not as good as I have been, but that's understandable under the circs.

Watched the Peter Finch Oscar. Christ he was excellent. Terribly moving. The witty lines excellently thrown away. How will I ever beat that? Lionel Jeffries splendid too.* Very painful.

So far we have 69,009 words for the novel. Have written a diary entry for the queeny character Oliver Mills who gets 'cured' by Davey rather as the horse did. Decided against actually writing the scene itself.

The thing seems to be taking shape. Oh God, it's so hard to tell any more. When you're inside something for so long, what do you really know about it?

Humpy-hip. Beddly-poos.

* As Wilde's nemesis, the Marquess of Queensberry.

Monday, 20 September 1993

More work. What else can a chap do? Again, seems to be proceeding all right. But Christ knows if it means anything.

My taxi returned from the garage, new radio and cassette fitted, the kind with a removable front. They've done a lovely job on the cab itself, but the fucking radio is dead. Boo.

At six-ish Kim came round, with a line of coke for us each to enjoy before the theatre. While he was chopping up I printed out the horse-fucking scene for him to read. He seemed to take to it well: really liked it I think.

Fortified artistically and nasally, we trolled to the Duke of York's for the first night of *Oleanna*. Rather ordinary first act, which disappointed me and then – kerboom! – the thing exploded and you had the ordinary nature of the pre-interval set-up reinterpreted in front of your eyes. Wonderful stuff.

Never seen so many people streaming out of a theatre *talking*. Everyone had something to say. I discovered that I was sitting next to Edwina Curry of all people. She, naturally, had *very* firm ideas about it all. Piffle, as you would expect. 'He failed her.' What, so he deserved to lose his wife, house and job, did he? What would Edwina's life be like if she was punished for a sexual indiscretion of that kind?*

---

* Ha! We didn't know at the time that she had had an affair with the future Prime Minister, John Major, in the mid-1980s.

We avoided the party afterwards and wound our way to the Brixtonian in Neal's Yard, where Alastair's friend Ian Poitier was having a birthday party. A sweet poppet from the W. Indies, Ian was at Oxf. with Al. and says he's a cousin or nephew of the great Sidney. We left there, however, and went to the Ivy actually to eat. Bumped into Simon Gray who, natch, hated *Oleanna*. Then home for kip.

Tuesday, 21 September 1993

Sat for Maggi *again* all morning. She has started the big oil now and I hope will be done by Friday. It's fun but intense. Nipped back home for a spot of work and then off to Mount Street to see Dougie Hayward the tailor to be measured for a suit. He's going to make a dark blue job. Never had one that colour before, but it could work. He makes for Michael Caine and John Cleese (who recommended him) very much *the* man of the 60s along with Tommy Nutter, tailoring for Terence Stamp and those kind of people. Not sure my bulk will bring out the best in his snipping, but we'll see.

At seven-thirty, after a lot of heavy writing, which went pretty well I think (did the scene in which Davey persuades the fourteen year old with a brace on her teeth to give him a blow-job) I taxi-ed to Ben's flat. He's in a bit of a state, poor love. His psoriasis is spreading vilely. He's trying this Chinese figure, Tong, who did so well for Jo Laurie, but so far no success. He's told Ben to steer clear of yeast, which means no beer, which Ben hates. But if tension is a cause, then it's amazing Ben hasn't got it worse, frankly. Neil and Glenys Kinnock came round and we walked to the Bombay Brasserie. Both N & G in excellent form. I was delighted and amazed to hear that they had come to the same conclusion as me, which I would never have dared raise otherwise, thinking it sacrilege ... viz. it's time the Lib Dems and Labour got to-bloody-gether and prepared to kick the Tories out. Very good fun.

Trailed back home at one-ish.

Wednesday, 22 September 1993

A frustrating day, if the truth be told. Not enough chance to work. David Tomlinson* had invited me to lunch at Carluccio's restaurant in Neal Street. Wonderful place, fabulous funghi, good wine and the company of David, Richard Ingrams, his assistant at the *Oldie* Isabelle, and Beryl Bainbridge, who's always a lark. But too much incredibly fine whisky. Woozily wandered home and got into the cab to go for a costume fitting for the Juvenal thing I'm doing next week. Cabbed back, fell asleep for half an hour and then had to get ready for the theatre. Went to see Simon Donald's new play at the Donmar *The Life of Stuff*: started badly but perked up. Very much a young inexperienced playwright's work, but full of heart and shocks and

* *Mary Poppins, Bedknobs and Broomsticks* and so forth.

some wit (mostly derivative and inconsistent if the truth be told). Was with Lo and Christian (Simon's a client of Lo's) as well as someone called Sarah and her boyfriend Dominic Minghella, brother of Anthony, also a writer apparently. They've built some whole new complex by the theatre called Thomas Neal's, sort of mall really. We dined at a new Mezzaluna there, part of the same chain you find in LA and New York. Then off home again.

Thursday, 23 September 1993

More productive day. 77,000 words done! Gosh I hope it's all right. Did a VO for Matchmakers at 11.00, with John Junkin of all people. Stout fellow, friendly, not sour, curmudgeonly and feeling passed over like so many his age . . . Barry Took etc.

I'm writing this at 4.45. Have to shower and change for the premiere of *The Fugitive*. I'm taking Alyce Faye: sending a stretch limo round to pick her up, the works. It's at the refurbished Warner West End, thence we go to a party at the Savoy, though we've also been invited to a party Michael and Shakira Caine are giving, so we might pop there first for an hour or so. I'll tell you all about it tomorrow, Daisy Dear. (Daisy is short for Daisy Diary, it's what the character Oliver Mills calls his diary in *The Hippopotamus* – that's definitely the title, I'm sure of it now). Must go and dress for tonight. Tell you about it tomorrow.

Friday, 24 September 1993

Well, last night was amusing enough. The limo that arrived was longer than a cricket pitch and whiter than a cricket boot. Alyce Faye highly amused. We had a voddie together and then hit Leicester Square. Absolutely *thousands* of people. What are they all *doing*? Most peculiar. In the foyer, hundreds milling about and, on TV screens, an in-house *Ent. Tonight* style show with comedian Andrew O'Connor, some bint called Amanda and good old Iain Johnstone all conducting interviews, with street people, celebs and film people respectively. Highly embarrassing. We went in and took our seats early. Only to discover that actually we were in cinema number 5, out of 11. *The Fugitive* was being shown in 9 of them. We were *not* in the same one as Princess Di and the A list. Feel acutely embarrassed and hope Alyce Faye isn't affronted. Doubt-less John Cleese, had he come, would have been in amongst the big nobs. They are showing the TV celeb show on the screen. Insane. Baz Bamigboye appears and says that only the nobodies would have turned up this early . . . glunk.

Anyway, film happens: damned good thriller. Tommy Lee Jones absolutely top hole. We streak for the exit. See a big white limo passing, but being moved on to do another circuit. I go out to stop it. Huge cheer from crowd.

It's not our limo. I walk back to the foyer: huge laugh

from crowd. Get trapped by a genuine TV crew and chat to the interviewer for a bit. Limo comes and we go. Weird feeling being pressed upon at all sides. People think it might be Madonna inside.*

We go first to the Hyde Park hotel to Michael Caine's and Marco Pierre White's new restaurant. We're in time for wine and *friandises* ... very fond of Shakira Caine. Michael is fine, but seems a bit pissed. Very sharp man in his own way but often cross and bitter. What he has to be resentful of I can't quite guess. I think he still feels the British class system held him back. Seeing that he and Sean Connery are far and away the biggest film stars we have produced since the war, with maybe the exception of Richard Burton who's hardly aristocratic either, I don't quite get it. But Caine can do no wrong in my eyes. He was Harry Palmer in *The Ipcress File* for heaven's sake.

We get back in the limo and head for the Savoy. More interviews on camera and then I'm left in peace. Gobble some lobster, command a table and some wine. Chat to Mo and Iain Johnstone. Michael White† and Jerry Hall pop by. We decide to leave. Home by 2.00.

Why does one attend such things? Well, it's honestly the only time I ever go to a cinema. You can just about

---

* I simply don't know *what* I was thinking of. A white stretch limo? Maybe they weren't so hen-party back then. But still . . .

† Producer of the first Monty Python film and impresario responsible for popularity of *Oh, Calcutta!*, *The Rocky Horror Show* and too many others to mention. Mad on tennis.

guarantee that people will behave at premieres and they certainly won't ask for your autograph or giggle. I don't think I've got many more in me though.

This morning up early, not hung over, another sitting with Maggi. Goes all right. Leave her place after four solid hours of standing and drive off to do some shopping for dinner on Sunday. Did I mention that Nigel Short and his wife Rhea and Dominic and Rosa Lawson and Kim Harris are popping in for dinner then?* Can't shop tomorrow because I'm off to Cambridge.

Anyway shopped and got back to the flat. No real concentration enough to work on the penultimate chapter, which is where I'm at. The Ryder Cup has started, for one thing. Oh – Manchester has lost its Olympic Bid.† No real surprise. Absolutely typical John Major failure, however. Australia, the Lucky Country . . .

Anyway spent most of the afternoon half-watching the golf and going back to clean up and rewrite the last few sections. 78,685 words. Lumme. When I think back to how depressed I was on the first Monday at Grayshott. How within an ace of calling it all off I was . . . not that it's necessarily *any good* what I've got. I have to keep reminding myself of that.

Well, it's 11:03 now, best be making an early night of it. We'll chat tomorrow, 'if I'm spared' . . .

---

*No, Stephen, it would appear that you didn't.
†For the 2000 Summer Games.

Saturday, 25 September 1993

Strange kind of a day. Had agreed, somewhere back in the mists of time, that I would drive to Cambridge and appear in a kind of 'celebrity' *University Challenge* game, hosted by Bamber Gascoigne. It was for the Alumni Weekend, which rather American sounding thing is an innovation. I arrived in time to do some shopping before the lunch. Bugger me Cambridge gets crowded these days: it's almost an unworkable city now. You have never seen such crowds, and if London had to put up with that kind of traffic there would be riots. Riots. Bought some books on equine anatomy and health to see if I can get Lilac's disease right in the novel. Also finally bought Donna Tartt's *Secret History* which everyone has been going on about and I suppose I ought to read. No sign of a book called *Trainspotting* which Simon Donald had told me to catch up on. By a Scot called Irvin(e) Wels(c)h I think the name is.

Got to the Grad Pad* in time for the lunch. I was on the Vice Chancellor's table, opposite Bamber and Germaine Greer and wedged between a couple of dons. Nice guy called Harcourt, Australian economist, on my right, zoologist called, I think, William Foster on my left. Sebastian Faulks was there too, which is good because I've just started on his novel *Birdsong*. Our team was completed by Valerie Grove.

The actual game was played in the Lady Mitchell Hall

* Deeply unpleasant soubriquet for Cambridge's Graduate Centre.

on the Sidgwick Site. Needless to say we *trashed* them. Germaine Greer said to me afterwards 'Jeez, you're so *competitive*' which I thought was *highly* revealing. She's a good stick though, for all that. It's clear in her conversation however that she still feels the need to prove herself all the time, which given her intelligence and confident eloquence is odd. No it isn't. We're all like that, eloquent or not. We just show it in different ways. Kept back for a few interviews and the like, one for *CAM* magazine, some graduate thing, and another for Varsity.

Drove back home listening to Day 2 of the Ryder Cup. It's going to be *fucking* close. Bit of telly, some small amount of work on the novel. London is not as good as Grayshott . . .

Ner-night.

Sunday, 26 September 1993

Up fairly late, tiny bit of novelizing, but most of the day spent chewing my nails at the Ryder Cup. We lost, boo-hoo. All a bit embarrassing, because it was down to Barry Lane chucking a three hole lead and turning it into a one hole loss all in the course of the last five holes. Also Costantino Rocca fucked up. All a bit of a shame. More English Majorite loss and gloom.

In the afternoon prepared dinner, just about got everything ready in time for Kim, Dominic Lawson, Nigel and Rhea Short and Dr Robert Hübner. Nigel in tremendous spirits considering he is on the brink of another famous English defeat. Well, not yet on the brink, but he was seriously outplayed by Kasparov on Saturday. A good evening though. Kim on good form, we talked a little about the chess. Then we got into a stupid argument with the rather vain figure of Hübner on the subject of whether or not things are altered by one's perception of them. He was poo-pooing any kind of thinking which veered from his *Ding an sich* Germanism. Bit of a prat, if the truth be told. After all, Schrödinger was just as German.* And Heisenberg. And they proposed that things are certainly altered by our perception. Certainly at the quantum level.

Kim and I promised we'd go next week to one of Nigel's games. I suspect we'll make it Saturday, when he'll be white and have a chance. They left and Kim and I stayed up for another hour. Kim had to shog, because tomorrow is the first day of *Frankenstein* rehearsals at Shepperton.

Monday, 27 September 1993

Day of some novel writing, but I'm finding it so hard to finish. Over 80,000 words done: never thought *that* day would dawn . . . but two chapters from the finishing post. Very hard to get them right. Didn't step out of the flat once. Rang a vet in Newmarket whose name was given to me by the Royal College of Veterinary Surgeons. Didn't seem to have much of a clue about an illness that could

---

* Well, all right, he was Austrian, but you know what I mean.

be misdiagnosed. Pathetic. I'm going to have to find a vet I can take out to dinner so I can explain it properly.

Watched Robbie's new series, *Cracker*, damned good stuff. He's on excellent form, really good. Not overacting, just perfect. Then wrote this. Highly dull, I'm afraid.

Time for boo-boos.

Tuesday, 28 September 1993

Oh Nigel. Oh Nigel, Nigel, Nigel. He missed a win. He missed his first great win. Oh damn, damn, double damn. Just been watching it on TV. He could have had Kasparov right there on the ropey-rope ropes. He fluffed it. Poor sod, he must be sicker than sick. He made a gigantically wonderful queen sacrifice and should have won. It's so clear that he should have won. Even I could fucking see it. Blastly damington. What a year for British sport. Is there a chance we can beat Holland to get into the World Cup finals? If there is it's far from a fat one. Poo and miz and boo and horridy-horridy-horrid.

Another day spent entirely in the flat. Not a breath of outside air. Getting unshaven and foetid so I lit some joss-sticks or 'incense sticks' as everyone now insists on calling them, but the novel proceeded better today. Now up to round about the 86,000 words mark. Man from the Newmarket vet rang today and suggested timpanic colic, which can be diagnosed as spasmodic colic which is worse. Might suffice, we shall see.

I shall watch *Tales of the City* which starts in half an hour on C4 and then go to bed. Boo-hoo.

Wednesday, 29 September 1993

90,113 words! Had a sudden and depressing realization last night at one in the morning that everything I'd written yesterday was wrong. Well, not everything, but nearly. I realized the final chapter had to run on immediately from the previous. Yesterday I'd set it the following morning and had the show-down in which Ted reveals the fruits of his researches taking place after lunch. As it is, it now takes place at dinner, which I think is better.

Got up early-ish, worked a bit and then did a voice over at ten. Got back, buying a pair of Doc Marten's on the way, and wrote till 6.00. Had a meeting with Dave Jeffcock at the Groucho Club at 6.30. He's producing the Juvenal thing I'm doing tomorrow and Friday and which, dear Daisy Diary, you will hear all about. Wish I wasn't doing it, though. I could bloody finish the novel this week otherwise. Drank one and a half glasses of red wine. No more. Came back, titivated a bit and counted the words. The novel is now longer than *The Liar* already. As if that makes a fucking bit of difference, Stephen, you total arsehole.

Really enjoyed *Tales of the City* last night. Damned fine. Followed by a highly depressing documentary on ITV about child abuse. The horror of it all.

John Smith has won his vote on OMOV today, thank Christ. Very, very close. The TUC loses its block vote.

Heigh ho. Better go and learn my lines.

HORRIFIED POSTSCRIPT: after doing this diary entry I decided to do some backing up of work on *The Hippo*. After my return from the Grouch I had worked for 2.5 hours rewriting the work of the day. Saved the wrong file and overwrote the rewrites, if that makes sense. So I might as well have stayed all night at the Grouch. Lost all my rewriting. Piss and fuck.

Thursday, 30 September 1993

Well, bugger me with a cocktail onion, what a day. What a day. Up earlyish and then a walk to the Groucho Club where the BBC had set up base camp.

The programme is called *Laughter and Loathing*, it's presented by Ian Hislop and purposes to analyse and document satire. Programme One, pilot and first ep., is all about Juvenal, played by me. Well, as you can imadge, the only way to play Juve is to get yourself dolled up in a toga and pace the streets of London, declaiming satires. No point doing it in a Tuscan Doric decorated studio looking like a historical figure. Juve was very much now and in the streets. There can be nothing in the world more embarrassing than standing outside the Bank of England in a toga, with a camera crew on a long lens miles away, shouting irate verse into a hidden radio mike. Tourists think you're a guide of some sort, punters who recognize you come up and nudge you or hound you for autographs. Unspeakable shame. Add to this a pair of thin boot/sandals and the rainiest late September day in living memory and you have a recipe for disgrace and horror. Filmed all morning in the City, Bank underground station and, mercifully, in the Conway Hall.

The evening was taken up with this party: brainchild of our prod./dir. Dave Jeffcock, the idea was that in the Gennaro Room of the Groucho a load of celebs and liggers would turn up for a free party in which self would be filmed (still in toga) being rejected and cold-shouldered by these media types. This would be edited with a VO of self reciting a Juve satire in which the poet complains about being a reject who has to go to smart parties and be ignored, just in order to eat. As we started filming the mood came upon me and – *eheu fugaces* – I asked Liam Carson whether or not he might be able to find me a couple of grams of Devil's Dandruff. This he duly did and I spent most of the party slightly wired. The guests included Clive James, Jeremy Paxman, Charles Kennedy the leader of the Liberal Democrats, a man who likes a drink, Angus Deayton, Danny Baker and Melvyn Bragg, the latter turning up with Cate his wife. The filming finished and I stayed on for a while.

Danny introduced me to a man with long hair that I realized was Rob Newman of Newman and Baddiel infamy. They had been a year or two below us at Cambridge but we never knew them. This frightening pair have been so rude about everyone I love and like that I assumed that he would snub me. In fact he was rather sweet and naturally I told him that I thought his show, currently on BBC2, was splendid. Haven't actually seen any of it and am sure it isn't quite my tasse d'oolong.

After this played Perudo* with Liam and a couple of other degenerates and flew off home when I realized that Tina Time had stolen some hours from me and it was twenty past one in the fuck-mothering morning.

Not ending September as I began it. Wine, coke, late nights. Shucks.

Friday, 1 October 1993

Pinch, punch – yeah, yeah, yeah. Another supremely embarrassing day, filming in Soho and Covent Garden in a toga and rain. Used up the lunchtime buying birthday presents for Nick Symons and Griff Rhys Jones, both of whom had parties tonight.

Finished filming at 8.00-ish and biffed off to Primrose Hill for Nick's party. Hugh was there and Paul Shearer and Kim and Alastair. Helen Napper and Jon Canter too. Had a gram and a half left over from the previous night.

Nick's party finished at eleven thirty and I cabbed it to Clerkenwell for Griff's. Usual suspects present and incorrect. Angus, Phil Pope, Helen A-W, Clive Anderson, Nick Mason (drummer from Pink Floyd) those sort. Mel Smith

---

*Perudo is a dice game that uses bluff, often called the Liar's Dice of the Andes. I described it as the second most addictive thing to come out of South America.

in US filming, but his wife Pamela in attendance. Got coked and drunk and at three-ish managed to retain the sense to call for a cab which I shared with Simon Bell to the centre of town: dropped him in Soho and fell into bed. Oh dear, Stephen, what a case you are.

Saturday, 2 October 1993

Up at 10.30, in no mood to work. Filled in time watching videos and then Kim arrived to accompany me to the Savoy Theatre to watch Nigel playing Gazza Kasp. We cabbed it after a cup of tea and arrived half an hour early. Sat in the front row and chatted. Rhea, Nigel's wife fetched up and we watched the first three quarters of an hour unfold. Nigel was white and it developed, as always, into a Najdorf Sicilian, with Nigel playing the Fischer favourite, Bishop c4. Kasp unwound a piece of preparation beginning with Nc6, and had taken 11 minutes to Nigel's 52 by the time we left the hall and went to Simpson's in the Strand where the grand-master's analysis room was. Most of the GMs in agreement that Nigel was in trouble. Kim had accurately predicted the course of the game and reckoned that Nigel stood all right, considering how taken by surprise he was. Tony Miles, ex-England #1 was presiding at the roundtable of GM's and making bitter foolish remarks about N's play. Dominic Lawson explained how completely asinine and childish Miles is. He cannot bear the fact that Short is so much better than him and has always beaten him. At one point he laughed out loud at a move of Nigel's which was absolutely necessary, precise and accurate. Really sad. He's spent some time in a funny farm, so one mustn't hate. Speelman turned up and was friendly. Chatted to Ray Keene and others. Nigel managed a draw and acquitted himself well over the board. Beaten in preparation perhaps, but excellently played.

Alastair then arrived and we had a drink and stepped over to Joe Allen's for dinz. Saw Maggi Hambling and, of all people, Amanda Barry* sitting at a table with Percy, Maggi's terrier. Then came home, drank a bottle of red wine and wrote this.

Now must bed myself. Off to Wyton† tomorrow for Jo (sister) and Richard's christening party for my nephew George.

Sunday, 3 October 1993

Drove to RAF Wyton. You have to report to the guardhouse and get a chit which you stick on your dashboard. Found Jo and Richard's quarters. Arrived same time as Roger, Ruthie, Ben and William. Ben and William v. affectionate and sweet. Jo looking fearfully well and George bouncing fit to bust. Splendid fellow. None of the usual stickiness you expect from these family affairs.

---

* *Carry on Cabby*, *Coronation Street*. Once I'd got to know her better it wasn't that surprising she was in Maggi's company.
†RAF station where Richard, husband to Jo and father to George, was based.

Almost frighteningly English. The X'ening itself took place in the church on the station, a rather cute little affair with shiny rafters. Simply *ghastly* ASB (Alternative Service Book) form of Christening. Even the Lord's Prayer was tampered with. Nice padre, but v. low. Came back for buns and cake.

Got away sharpish and returned to London, spot of TV and bed.

Monday, 4 October 1993

Well, a day spent entirely in the flat once more, and a day that has seen me finish the novel. Well, I say that, but when is a novel ever finished? I dotted the *point final* as the French say at round about six-thirty and ever since have been combing through the main body, rewriting. I suspect the length will be round about 96,000 words when we're done (Stephen, you are *such* a size queen).

Stopped off to watch the second ep. of Robbie Coltrane's *Cracker*, even better than the first, simply spot on. This was followed by *News at Ten* with all the pictures of Moscow's new October Revolution. It'll all drift into dim memory in a fortnight or so, but what a day . . . tanks blasting holes in the side of the Parliament building, hundreds killed. Could it happen here, we wonder?

Only worrying thing is that I somehow succumbed and opened a bottle of wine at nine-ish, most of which

I've consumed. Really must get into the habit of passing through a day without any alcohol.

Heigh ho. Up earlyish tomorrow please, Stephen, and perhaps it will all be really, really, really done.

Ner-night.

Tuesday, 5 October 1993

FINISHED ... well perhaps there's more work to do, but I've printed it out, sent a copy to Hugh Laurie and feel that it's out.

Immediately rang Sue, but she's at the Frankfurt Book Fair and so I won't send it to her until tomorrow or Monday even as she won't be back for the rest of the week. Rang the Lauries though and have cabbed it off to Hugh.

God knows what it's like. Feel hot and cold about it.

The evening saw a dinner at W. H. Smith's headquarters in Holbein Place off Sloane Square. Sir Simon Hornby, the chairman had invited me to dinner. Turned up in time, after a couple of lines, still left over from Liam's kind sale on Thursday. Drove the taxi. Interesting people there: the Roux bros., Hugh Johnson the wine writer, Edward Cazalet, Plum Wodehouse's grandson and others. Strangely serendipitous going to a Smith's dinner on the very day I finished the nov. They served Chateau La Tour and Meursault. Highly enjoyable, I got very drunk indeed.

Wednesday, 6 October 1993

Spent the day sorting out all the correspondence that had built up over the weeks since I'd been concentrating on *The Hippo*. Then I posted it and went shopping. Had lunch with Lo and Christian at the agency. Then . . . walked to Mortimer Street and bought an Apple Newton. Wow! What a piece of kit. It's going to take a little time before it can read my handwriting, but this is the way technology is going, no question.*

In the evening went to Victoria Wood's concert at the Royal Albert Hall. Met up with Hugh and Ben Elton: Ben's manager Phil McIntyre is the promoter of VW and arranged a good box for us. Afterwards we trotted off to the Bombay Brasserie (where Ben and I and the Kinnocks dined the other night) and spent a wondrous evening chatting. Hugh is reading Ben's novel as well as mine at the moment, so I've got a fluttery tummy. Especially as I've suddenly lost confidence in *The Hippo* and wonder what on earth I was at writing such a hard-to-define novel.

Thursday, 7 October 1993

Hugh came round this morning to start writing on the next series of *A Bit of Fry and Laurie*: no two week holiday after the intensity of *The Hippo* and all else. Come to think

---

* Sadly the Newton was somewhat before its time, but it was indeed the way technology was going. Hand held, touch screen (although with a stylus) . . . many things to like and admire in it.

of it when did I *ever* have a holiday? We didn't get much done, but it was *so* good to have him here. In the afternoon, Griff Rhys Jones rang up to invite me to a poker game at the Groucho.

After Hugh left I wandered to the G and the game happened. You have never seen so much coke in your life, how Griff resists it I do not know. XY was there too and the white powder simply flowed. I played poker pretty well, despite some very bad hands and managed to exploit what little luck I had. The effect of the C and a lot of red wine began to take its toll on me (but on no one else) and towards the end of the evening I (embarrassingly) threw up out of the window onto Dean Street below. Liam had a look and said there was no one there, no policemen, no unfortunate victim of the chunder. Shame, indignation and horror. It reminds me of the time when I was with *insert names of huge rock star, huge acting name, huge producer name here* in the back office of the 24 hours café in Kingly Street and we decided to have a Longest Line Competition. Each of us chopped out a line, mine being the longest. But the point was we had to take it up in one. A vile version of the shot-glasses down-in-one horror. On that occasion I took the line up my nose, it must have been seven foot long, but thin, hoovered it up, and as I got to the end of the table opened my mouth and let out gallons of pure, bright red vomit.

Not quite as bad as that this evening. Everybody very

nice about it, but what a humiliation. Struggled home somehow.

Friday, 8 October 1993

Quieter day. Hugh arrived late and we worked a bit. I wrote a sketch of appalling double entendre quality* and then he left. Played with the new Newton, watched a few videos and then went to bed.

Saturday, 9 October 1993

Bought some French videos to watch actors for the movie *Bachelors Anonymous* that I've been asked to direct next year. The Lauries invited me to dinner and I popped over. Nigel Short lost his match today, for the first time for weeks. Big shame. Came home, got a bit drunk and wrote up these last few days. Forgive my brevity of late.

Ner-night.

Sunday, 10 October 1993

Woke up good and dominically† late. Had a lunch at the Ivy with John Reid, Elton John's manager, and Arlene Phillips the choreographer. They had asked me some

---

*Known as 'The Understanding Barman'. Quite proud of it now. I think we thought it was a satire on Ronnie Barker-style innuendo, but of course such innuendo is funny: https://www.youtube.com/watch?v=U8ko2nCk_hE.

†My electronic calendar confirms that 10 October 1993 was indeed a Sunday.

time ago to see if I couldn't come up with a narrative framework for Elton's songs, with a view to putting on a West End Show. I wrote the book in February/March this year. Reid and Arlene like it, John R. has just come back from LA where he showed it to Bernie Taupin, Elton's lyricist who, as I suspected, did not like AT ALL. Accused it of being cliché-ridden, which is true, but inevitable for a West End/Broadway musical, and Elton's early life of transgressive sex, excess, drugs, rock and roll *was* frankly cliché-ridden. Still John and Arlene want to go ahead, so I'm to ring Sam Mendes tomorrow, as John likes the idea of his being the director. John, who'll produce, will see Sam when John gets back from Hong Kong next week. As well as being Elton's manager, he's also Billy Connolly's (and until a month or so ago, Barry Humphries').

Well, it may or may not take. The story is full of gay stuff, which will at least make it different. It's unhip and uncool, which is what Taupin dislikes, naturally. Taupin thinks of himself as some kind of hep Village guy from the 60's. Sort of Neurotica-Beat generation cool dude poet. Still trying to escape the fact that he's a Lincolnshire farm lad gone middle-aged and millionairoid.*

Came back, watched TV and wrote this. Still haven't watched any French stuff to see what I think of French

---

* This is awful. I met Bernie Taupin a year or so later and found him to be just about the most endearing fellow you could ever encounter, not in the least self-deluded or spoiled by his enormous success with Elton.

actors for *Bachelors Anonymous*. Hugh round again tomorrow for more *F&L* writing. Glunk.

Monday, 11 October 1993

I'm a bit behind diary-wise and I'm writing this later. Damned if I can remember what happened today. Wrote with Hugh in the morning and afternoon and then what . . . ?

Tuesday, 12 October 1993

More writing with Hugh during the day and then popped over to the Groucho to see if I could find some coke to ingest before dinner at L'Escargot with Pnina my second cousin's wife and Liora, her daughter. They were alright actually, could have been a lot worse. Desperate to know what the rest of the world thought of Israel's peace moment with the PLO. L'Escargot just recently reopened and Jimmy Lahoud, the new owner, was absolutely thrilled to see me there and stood me cognacs and all the rest of it. Okay evening. Walked home nearly sober.

Wednesday, 13 October 1993

Strange day. Wrote with Hugh up until about 5.00 when Mother came round to pick up a copy of *The Hippo* which she wants to read. We gossiped for a while and then I had to change for the evening. Tristan Garel-Jones had invited me to dinner. Arrived first at his Catherine Place address. Highly bonhomous cove, far too civilized to be a convincing Tory. Other guests included the Chancellor of the Exchequer, Kenneth Clarke, the Chief Whip Richard Ryder and assorted sprigs of the nobility, chiefly female (Leonora Lichfield, Jane Grosvenor that kind of thing). Had damn good chat with them all and raised the subject of tomorrow's debate at the Cambridge Union, viz. the age of consent. Tris was all for a free vote if ever it gets to the House of Commons, Richard Ryder (Ma and Pa's local MP in Norfolk as it happens) was being very tricksy about it. This horrific shite that the government have been spewing about 'family values' recently, since Blackpool in fact, may mean that they are not interested in things like justice and equality at the expense of the blue hair vote.

Left the dinner early because Griff had invited me to a card game at the Groucho. Eventually it took place: rather knackering business, lots of C. Managed to struggle home at two-ish.

Thursday, 14 October 1993

Had to be up very early in time for the *Today* programme on the consent and Cambridge debate issue. Felt like shit, as you can imagine after the excesses of the evening before. Eventually, after a great deal of hanging about, I got to the studio where Anna Ford and Brian Redhead were at their microphones. I was to deliberate with a

Conservative MP, David Wilshire, a sponsor of the Clause 28. In fact he said nothing I disagreed with: he made a libertarian point about it not being the law's business to interfere with what people do in private and left it at that. No debate to speak of at all.

Got back and dozed until Hugh arrived for writing. Spent a lot of the day not writing but thinking about what I was going to say in the evening.

Jon Plowman turned up at 12.30. He and Bob Spiers, I hope, are going to produce and direct respectively the next *Fry & Laurie*.* We lunched at Langan's, once we had tracked down poor Bob Spiers who was lost and wandering desperately around St James's. I think they would be perfect those two and I believe Hugh thinks so too. Highly amiable and capable of delivering much higher production values. Lunch was fine and fun. Mostly gossip, but we agreed that we should proceed.

Sir Ian McKellen (or Serena McKellen as Kim told me he should more properly be addressed) showed up at about half-four, as did Michael Bywater who is on the opposition benches, opposing the motion 'This House Believes in an Equal Age of Consent for Homosexual

---

* Indeed they did. Bob Spiers, now deceased sadly, was an old hand from the Golden Age who had directed dozens of episodes of *Dad's Army*, *Are You Being Served?*, *It Ain't Half Hot, Mum* and, crucially, the second series of *Fawlty Towers*, which rendered him holy. Jon Plowman: an old friend from Granada *Alfresco* days who would go on to be probably the BBC's longest-serving head of comedy, ushering in *Ab Fab*, *The Office*, *Little Britain*, etc.

and Heterosexual Acts'. Poor old Michael agreed to do the debate without knowing that he was going to oppose. Claims he can't think of anything to say against the idea.

Drove to Cambridge, traffic in London bad, arrived a little late for the pre-debate drinks and dinner. There was already a hell of a queue leading into the union building.

Dinner was fine: not a culinary excitement, but fine. The President was an elegant girl called Lucy Frazer and to my left was a sporting chappie called something or other, he was from King's and reading Theology. Why have I forgotten his name already? Also there was Tristram Hunt, who is the son of the Hunts who live plumb spang next door to Hugh and Jo Laurie. Simply a poppet, he was speaking on our behalf.*

Anyway, eventually time to debate: we marched into the chamber, with *Newsnight* cameras on our heels. HUGE cheer for me. They just wouldn't stop, it was awfully sweet. Felt like blubbing. The President got things off to some kind of start, and Tristram Hunt opened the debate for us. Four speakers on each side, Tristram, Serena McKellen, Angela Mason (of Stonewall Group) and self proposing, and two undergraduates (including the one whose name I've forgotten), Stephen Green of the Conservative Family Campaign and Michael Bywater opposing.

Tristram put the case pretty ably, bless him. Our first undergraduate opposer was a cheery Scottish conservative,

* Now a Labour MP and dashing broadcaster who makes fine documentaries on history.

classic stout gingery politico. He was an indication of things to come, for it was clear that he did not believe in the position he had to take up at all. Serena then spoke, quite wonderfully, very moving indeed, ending up with a recitation from Housman's poem about the laws of God and man. Then the student whose name I can't remember: he was so disrespectful to the idea of the motion that Stephen Green got up and walked out! 'I'll come back when he's finished' he said. Highly entertaining.

Angela Mason next, she's the very extraordinary lesbotic campaigner who runs Stonewall. Used to be a member of the Angry Brigade, narrowly escaped conviction at some bombing trial. Oo-er. She was, as you would expect, dull and uninspired as a debater.

Then Stephen Green. What a ghastly and unfortunate specimen. Simply HOPELESS performance. Witless, graceless and useless. Didn't even try and present his real point of view, which is that he abominates anything to do with whoopsidom. Instead he tried to make some feeble, pettyfogging legal point about the age of consent which made no sense at all. He presented his book *The Sexual Dead End* some magisterial work, we are given to believe, outlining the dreadfulness of being a bottomite. Poor man. Sat down to, at the most, polite splatters of applause.

Then it was time for the floor debate. Oh yes, Stephen as usual, has to wait and wait and wait before he can speak. Undergraduates on this side and that spoke. Finally it was my turn. I had jotted a few things down on the back of an envelope as it were during the debate, but otherwise entirely busked, which is definitely the best way of doing things I think. Told them all about Cambridge and what kind of a place they were attending, the history of its alumni and what they stood for: contrasted this with the adulterers, closet cases and corrupt canters who get up at Tory Party Conferences and dare presume to talk about 'family values'.

The long and the short of it was that I got a standing ovation, which made me all trembly. They just wouldn't stop applauding me and cheering and all the rest. Very exciting. Michael Bywater spoke next and said he opposed the motion because he believed that the age of consent should not be equal: *hetero*sexual love was far too complex and difficult a thing to allow 16 year olds to engage in it. Homosexual love was fine: it was a matter for equals and those who know each other and should happily be set at 16. He ended by saying 'I'm sitting with the faggots' . . . crossed the bench and sat with us.

Well, as you can imagine, we carried the day. 693 votes to 30. Of the 30 it was mostly those who found the queue into the Aye door too long and voted by filing through the No. Was kept for at least an hour signing autographs in a great crush of undergraduacy. For the large part not the most bouncily charming bunch: 'Rory', 'Nicole', 'John' would be shouted at me as an order paper was put under my nose to be signed. Very few pleases or thank yous. One can overlook a lot by imagining that they were shy or nervous, but generally speaking a disappointing set. There is no point in being shiny, attractive, intelligent and young unless you beam it out, whatever your gender, to those older than you.

Eventually managed to get through to the room where drinks were supposed to be served. Bar had closed by that time, natch. No bad thing, since I was driving home. This we did once Serena, Michael and a couple of others could be prised away. I got home and to bed by about two-thirty. Long day. Little sleep lately.

Friday, 15 October 1993

Woke up early enough to do a Voice Over at 9.00 . . . really that's so many late nights now, I'm beginning to think all the work of Grayshott is being undone. Pretty feeble ads for Croft sherry. Got back in time for Hugh to come round and we stuck at it all day. Anthony Goff (my lit. agent) rang to say that he really loved *The Hippo*, which was a huge relief. I do honestly think he meant it.

Robin Hardy came round at 5.30 and we chewed the fat on the subj. of *Bachelors Anonymous*. I told him that Thierry Lhermitte was my certain favourite for the lead. He seemed to think this was a good idea and promised to try and see if he could book him. At 7.00 I biffed to the Groucho to see if I could spot a dealer of any kind. BW introduced me to a chap called Jethro who sold me a gram. Then I loped off to Hugh's and Jo's for dinner. Alastair and Kim were there and we had a jolly dinner before I ripped off home again, by way of the Grouch. I am back to my bad old ways with a vengeance.

Saturday, 16 October 1993

Signing tour. Up early for a car to Euston station, where I met Rebecca Salt of Mandarin books and we got on the train for Chester. Late, unfortunately, trouble at Watford. This meant we were late for Chester and only just arrived in time for my 'performance'. This involved a reading and chat on stage at the Gateway theatre. Read the Sherlock Holmes story from *Paperweight** and then took questions. Very good fun, really: seemed to go well. Then we grabbed a late lunch and signed some stock in a couple of book-shops in the Chester 'Rows'. Beautiful city, quite entrancing. Car from Chester to Liverpool where we signed again and leapt on a train for London. Did some fatuous IQ test for *Esquire* magazine on the way.

Went straight to the Groucho and hung around for a while. Jethro showed up and I bought 2 grams. Finally fell into bed in some kind of a state at 3.00.

Sunday, 17 October 1993

Lunch with Ferdy Fairfax† in Clapham. Charles Sturridge

---

*An earlier book of mine, a salmagundi of writings that you are sure to find delightful and a perfect gift too, for a hated one.
†Director of two series of *Jeeves and Wooster*, also now sadly no longer with us.

and Phoebe* showed up, Robert Fox† those sort of people. Rather fine affair, hearty Sunday lunch food, lots of children, very bright sunny autumn day, splendid.

Home at 6.00 watched telly and went to bed sober and early.

Monday, 18 October 1993

Press launch of *Stalag Luft*, screening and photo-call and all that. Took place at the Imperial War Museum. Watched it. *Think* it's alright. Hard to tell. It's a good story, so it should work well. I was fat, naturally. Nick Lyndhurst and I had to fend questions from the press. They were all dead keen to know about the Elton John musical, much to the distress of the poor popsy from the press office. Tore myself away at one thirty, just in time to get home before Hugh showed up at 2.00 for writing.

Met Chris Pye of Anglia and Anthony Horowitz, the writer, for drinks and a chat about a new detective series they want me to do. At the Groucho, naturally. Who was there but David Reynolds, the producer of *Stalag Luft* and some colleagues? They had been there since the screening finished. TV people, crumbs. Meeting went okay, then John Sessions showed up with some actress who plays a nurse in *Casualty*.

Home a bit pissed and fell into bed. What a week.

---

* Charles directed *Brideshead Revisited* at some preposterously young age and married Phoebe Nicholls, who played Cordelia (quite brilliantly).
† Producer brother of actors James and Edward.

Tuesday, 19 October 1993

Up and just about capable when Hugh came round. Jo (sister) popped over from Huntingdon to lunch with me and James Penny, my 'personal banker'. They use some phrase like 'wealth management' that makes me so embarrassed I could scream. We lunched there. Dear, dear. Have you really come to this, Stephen? All very flattering. You are ushered in by Jeeves-dressed Messengers, all striped trousers and tail-coats. There was Bruce, the manager of the Langham Street branch where I had banked before, and there was James Penny, who looks about 10, but knows his financial onions and his commercial shallots.

Downstairs in one of the dining rooms we lunched and supped burgundy while Penny told me that my money was useless as cash and that I really should do things with it. Gilts, he felt. I have always been dodgy about all this. If I earn the money I don't see why I then have to make money out of money. But you know what it's like, they look at you as if you're mad. So I suppose I'll sink something into shares, something into gilts. The good thing is that I can afford to stop working and travel the world for a couple of years or whatever, if I felt like it, without worrying about taxes for the previous years.

The private bank is open from 8.00–8.00 and can make any 'arrangements'. If I want cash they bring it to me on a salver . . .

Came back to write with Hugh. He's written a couple of fabulous songs lately. He left and I toddled to the Groucho for a meeting with Alex Hippisley-Cox (sic) a girl who will be doing the publicity for *The Hippo*. She likes the book, which is great. People at Hutchinson who've read it seem to think it's better than *The Liar*, which is wonderful – if they're right. Stayed on upstairs to watch Norwich beat Bayern Munich 2-1 . . . unbelievable. Wonderful stuff. A goal from Jeremy Goss that will live long in legend and song. Spike Denton, the Radio London film critic was there, and Rory McGrath and Charles Fontaine the owner chef of the Quality Chop House. Spotted Jethro and nipped off to do some rather decent coke I'm sorry to say. This is going to have to stop soon. Home at 2.00.

Wednesday, 20 October 1993

Up reasonably early to go to Doug Hayward, the tailor, for another fitting. The blue whistle and flute is emerging. Hugh was round a bit late, looking at new cars and tiles for my kitchen with his wife Jo who's designing it, bless her from crown to toe.

Wrote during the day as usual, then stayed in till 10.00. Watched a video of Bill Humble's *Royal Celebration*, which was directed by Ferdy Fairfax. Very good performance from Rupert Graves. Watched a vid. of Monday's episode of *Cracker*, Robbie really is giving the performance of his life. Fabulous.

At 10.00 off to the Groucho, I'd agreed to play Perudo with Keith Allen for some programme he's making in which he's being followed around London for a day. Silly but fun. The cameras whizzed about us: God knows what they saw.

Thursday, 21 October 1993

Voice Over at 9.30. With John Gordon Sinclair. He seems in fine shape. More writing with Hugh all morning and then at 7.00 I arrived at the Tallow Chandlers' Hall for a Bowyer's Dinner, guest of old John Perkins. Most extraordinary evening. Never been at a Livery Dinner before. A lot of City figures in ermine and gowns. Fairly clear that they would never otherwise have been able to earn the right to such accoutrements, for these were bears, so far as I could see, of very little brain. A lot of pompous people in spectacles for the most part. Simply dreadful. But Perkins is such a nice man. There was the whole business of the Loving Cup and so forth, and a load of exceptionally bad oratory.

Perkins had to be back in Norfolk, so we left round about tennish and I got dropped at the Groucho for a card game. Played poker with Griff and Rory and others for about three hours and ingested rather a lot of the old Bolivian marching powder.

Friday, 22 October 1993

Writing in the morning and afternoon. Quick pop off to the Grouch for supper. Had a long chat with Bob Mortimer of Reeves and Mortimer fame. Turns out they've got a signing gig tomorrow as well, also to Leeds, but at a different time. Bumped into Z, who is worried that his C habit has been going on for too long. Takes it during the day. Bad idea. Got home reasonably early a little chastened by the thought of Z, but cheered too, to think that I wasn't in such a parlous state as he was.

Saturday, 23 October 1993

Up earlyish for King's X station. Train to Leeds, signing. Car to Sheffield, signing. Car to Nottingham, signing. The latter had such a big queue that it was as well that it hadn't been the first or I would have been late for all the others. Lots of people, all very friendly. Think *Paperweight* in paperback is doing really well, which is so heartening. Home by half past nine. Watched a bit of telly, fell into bed sober and knackered after a heavy week.

Sunday, 24 October 1993

Up at 11.00, which was really 12.00 because the clocks went back today. Spent the day preparing for the Palladium gig. This is a benefit for the Stonewall Group, part of the age of consent campaign which the Cambridge Union had been about as well.

Got to the Palladium round about half past six. Ian McKellen was organizing the affair and the usual suspects turned up, Jo Brand, Julian Clary, Pet Shop Boys and so forth. I had invited Christian Hodell to come along and mix with the merry throng. He seemed to enjoy himself mightily.

At the end of the show, walking to the party, I discovered my cab had gone from the street where it had been parked. Christ I hope it was towed away, not stolen. We strolled on Christian and I to the Edge in Soho Square. I took about an hour of it before the press of people finally wore me out and I walked home and tumbled into bed after a couple more lines and some diet coke. What an arse I am.*

Monday, 25 October 1993

Before I go any further, I must register Gary Wilkinson's 71 clearance to beat Steve James to a quarter final place in the Skoda Classic. I know this looks naff, but it was one of the great sporting contests. You, dear reader, will wonder why on earth I am going on about such a strange thing as snooker, but as the old saying has it, 'you had to be there'. Four incredible hard final reds and an on-their-

---

*Just the Diet Coke would now keep me awake for hours, let alone the Naughty Coke.

spot-clearance to follow. I was happy to witness such a moment.

Work with Hugh then lunch with Max Hastings at Wilton's. Max arrived late, and at the neighbouring table while waiting I bumped into Don Black* who was meeting John Barry, to whom I was introduced. Barry happens to be something of a hero, so I was v. excited to meet him. He turns out to be a very down-the-line Yorkshireman, weirdly thin fingers and hands, and very charming. Lots of gossip about Saltzman and Broccoli from the Bond days.

Max arrived and told me that if I demanded 200,000 a year he would happily pay me to provide a column. This is a strange position to be in. I could say 'yes' and 200 grand would be mine. We nattered about the Tories and he said that Major, whom he fairly regularly sees, is a paranoid figure who believes his current unpopularity is entirely down to a conspiracy of a) Thatcherite mavericks and renegades and b) media enemies. Even if Major is *right* this attitude should be hidden. A real leader would surely kick arse and establish himself? We also chatted about Lamont's bitterness over his sacking. When it was time to leave the restaurant we discovered that Lamont was sitting at the neighbouring booth. Whoops! Don't *think* he was listening. Max turns out to be genuinely anti-Murdoch. He thinks him a completely evil and appalling man. Why isn't this made more plain in the

---

* Astoundingly prolific and successful lyricist, often in collaboration with John Barry.

pages of the *Telegraph*? Murdoch has announced his intention to destroy the *Telegraph* within the next five years.

Got back to the flat at 2.40 and wrote some more stuff, then Hugh left. Slept for an hour before driving off to Fulham for dinner with Matthew Rice and Emma Bridgewater, his wife. Chap called Jonathan Cavendish was my neighbour at table, he produced *Into the West* and *The Severed Bride* and so forth. Turns out he's doing an Oscar Wilde movie with Alfred Molina. Bollocks. Home in time to watch video *Cracker* and *Film '93*. Barry Norman wonderfully vituperative about *Dirty Weekend*, which is clearly drivel like every Winner movie. Time for bed.

Tuesday, 26 October 1993

Voice Over in the morning, just redoing the old Croft LBV port thing. Hugh and I worked again during the day and then at 8.00 I toddled over to the House of Commons to dine with an MP.

This man had written to me last month telling me how much he loved *The Liar* and inviting me to dine with him. Intrigued I accepted. But . . .

If this is the quality of MP that the Tory party is relying on then I am happy to say that they are not long for this world. Absurd looking man with the oddest manner you've ever seen. Sounds very ungracious after I have eaten his bread, but truly . . . Very right wing in a thought-less, 'I made it by the sweat of my brow' kind of way. Anyway, went and had a line in the loo.*

Wednesday, 27 October 1993

Spent the morning being painted again by Maggi H. Not too clever at 8.30, but I warmed up and started to enjoy it. She finished off by doing two drawings of me asleep, which was wonderful! She is the most extraordinary woman. Her company is more stimulating than cocaine, but her gruffness of manner and hard glare are apt to frighten off those who don't know that she has a heart of marshmallow. She would probably retch at me saying that. Being painted by a true artist is an extraordinary experience. She's so *athletic*: all the time I heard the snap of breaking charcoal or the sweep of it on cartridge paper and the stamp of her feet constantly (and uncon-sciously it seems) readjusting her stance as, like an athlete or a cheetah, her body moved while her eyes and head kept deadly still.

Home via the Groucho, where I was supposed to meet Jethro. Unfortunately he was late, so I left without him or any C. Back at the flat Jo and Charlie were there, Charlie typed out a message for me on the computer and was generally a poppet. He's five now. Weird to think that

---

*See earlier.

unless I top myself, OD or get run over by a bus, I'll live to see him make 25.*

Tried to sketch up† after they went, not easy. Went off to the Groucho again to meet Jethro . . . missed him *again* as I had to get back in time to meet Anthony and Sue F. for a dinner party to celebrate the delivery of *The Hippo*, which they really seem to like. I felt a bit odd, wine and ciggies tasted strange in the mouth.

They were interested in the planning and structure of the novel and I told them that I had been writing this diary through some of it and that it would show how late certain key ideas came to me . . . Simon's role for instance and lots else besides. They genuinely didn't believe me. 'It must have all been in your head . . .' Perhaps it was, but I was buggered if I could get it out, as a glance through September will show.

Bed at half past one. Too many armagnacs.

Thursday, 28 October 1993

Up feeling v. queer. Simply not well at all. Flucy and peculiar. Lurched over to Gresse Street for a VO. Managed it somehow and then staggered back to receive Hugh for a day's work. Not very capable for most of the day, but I managed to bang down a couple of sketches: slept for

---

*Which he has comfortably done. Well on his way to thirty now. Still a
poppet.
†i.e. Write a sketch.

two hours on the sofa round about mid-day. That helped a little I suppose.

At six thirty I trotted over to the Paris theatre (just two minutes walk, God bless where I live) for the *News Quiz*. Me and Alan Coren v. Richard Ingrams and Peter Cook. Alan and I won convincingly, the biggest win of the series, 20 points to 6. Quite a lark really, I managed to say the word clitoris a number of times, which is always pleasing. Then struggled over to the Groucho to see if some poker and coke wouldn't help push me out of my flu. Funnily enough it did. Won convincingly and we broke up at 12.30-ish, highly civilized. Met a fellow called, intriguingly and very Soho 50sly Nick the Basque. Home and asleep by 1.00.

Friday, 29 October 1993

Felt very bouncy and much improved by the time Hugh came round at 10.30. Worked and fiddled at sketches and then, at 6.00 Robin Hardy came round to go through the script of *Bachelors Anonymous*, the idea being to see if there was any chance of working out a rough and ready schedule. How many days shooting in France, how many in studio, how many on location, that kind of thing. Pleasant enough time chatting it through until 9.00. Then I bunged myself over to 2 Brydges Place for a dinner with Ian Brown,* Alfredo† and

---

* Ian Brown, film producer friend.
† Alfredo Fernandino, Peruvian founder of the club situated in the almost unbelievably narrow passageway next to the Coliseum Theatre in

Cosmo Fry. Turned out that on Booker night Roddy
Doyle and party had come over after the award to continue their celebrations. Then who turned up but
Salman Rushdie? *On his own.* Highly risky you'd've
thought.*

Pleasant dinner, followed by two rounds of Perudo.
Then, bother it, it was 2.00 suddenly. And I have to be up
at the crack tomorrow to take a train to Bath. Poo.

Saturday, 30 October 1993

Struggled out of bed at 7.30 after three hours sleep, into
a car driven by some maniac who wanted to tell me about
his idea for a novel, 'I asked if I could be given this job
specially . . .' I dare say I'll hear from him again some
time.

Was being towed around by a girl called Alex Lankester,
who seemed very sweet; the usual pretty leggy thing that
they employ for these gigs. That sounds very sexist but it
can't be a coincidence, surely? We arrived in Bristol and
were met by a charming Reed Publishers rep called
Andrew Whitaker. Snatched a cup of coffee in the Bristol
Waterstone's and went out to meet the queue. A lot of
signing, but very friendly. The manager said it was a record

London's St Martin's Lane. From a powerful Peruvian family, he intro-
duced Perudo to Britain and marketed it with his friend Cosmo Fry.
Cosmo Fry, elegant playboy, distant cousin, chocolate heir.
*The fatwa still very much in place then.

attendance, most books sold in such a session ever.* Gratifying. Then we went off to another Waterstone's in Bristol where I was interviewed by a TV crew and signed some stock.

Then we drove off to Bath where the queue was *astronomical*, really wore my hand out. Two very strange psycho-fans turned up. Trembling, barely able to speak, one of them said 'oh my God, I'm coming, I'm *coming*.' Whoops. Finally got through it all, biffed off to W. H. Smith's to sign some stock and then back to London.

Arrived at 7.00 in time to snadge over to 2 Brydges Place again for Kim's birthday party. Highly agreeable. Chatted to Shawn Slovo† a lot and to Jo Laurie and Kim and lots of other poppets. Greg was on excellent form and Hugh left at one point to pick up his nephew Hugh Lassen from the airport and bring him back on his motorbike. Rather snazzy for a 17 year old, I should imagine, being whisked through town on the pillion of a Triumph by your famous uncle. Left at 1.00-ish and tumbled tired but stupid, into bed.

---

*I think I'm right in saying that the student Derren Brown was in this queue and that I encouraged him to work hard at practising his magic. Oh dear. Condescending or what?

†The screenwriter daughter of Joe Slovo, a leading anti-apartheid voice. As a Communist Jew, Joe Slovo was one of the Afrikaner right wing's most hated figures. He became a minister under Mandela and died in 1995.

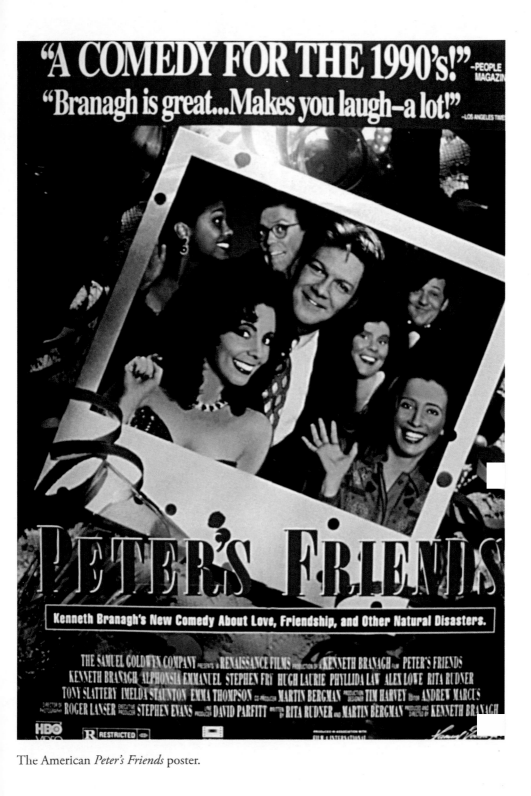

The American *Peter's Friends* poster.

Peter's Friends publicity shot. From left: Emma, self, Hugh, Rita, Alphonsia – it's clear I'm thinking about the *Time Out* critic.

Full cast of *Peter's Friends*, 1992. From left: Rita Rudner, Ken Branagh, Alex Lowe, Emma Thompson, self, Alphonsia Emmanuel, Imelda Staunton, Tony Slattery, Hugh, Phyllida Law.

Publicity still for *Hysteria*, 1992. I have no words.

Self.

Labour Party fundraising gala. Next to Dickie Attenborough and Melvyn Bragg.

Sir Paul Fox, the
Prince of Wales,
self, Alyce Faye
Cleese: premiere
of *The Man
Without a Face*.

With Alyce
Faye Cleese at
*The Man Without
a Face* premiere.

Publicity for Comic Relief, April 1991 – m'colleague, Hugh Laurie and Emma Freud, self, Jennifer Saunders, Tony Slattery.

Note where I'm playing from.
Total duffer. Inverness, 1994.

Jo and my third nephew,
the most excellent George.

Carla Powell checking to see if my beard is real. It is.

I can't quite explain why I'm sitting like that: I'm going to say in order to keep the jacket smooth . . .

Sunday, 31 October 1993

It was all going to fizzle out into a placido domingo* ...
got up very late, shopped a little, got the papers and the
New Avenger's tapes and snuggled in for the day.

Then Kim rang to remind me that I had left a bag
behind at Brydges Place. He and Al would pop round
some time to deliver it to me. Fair enough. Then of
course, it gets later and later in the afternoon, so Kim
and Al suggest we meet at Joe Allen's for the handing
over of the bag.

No sooner sat down at Joe's than the waiter brings me
an enormous Armagnac, courtesy of a rather cute young
boy sitting elsewhere. Kim and Al very amused. We chat,
we chew the fat, we nibble dinner and time passes. The
little chap comes over to our table. About eighteen I suppose and very sweet.

'I'm sorry to be gauche,' he says ... pronouncing it
'gorsh' rather divinely. We've all done that with words
we've only seen written down: mīsl'd and ímpious for
example instead of misléd and impīous. He hands me a
note and trots out. The note gives his name; he admires
my writings and stance on the age of consent and gives a
telephone number. Do call. Oh my.

Alastair drove me home and I invited them in for a
drink. Alastair didn't want to but Kim did so we cheerfully

* Spanish for a quiet Sunday, but you knew that.

bade him farewell and stayed up for hours and hours. We can talk forever, which is so happy-making.

And so the month ends.

Monday, 1 November 1993

Up in time for a Voice Over. Sanatogen Multivitamins 'Do you feel all right?' Good bloody question. Struggled back in time for work with Hugh only to discover that the *Spectator* needed my copy for the diary today. Had completely forgotten the whole damned thing. Agreed months ago during a *Spectator* lunch that I would do the Diary column for a couple of weeks. Therefore spent most of the day writing that instead of a sketch. I'm a bad bunny. Got it done anyway. Think it's OK.

Dreadful news broke about River Phoenix dying. Mortifying. So adored him. I remember changing a line in *Peter's Friends* to make a mention of him. When Emma's character in the movie tries to seduce me I tell her that I'm sort of bisexual but that I don't do anything with anyone at the moment, but if I did, she would be 'right there at the top of my wish-list along with Michelle Pfeiffer and River Phoenix'. Always got a huge laugh. Such a sweet boy. Looks as if his death might be drug-related, which is bizarre because I always thought he was a terribly straight sort of chap, all environmental concern and poppety prudishness. Oh cripes. I remember choosing him as a pin-up for the *Oldie*. 'Yum yum' I had written

... And there on the wall is a photograph of him, just above the desk where Hugh works when we're sketch writing. I'm looking at him now, so earnestly beautiful. *Running on Empty* my favourite film of his. I love all Sidney Lumet's work and he brought out the absolute best in the Phoenix who will never rise from the ashes. Oh dear, I'm actually a bit damp eyed. Bit like when Bobby Moore died earlier this year.

In the evening hastened to the Garrick for a dinner given by Lord Alexander, the chairman of the Nat West Bank. This had been arranged courtesy of Charles Powell. Arrived in good time to be greeted by Lord A, Bob as he is known to his chums. Thoroughly charming fellow: his wife Marie I had sat next to at Charles and Carla's wedding, or rather the wedding of their son Hugh. She's a lawyer with a lovely soft Irish voice and nice soft views to go with them. Then Dennis Thatcher turned up and a strange woman called Bishoff, very nice, but oddly shy or neurotic or something.

Dennis, I have to confess I took to enormously. Right wing, natch, but very wonderful. Much better read than I had ever imagined. Loves history, knows a great deal about it too and was, I think, pleased to talk to someone of my age who wasn't pig ignorant. Went so far as to describe me as a 'brilliant conversationalist'. Lumme.

Home reasonably early. Few lines, bed.

Tuesday, 2 November 1993

Up early and round to the Lauries'. We are to drive off and inspect the kitchen of my house in Norfolk. Jo has been superintendent in charge of a massive rebuilding project, of a kind that would make a Pharaoh think twice.

Hugh accompanies and we drive through a grey day to West Bilney. Amazing job has been done so far, I just didn't recognize anything. The carpentry, the roof lowering, the floor. Incredible. Simply incredible.

Spent a few hours there chatting to Brendan the builder. The architect Nigel Harding hasn't made provision for facilities for rubbish. Stupid little details, but fantastically important. I compile what I'm told is a 'snagging list'. Cannot believe Jo L's skill, commitment and kindness in giving me all this time and talent. Wound our way back, via A.J.'s family restaurant and an enormous burger.

Back at the flat waited for Sam Mendes to come round and talk about the Elton John musical. He likes the script but wouldn't want to work on anything unless it was much more interesting and dangerous and sharp. Quite right and makes me feel a prune for being involved in the thing as it stands. He'll talk to John Reid. If I had a couple of months to make it far more original then he would have loved to have done it. The swine is absolutely right. Not a swine of course. Thoroughly good man. Still only 28 and one of our best directors. Handsome too and brilliant at cricket. Tchah! Some people.

Went with him to the Groucho and we bumped into Griff there. Griff and I proposed and seconded him for the Grouch and we wandered in for sustenance. Old Jim Moir was there (aka Vic Reeves) and he joined us for merriment. Bought a couple of grams from Jethro and wandered home in rather a wired condition to watch *Stalag Luft* as it aired. Then bedness and blankness.

Wednesday, 3 November 1993

Hugh called in early this morning to report sick: or rather Jo did on his behalf. Flu, sinus, that kind of nonsense. This has left me with the day to myself. A chance to 'clear my desk' of plenty of correspondence and other dribble. A sketch didn't come though, so I biked off a mock sketch to Hugh detailing how difficult it is to write a sketch.

A car came at sevenish to take me to Alyce Faye Cleese's. We're off together to The Canteen, the Marco Pierre White restaurant, as guests of Michael and Shakira Caine. Arrive in time for a glass of wine with A F. Cleese himself is 'tired' as always and not up for fun and larks . . . hence my role as walker to A F.

We arrive at Chelsea Harbour and I watch glued at the bar as Norwich keep Bayern M. to a 1-1 draw and go through 3-2 on aggregate. Yippee. Michael and Shakira join us . . . Michael grew up in North Runcton, near King's Lynn so he harbours a secret love of Norwich City. Then David and Carina Frost turn up and we watch until the match is over. David was a fine footballer as a youth and trialled for Norwich, so he supports them too. Good dinner. I sat between Carina and Shakira. The latter is absolutely delightful, and almost impossibly beautiful. Carina is just as delightful in a quite splendidly batty way. Terribly enthusiastic about all her friends. Get quietly sozzled. Just one line in the bog, otherwise full behaviour. Tomasz Starzewski* was at another table and full of beans. Told him to be sure and turn up to the Perudo evening. Home at one-ish and straight to bed.

Thursday, 4 November 1993

Up fit and ready for the day thanks to the previous night's moderation. Jo phoned in to say that Hugh would be staying in bed most of the morning and joining me for an afternoon's Alliance and Leicester VO.

So I had to face Chris and Jeff from the Labour Party on my own. H. and I have agreed to do a Party Political broadcast for Walworth Road.† Jeff Stark is the director. We're doing it because it's actually rather a fun script. Jeff wants us to play all the parts in it, but I think it's best if we don't. For a start it'll be less work on the day and there is also the extra element of comedy to be considered that some good and unexpected luvvies will be able to add.

---

* Polish-born but British couturier, whose frocks were much favoured by Princess Diana.
† Where the headquarters of the Labour Party were then situated.

Brimped off for the VO. Hugh looking a bit pale and yucky, a bit drawn and wobbly. All went okay and I returned to the flat to climb into my best bib and tucker. Zimmed round to Emma's house. I am her date for the preview of *Remains of the Day* which also opens the London Film Festival. Em being made up by some private m/u artist, so I drink and chat to her. She then climbs into the most *stunning* top I've ever seen. Its quality is somewhat shat on by the news that it is Armani and costs £6,000. Not even a dress, for the lord's sake. Em hasn't *bought* it, you understand, they've *lent* it to her. This is what happens when you win an Oscar. Into the limo and ho for the Odeon Leicester Square. Huge crowds as always, somewhat amused to see me instead of Ken dismounting. Em, like Princess Di, leaps for the crash barriers and chats to the waiting throng. I stand on one leg looking like an arse until she joins me. Bit of posing for the paps, and then inside. Em has to wait downstairs because she'll be appearing on stage for the opening speeches and so on. I go up and find myself next to Jenny Hopkins, wife of Tony (also starring in the movie) and Greta Scacchi. Film highly enjoyable, perhaps a leeetle too long, but some stunning performances from Em and Tony. Then we trot off to the Café Royal for the party. Manage to get a line in the loo before joining the table where Kim and Shawn Slovo are already there. Slovo *hated* it, natch and Kim was less than thrilled I think. Hugh Grant and his ravishing lady are present. I quiz him on *Four Weddings and a Funeral* which he has just made. He loathed doing it, thinks he's crap in it and wanted to punch Mike Newell most of the time. Bet he's brilliant though. Also asked him about the rumour that Madonna wanted to shag him. Turns out it's true. James Fox also present: what an absolute *sweetie*. Adorable chap. Very good in the film too, in that wonderful mournful weak way he has.

Sir Dickie (Lord Dickie, I beg his pardon) came up and took both my arms and gazed lovingly into my eyes in that way he has and told me I must see *Shadowlands* . . . usual suspects also present included Kenith Trodd,* Ben Kingsley and assorted baggages. Walked home pissed but reasonably cheerful round about the two o'clock mark.

Friday, 5 November 1993

Voice Over at 10.00 for Biactol, followed by writing with Hugh all day until biffing off to the Garrick for a drink with Robin Bailey.† He had rung me up with some story about a taxi driver whose first wife had been a waitress at the Chelsea Arts Club: a painting of her hung in the bar. Would I as a member take Robin to see if it was there? I said yes, let's dine there. He suggested meet-

---

* BBC producer (yes he does spell his forename like that) best known for his collaborations with Dennis Potter and Simon Gray.
† The actor who played Uncle Mort in *I Didn't Know You Cared*, way back before you were born. Also the narrator in *Tales from the Long Room*. We had both been in the happy West End flop *Look, Look!* the year before.

ing first at the Garrick for a snort.* He turned up over an hour late. I think he's gone a bit potty. Incapable of anything other than weird conversation, acting out pretend bitterness at his career. Bit sad. We dribbled off to the Chelsea Arts and awaited Johnny Sessions who was to join us. He arrived, thank God and injected some sanity and wit into the proceedings. Drunken dinner which I hated: had forgotten what a ridiculous place the C.A.C. is. Good initials. Home late.

Saturday, 6 November 1993

Robin Hardy came round at 10.30 and we worked for hours on the script of *Bachelors Anonymous*. Ended up feeling more cheerful about it than I had for weeks. Managed to persuade him to cut a number of dodgy scenes and take a more serious view of the love story. Then shopped a bit at Fortnum's and spent the evening in front of the telly. Mm. Sober and sweet at bed-time.

Sunday, 7 November 1993

Up at 11.15 just in time to climb into a suit for Sir Charles and Lady Powell to pop round and pick me up. We were all going to a lunch at Josephine (*née* Hart)† and Maurice

---

*In its old-fashioned sense of 'gargle' or 'snifter'. A drink in other words.
†Novelist wife of Maurice Saatchi, now sadly deceased. Known for powerful, rather shocking short novels with one word titles: *Damage, Sin, Oblivion* . . .

Saatchi's house in Sussex. *Very* grand. The world and his wife were there. Nicholas Soames, bless him, and his intended, Serena, Melvyn Bragg, Simon Callow and his friend Christopher,* Sir Norman Fowler, Michael Howard the Home Sec., John and Jane Birt, Alan Yentob, Christopher Bland,† Paul Johnson, Simon Jenkins, Gayle Hunnicutt, Alastair Goodlad, Grey Gowrie, Pamela Harlech and others too splendid to mention. Wine and chat flowed, all rather good fun. Signed a copy of *Paperweight* for the Saatchi child, Edmund, who is eight and very bright clearly. Josephine told me she had gone into his room last night and found him reading *P'weight*. He asked 'Mummy, what does "biopsy" mean?' Sweet.

Rode back with the Powells again and home in time for telly and bed. Without coke again. That's two nights in a row. It's becoming a habit.

Monday, 8 November 1993

Hugh couldn't come round today: meetings for his advert next week. I messed around doing correspondence and sorting things out generally. Voice Over in the morning, followed by a researcher popping round for the Clive Anderson I'm doing on Thursday. While chatting to her Alyce Faye

---

* Christopher Wood, designer. Now attached to Johnnie Shand Kydd, the photographer.
† BT chief, chairman of endless boards – BBC Governors, Royal Shakespeare Company, etc. Good egg.

rang up and asked me whether I would like her tickets for *The Meistersingers* currently wowing them at the ROH. I squeaked *Yes!* with great excitement, said to be a great production. Immediately rang up Johnny Sessions to see if he could come. Starts at 5.00 of course. He replied with equal alacrity and I spent the rest of the day in a fever waiting for the tickets to be biked round. Bathed and climbed into a suit and Johnny appeared at 4.00. We cabbed in to the Garden and ordered our first interval drinks. Sir Kenneth Bloomfield (Bromfield?) was there: a governor of the BBC, Ulster Civil Servant. I'd met him at Birt evenings, proms that kind of thing. Simon Hornby* also present.

Then the music drama itself. An absolutely knock-out production by Graham Vick, with Bernard Haitink on unbelievable form in the pit. Just sensational. Thomas Allen a fabulous Beckmesser, possibly the best acting performance in London at the moment, never mind the singing. And John Tomlinson a sensationally dignified and wonderfully voiced Sachs. Oh, I can't tell you Daisy dear, the best evening I've had in years and years. One forgets just what a great man Wagner was. This was Art, this was total magical real uncompromising Art. Genius is, I'm afraid, the only word. Unparalleled genius.

We stumbled out into the light and headed for Orso for our dinner. Ned Sherrin was there, natch, chatted to him awhile and chewed the fat. I tried to explain to Hegel

---

* Head honcho at W. H. Smith as mentioned earlier: the last family member to lead the company.

to Johnny: he said it was fascinating but that he knew he would forget every detail of it the moment I had stopped speaking. I know what he means. That's why I love talking and teaching: the act of reproducing ideas out loud reinforces them in the head. If, every time you read a complex book or idea, you had to explain it to someone else, you'd never forget it.

We shogged back to my place a little drunk and stayed up for hours. Johnny stayed in the spare room and I fell into bed, unable to sleep till way past four.

Tuesday, 9 November 1993

Woke Johnny at 8.15 and fell back to slumber. Dimly remember J. bidding me farewell. Jo forwarded me a letter to tell me that a set had become available in Albany. Then other Jo, Jo Laurie, rang to say that I had to go round a bed shop in Chelsea with her to choose 5 new beds for West Bilney. She turned up in a cab with Hugh. Hugh went in to work and I zipped off with Jo.

In an hour I spent £11,750 odd quid on some beautiful beds and six hundred quid on material to upholster one of them. Stunning stuff though.

Then back, through terrible traffic (State visit of TM the King and Queen of Malaysia or somesuch) to the flat. Hugh stayed for a while and then went off to interview a headmaster for the boys' prep school. I rang the secretary of the Albany trustees and arranged to see it this afternoon. Set up a meeting too with Jethro at the Grouch at 5.00.

Messed about, then the copy-edited proofs of *The Hippo* arrived and I went through them. Off to the Albany next. I think the set has great potential. I'd need to redecorate quite substantially. Definitely an exciting prospect. No children, no dogs, no noise, no publicity are their rules.

Then to the Groucho for an hour or so: scored a couple of grams off Jethro and popped upstairs for a wine-tasting, which was charming. Back home to meet one Sir Peter Ratcliffe, who is in charge of the charity for which I'm speaking at the premiere of *The Man Without a Face* next week. He told me all the stuff about the evening and when I was to make my address. 'The Prince of Wales is *delighted* that you are speaking . . .' all that sort of thing. I'm going to have to be rather good I fear.

Then to the Groucho again, bit more wine-tasting and down Old Compton Street to the Ivy, where I was due to have dinner with Tomasz Starzewski. There was a sign on his doorbell which said '9.10 Stephen . . . gone to the Ivy.' This rather confused me as my watch assured me that it was only 8.30.

Toddled to the Ivy, no sign of the man. Then he turned up. The sign was left over from yesterday . . . doh! He thought he had arranged to see me on Monday . . . in fact it was definitely Tuesday. Anyway, no harm done. Charming evening, all well. He lent me *The Witkiewicz Reader*. Back home by one ish. Read in bed.

Wednesday, 10 November 1993

Somehow an incredibly busy day on the phone. Sorting out the Perudo evening on the 17th, who's to be on my table, that kind of thing. Also, I have taken the more or less momentous decision to go for the Albany set that I saw yesterday. A lot of work needed: forward Jo Laurie and her team, but it could be something, I think.

Rang around the place trying to get references for the Albany Trustees. Banker plus two personal. Tried to get hold of Charles Powell, but he's all over the place, obviously. Managed to get John Birt's secretary: she said he'd ring back . . . which he did pretty quickly. Frankly, whatever else they say about him, he's always been an absolute poppy to me. Spoke to Carla and she invited me to a black tie dinner she's holding in honour of Colin Powell, the US Chief of Staff during the Gulf War. She's a firm friend and is inviting just about everyone in the world, so I'm *rather* honoured. What a couple.

She told me an *extraordinary* thing. Paul Johnson, whom I've only met twice (and on both occasions he has been rather scowly), and Carla were in their Catholic church this morning, Carla to pray for Nicky her son, who's having a brain scan ('too much bonking, darling. I know it. He's my beautiful son, but he does bonk too many girls.') and Paul because he's *always* in there apparently. Paul said that his wife Marigold, who was with him at the Saatchi's lunch on Sunday, is a great fan of mine and would love to get to know me better. Paul, on the other hand, when Carla told *him* that she liked me too, growled 'But he's a socialist, isn't he?' To which Carla promptly replied, 'but so were you darling, when you were his age!' Paul then agreed and said that they should pray for my deliverance from socialism. So. Carla and Paul Johnson get down in a Catholic church in London and pray for me to be converted to Conservatism. Most peculiar.

Carla was howling with laughter as she told me: well, she's Italian and has a splendid attitude to everything. Dear me, however.

Anyway, she thought Charles would be delighted to write a reference for me. He's a busy man however, so I might get a back up reference from Max Hastings.

Managed to write a small sketch: Hugh was away all day on a recce for his commercial. Then I turned to the copy-edited version of *The Hippo*. This has to be in today in order to get the thing fully done in time for proof copies to be out in December. The copy editor (Hugo de Klee . . . splendid name) has done an excellent job I think. Somewhat pernickity about the shooting scene, but very attentive. So I spent three or four hours going through that and reminding myself of it.

Six o'clock and off to the Savoy to meet Kim before the first night of *Eurovision*.* We sat and supped Old Fashioneds, said 'hi' to Neil Tennant and Julian Lloyd-

---

* A stage musical, not the peculiar television event.

Webber and others who were there then toddled to the theatre. Jo in attendance, waiting for Hugh, whom she hadn't seen all day. He fetched up at last, having forgotten all about it and only realized when he had got home and found Melissa their nanny baby-sitting.

The show was about the campest thing you could ever imagine. In fact, not very good. Made tolerable only by one astonishing performance from an actor called Julian Dreyfus.* One to watch without question. The whole 'drama' was incredibly amateurish and lumpen in structure. Some excellent farce scenes involving, of all things, the ghosts of Hadrian and Antinoüs, but somehow it was all a bit stupid. It won't appeal that much to gay audiences because they will have seen it all before at Madame Jo Jo's and a million nightclubs and gay theatre happenings up and down the country. The person in our party who enjoyed it most, as it happens, was Jo Laurie. She didn't like it when it started going on about love in the second act, however.

The Ivy afterwards for dinz. I coked up in the loo, which I have no doubt Hugh and Jo noticed. Oh dear I am an arse. I expect there'll be what I believe is called an 'intervention' soon. I keep picturing it. All my friends bearing down on me and me denying everything until my pockets are emptied. Oh the shame. Lots of wine and coffee and home by quarter to one. Then stupidly sat and gazed at the

---

*I meant James Dreyfus, unless he subsequently changed his name. Later to achieve fame in the immortal *Gimme Gimme Gimme*.

TV while doing the crossword and chopping more lines. Bed by half past two. Stupid. Stupid, stupid, stupid.

Thursday, 11 November 1993

Poppy day, seventy fifth anniversary thereof. A day for sitting at home and working. Bad news popped in. The legal secretary of TVS who own the lease on the set in Albany rang up to say that there was a first-comer who has now definitely expressed an interest and she feels duty bound to give him first crack of the whip. Poo. I've amassed a startling collection of references, however. One from Sir Charles Powell, one from John Birt and one from Max Hastings. All very splendid. Charles begins his with the typically, but lovably, pompous 'Gentlemen . . .' Heigh ho. Unless this chap pulls out at the last moment or can't get the right references, it looks as though I shall have to wait more.

Car came at sevenish to take me to the studios for a *Clive Anderson Talks Back*. Bamber Gascoigne was another guest, plus a chap who gives (and is a walking example of) body piercing. He had studs in his tongue, a massive spike through his septum, one through his lower lip, nipple rings, and, though this was never shown, a Prince Albert. Crumbs. I think I was alright. A very startling reception from the audience, who appeared to be delighted to see me. Much whooping and cheering. Very gratifying, but I should imagine intensely irritating to the TV audience.

Spoke a bit about the horse scene in *The Hippo* and about politics. Did my 'family values' stuff, rather hard-hitting but well received from the audience.

Shifted it from the London Studios to the Groucho for a poker game. Griff and Bob (Ringo) and an actress called Caroline. She was very sweet but introduced a game called Anaconda which all but wiped me out. First time I've lost that heavily for years. That'll teach me. Much of cocaine. Bed at Two.

Friday, 12 November 1993

Up very early for a voice over. It was in Oxford Street so I shopped at M&S afterwards. Back for Hugh, some sketch writing and normal business and then I popped at seven round to Quaglino's for dinner with Alfredo and Patrick Kinmonth an old school chum whom I've only seen twice in the last twenty years. He's a splendour, however. Painter and now theatre designer. Very talented, very sweet. Had a good dinner, courtesy of Patrick who has Quag's luncheon vouchers, part payment for decorating one of the pillars in the main dining area.

Back to my place for chat. I disappeared into the loo every ten minutes but they didn't seem to notice and popped off at 3.00; I knew it was okay because for the first time in ages I could sleep in on Saturday as much as I liked.

Saturday, 13 November 1993

Awoke at 12.20 feeling much refreshed. Went out and bought some videos at Tower Records, shopped a little at Fortnum's and then came back to eat and watch telly. Bliss. First time in ages. At six thirty off to the Lauries' for dinz. Kim and Al and Nick and Sarah. Good fun. I eschewed coking up in their loo, I know they know and I know it upsets them. Home at half past one.

Sunday, 14 November 1993

A very busy day spent completing the *Spectator* diary for next week and writing the speech for the film premiere on Tuesday. Eventually got it all done and then watched a bit of telly before packing and cabbing it to Euston station for the sleeper to Dundee.* Drank a bit of Scotch and ate a couple of sandwiches. *Huge* mistake. For some reason it gave me the horriblesty pangs of indigestion you can imagine. Bloody nuisance, acid gnawing inside me and the train hammering through the night. Very little sleep.

Monday, 15 November 1993

Next stop Dundee station at five minutes to six. Abso-

*I was Rector of Dundee University: by this time I think I was partway through my second three-year tenure. The honorary post, unique to the ancient Scottish universities, involves looking after the interests of the students, who vote for their rector. I would come up by train to attend meetings of the University Court and hold 'surgeries'.

lutely bloody freezing on the platform and the train was ten minutes early, so I had to hang around until my welcoming party arrived to take me off to breakfast. The w.p. consisted of Jim Duncan (the Rector's Assessor), Ayesha the President of the Student's Association (DUSA) and Dougie the Senior Vice President. Amiable people. Ayesha is actually rather stylish and splendid, the best of the three I've known so far. I'm sure she could *walk* into any job as a researcher for Clive Anderson/J. Ross that kind of thing. Sweet and bubbly. Not a fool either.

Back to Jim's house, as is traditional, to consume a large breakfast cooked by his dear wife Hilda. Lots of orange juice, black pudding, bacon and so forth. Then there was the usual hour or so of sitting and chatting, catching up with whatever issues are prevalent in the University (none really at the moment, thank God) before our first 'visit'. I've instituted this custom whereby I'm shown round a couple of different departments of the university every Court day. Bit Prince of Walesey, but they all seem to like it, and I find it 'absolutely *fascinating*'.

Actually we stopped off at Ayesha's digs on the way because she had promised her flatmates that I would pop round. They were still in bed as it happened: a couple, blond and gorgeous and tousled and studenty. So sweet. Had a coffee while they degrogged. First port of call was the Accountancy and Business School. Not very exciting you might think, but Bob Lyon the dep. head was amiable and so were all the staff. Met a gang of absurdly UN international graduates: from Sri Lanka, Saudi, Bangladesh, that sort of thing. The computer whizz, a splendid hairy faced wonderment called Roz showed me the computers and we did some internetting, trying to chase a Douglas Adams thread. Coffee in the staff room and more chatting before we slid over to the school of Politics and Social Policy. Very amiable bunch of people. Nothing actually to *see* there, unlike visits on previous occasions to other departments where one can goggle at medical equipment, labs and so forth, but nonetheless a charming group of people. Rather left-leaning which is rare for Dundee. Charles Kennedy and George Roberston both products of that school, I believe. They weighed me down with books and pamphlets.

Midday now and time to visit the Principal, Michael Hamlin. Not looking too good: bit of fluid retention under the chin and puffiness about the eyes. Not a well man, I fancy. He's retiring at the end of the year. We chatted for three quarters of an hour, he calling me 'Simon' as usual.

Time for the pre-court lunch. Sat next to a bit of an ass, can't remember his name, usual rubber chicken and split mayonnaise. Bless them. Then, at 2.00, it couldn't be put off any longer, time for Court. I dropped off three times: the first time Jim Duncan, by my side woke me up; the next two times I was awoken by a change of voice or something else. There really is nothing on earth so arse-paralysingly drear as a committee of academics discussing university business. The only time I really perked up was to repudiate a letter written by an oncologist asking how the University could morally justify the setting aside of smoking rooms to 'feed student addictions'. Per-lease.

The court wound up in record time after two hours, and I had an hour to kill before my appointment at 5.00 to address the freshers. We went to 'Pete's Bar' upstairs in the association building and drank some scotch. Lots of studes clustering round: all very charming. Then at 5.00 in I went to the 'Dead Club' where hundreds of little freshers had assembled to hear their rector speak. I had only been told this was to happen this morning, so no chance to prepare: all busk therefore. I told them that there was nothing on earth less appealing than a young person putting on a hard cynical face and trying to look as if they saw through everything and knew the world for what it was. I told them it was their duty every morning to check their faces in the mirror and to make sure that they looked lovely and open and kind and smiley.

A full hour of talking: think it went all right. Then another hour in the bar before the dinner that had sweetly been laid on in my honour by the students themselves. They had drawn lots to see who could attend, because they wanted to keep the numbers manageable. As always there seemed to be some deep desire amongst the *corpus studenti* to get me completely hammered. It was my job to circulate around the table so that I sat with every group for a fair length of time. They were all very sweet actually and welcoming. At last, tottering and with the help of a couple of lines in the bog, I was escorted by Jim and Dougie (Ayesha being off her face by this time) to the station. Another huge whisky and then the train pulled in. We're talking 10.55 pm by this time. Managed to sleep straight away, which despite the lines (both railway and stimulant) is something of a miracle.

Tuesday, 16 November 1993

Woke up in Euston at 7.00. Cab to St James's and bed for two hours before struggling up again for a Voice Over. What a business. Got back at eleven, time for opening post and a cup of coffee before a cab to Whitfield Street for a four hour photography session for *The Hippo* cover and publicity materials.

Not too bad: charming snapper called Colin Thomas and Mark McCullum and Sue F.* were present, all old chums. Tried various poses, emerging from a bath with suds, that kind of thing. Hope it isn't all too vulgar. The book is not entirely of that nature, after all. At least *I* don't think it is . . .

Left at half-three-ish, me desperate to get back to the flat and prepare my speech. In the cab back to St James's I realize I've left my coat at the studio: it contains my keys. *Arse.*

I borrow the wonderful local barber's phone and we ask Colin T. to shove it all in a cab instanter. Sue and

*PR and editor respectively at Heinemann, publishers of *The Hippo*.

Mark and self then repair to the Red Lion pub for a half of Guinness and so forth. Cab turns up, I'm back in business.

The speech is all right I think. I don't have time to learn it, however, so I'll read. Not ideal, but suck it. At six forty-five-ish Alyce Faye turns up looking absolutely *stunning* in a Starzewski frock of limitless elegance and beauty. We have a gin and tonic and then pop in the car for the Odeon Leicester Square. Big crowds, natch. We are welcomed by a very charming old biddy called Shirley who takes me and Alyce F. round backstage. A lot of pacing about behind the screen from me as the trumpeter heralds warm up their instruments and the screen in front of us shows the celebs and eventually, the royal party arriving.

After the fanfare and national anthem I go out on stage and make my speech of welcome. Talk about the Cinema and Television Benevolent fund and their 'work'. Seems to go well. Then escorted round to my seat in the royal box for the film itself, which I have to say I liked a great deal. Very *written*, but none the poorer for that. Intelligent and humane for the most part and containing quite simply the best child performance I have ever seen. Really a brilliant boy called Nick Stahl: quite remarkable, as good as Jodie F. in *Taxi D*. Mel Gibson too, a fine performance and well directed. Not a big film, or a possible cult film, but a *good* film: to be proud of.

As soon as it was over I was whisked downstairs to

meet the P.o.W. He was very matey and said to me 'You *did* write that speech didn't you?' I said, 'indeed I did, sir.' He said, 'Mel Gibson asked me if you had written it yourself, and I said indignantly, "of *course* he did!"' Introduced him to Alyce Faye and they chatted a bit about Cleese and *Frankenstein*.

We got in the car after HRH had gone and went all the way to Planet Hollywood where the party was. Stayed for a voddie and then to the Ivy for dinz. Parties are so ghastly at Planet H. really. Nice dinner in fact. Chatted for a while. Alyce Faye said that she (and John) thought my short writings were better than my novels. I was very stung by this. I sensed that *The Liar* was just the sort of thing that Cleese would not like, because, despite, or perhaps because of, his comic genius he does not seem to understand the profound truth that comic things are more serious than serious things. More serious and truer. It's part of his guilt at being a comedian, and reflected in his absurdly high doctrine of abstract spiritualist writing like the *Tibetan Book of the Dead*, Gurdjieff, Coelho and that kind of bogus baloney. If he had ever read a true mystic like the Author of *The Cloud* or Mother Julian he would know that abstraction and unearthed thinking are foreign to true spirituality. I tried to get some of this across. I don't know if she understood. Annoyed with myself for being so stung, however. Bed lateish.

Wednesday, 17 November 1993

What a strange day. It began early. Horribly early. It began with *The Big Breakfast* for Channel 4. I had agreed that I would go on to help plug Perudo. Cosmo Fry had asked and I, softy that I am, had consented. Felt a bit grumpy on the way to . . . god rot it . . . *Bow*. I knew that when it was over I would have to charge off in another car to go all the way over to Wandsworth for another sitting with Maggi.

Once we arrived though, the frantic and friendly spirit of the programme cast all gloom away. You'd have to be very churlish not to be engaged and charmed by the silliness of the show's spirit. I played a little Perudo with Chris Evans the presenter and did some links. I gave a 'Showbiz Tip' about how to speak in cold weather without steam or vapour coming from your mouth. The technique is to suck an ice cube. They liked this very much and for the next link I was shown sucking some ice. I took it out of my mouth and – you'd better believe it – lots of vapour streamed out. Very stupid I felt.

Car took only fifty minutes to get to Maggi's in the end. Pretty good session in fact, probably the last this year. Maggi told me an amusing story about Margi Kinmonth, cousin of old schoolfriend Patrick Kinmonth. (This is going to be confusing: a Margi and a Maggi . . .) I'd met Margi at Ferdy Fairfax's* lunch not so long ago,

---

* Director of series 3 and 4 of *Jeeves and Wooster*, sadly snatched from the world way before his time.

anyway it turns out she's doing some kind of documentary with Dawn French. The purpose of this doc. is to show how wonderful it is to be fat. This will help Dawn sell her collection of clothes for the larger woman, as well as pushing this idea that being overweight should not be seen to be a stigma. Patrick had had a bit of a tiff with Margi about this previously: he had ventured the opinion that fatness is not wholly desirable and that there are sound reasons why we usually find it unpleasant to behold in both others and ourselves. Margi wouldn't hear this and trotted out all the usual 'Fat Is A Feminist Issue' arguments. Anyway, that's by the by. Margi yesterday approached Maggi Hambling and asked if Maggi H. would allow herself to be filmed while painting Dawn as part of this fatumentary.

Maggi, who is an artist and not like others, replied that a) she never allowed cameras to shoot over her shoulder while she worked and b) she usually paints women nude, but that presumably that would be what Dawn wanted? Well, slight ums and ahs from Margi K. at this. Nude? Um, as in *naked*? Well, says, Maggi, not deliberately trying to rootle out hypocrisy, surely the whole idea of this is that it's a celebration of *flesh* and plenty of it? Great gulps of embarrassment from Margi K. Poor old Dawn: if she refuses to be painted nude with her tummy spread out like a pool of lava she will look as if she doesn't really mean what she is saying. On the other hand, one can't really blame her for preferring to keep her clothes on, can one?

I, being far less beautiful than Dawn, kept my clothes very firmly on and we spent a merry four hours together.

At one o'clock a car came containing Rebecca Salt to take me off on a signing tour around town. What a week.

First port of c. was Waterstone's in the Charing X Rd. Good queue, not too many mad people, fairly amiable. Then across the road to Books Etc. for an informal stock signing. Round to Hatchard's in Piccadilly for more stock signing. *P'weight* is actually number one of all sellers in Hatchard's at the moment, which is rather pleasing. Afterwards we went off to the Strand: there was a shop there to sign at round about the 5.00 o'clock mark. It being 4.00 Rebecca (and Lynne Drew from Mandarin who had joined us) suggested we pop into the Waldorf for tea. They'd booked a table, knowing there would be this hour gap. I was secretly a bit miffed that they hadn't got the timing better and indeed the locations. Why not Hatchard's last so that I could just walk to the flat? Heigh ho.

Curiously the table we were shown to was for six. 'Ha ha,' I thinks, 'plots'. 'Is this the right table?' I wondered. 'Well, you never know who might turn up when you have tea at the Waldorf,' Rebecca said. Something definitely *up* I reasoned. Sure enough John Potter suddenly walks in, the *capo di tutti capi* at Reed Books. Followed by Helen Fraser, head of Heinemann, and Angela, managing editor. Well, well, well.

It was very sweet: they wanted to feast me for sales of *The Liar* passing the half million mark. I was very touched.

But then ... *then* ... Sister Jo walks in too! Quite wonderful and v. touching. They presented me with a leather bound, gold tooled, head and tail-banded, edition of *The Liar*. Very sweet: nearly cried. Gorged on tea and cakes and then Jo and I cabbed it to the flat. Just time to change and bath for the walk to Northumberland Street where the Perudo tournament was taking place. Hugh arrived at seven and off we trotted.

The Royal Commonwealth Hall or Institute or somesuch was the venue. It slowly filled up with all the usual suspects. Plenty of the cool and splendid crowd. Actually mostly sweet. It was in fact round about 8.30 before I could get to the microphone and address the company in the guise of The Gamesmaster. Fairly complicated tournament rules, but everyone playing with great spirit and dash and splendour. I was at a table with Peter Cook and Carla Powell and Alyce Faye and (hurrah!) Jethro, Spike and Jo and Hugh. H. was busy cutting his commercial in his head and went fairly soon. We played informally as we had a bye into the next round.

After nearly two and a half hours half the teams had lost and I was able to announce the pairings for the next round. But by this time it was half past eleven and frankly time to leave with Peter and Lin Cook and Alyce Faye and Tomasz and David Wilkinson and others for Peter's birthday party dinner, which was in Gran' Paradiso, Pimlico. Actually, a hell of a shame to have to leave: I would much rather have stayed. I scored a couple of grams from

Jethro and B. and would have happily remained. Not to be, however.

The Cook party was fine. Alyce Faye and I talked a bit about J. Cleese, a subject I can never tire of, him being such a comic hero and all. He had not come because he'd just completed a day's filming with Robert de Niro at Shepperton and felt he'd done badly.

'Ken was disappointed in me,' was his verdict. I tried to explain to A F that this was unlikely. Left at 1.15 and bed after the crossword.

Phew! It's been a strange old time. From the Big Breakfast to the Big Tea, to the Big Dinner. Non-stop since the sleeper to Dundee really.

Thursday, 18 November 1993

Not quite such a frantic day. Stayed in most of the morning: Hugh still editing his commercial. At 12.15 Mother popped round to take me out to Fortnum's for lunch. She is doing something in the House of Commons at 1.45. Something to do with Harriet Harman and a women's thing. Never quite got to the bottom of it. The state opening today, so traffic in London ghastly.

We had a very pleasant lunch and I put her in a cab at one thirty. Back to the flat: Hugh not able to come round because of editing and so forth. I rang Christie's because I had heard that a couple of Oscar Wilde letters were coming up for auction: put in a bid of five thousand for the first and fifteen for the second. Couldn't turn up for the sale itself. Stayed in till six and decided to pop round to the Groucho to see if there would be any poker. Keith Allen and Simon Bell were present so I sat and drank with them for a while, joined by Jim Moir (Vic Reeves) and a couple of others. At eight o'clock Keith, Liam, Simon and I went up to play. Keith's agent, known as T. kibbitzed happily. I won a fair bit, we all ingested a goodly quantity of white powder and I stayed sensible enough to bed myself at 1.00.

Friday, 19 November 1993

Car at 7.00 to take me to Shepperton. Hugh and I had agreed to film a Labour Party Political Broadcast. We play a couple of shady tax advisers, Weaver and Dodge who advise a procession of fat cats how to avoid tax. There was Roger Brierley (Glossop in the first two *Jeeves and Woosters*), Robin Bailey, Jeremy Child and Tim West. The idea was to demonstrate that Tory tax loopholes for the rich could save billions for the exchequer.

At lunchtime Robin Bailey, who hadn't shot yet, was in a foully cantankerous temper. A cuntankerous cuntmudgeon, in fact . . . ordering the producer's assistant and first AD around as if they were skivvies. Hugh took against this hugely and was (rightly) rather curt when Bailey tried to communicate with him. Bailey extremely sensitive to this and not pleased at all. He's barely sane at the moment and the whole thing was somewhat embarrassing. At last he went. By this time it was apparent that we would be shooting until late. Jo and Hugh had invited Greg, Kim and Alastair round for dinner and Hugh felt put upon, simply because he hadn't been warned that shooting would take so long. If the Labour Party is as inefficient as this when it comes to running the country, we're all for the basket as Georgette Heyer characters would say.

At three in the afternoon I learnt that my bid had been successful for the Oscar letters . . . asked to remain anonymous. Four thousand for the first, thirteen for the second. All told a total of £18,700 with commish. Gulp!

The filming dragged on and on. Jeremy Child a charming fellow, *seems* to be the absolute archetype of an Etonian baronet, which he is, but clearly – by volunteering for this gig – he does not vote along with most of his class. He told an amusing Jimbo Villiers* story. Jimbo had been talking about Simon Williams who had been having a ghastly time in a play and filming and visiting his mother (since died) in hospital. Driving about four hundred miles a day. 'I hope he isn't energizing himself with the ingestion

---

*The magnificent James Villiers (pronounced the smart way to rhyme with 'millers'). In the 1960s he was apparently twenty-somethingth in line of succession. John Osborne was said to have produced a typed list of the nineteen from the Queen downwards who came between Villiers and the throne. He had this list mimeographed and distributed to friends: 'If you meet anyone on it,' he ordered, 'kill them and before we know it Jimbo will be King and it will be Gin and Tonics for everyone for ever.'

of some kind of comical pastille,' Jimbo said. Splendid phrase. The time wore on and on: eventually we were released by 11.00. Hugh not best pleased, partly brought on by the knowledge that he had made himself look grouchy. 'Twenty people now hate me,' he said. Oh dear. Made me feel guilty for being by and large cheerful all day. Of course nobody hates Hugh. Can't be done.

Got to Tufnell Park, where Kim, Al and MU* were there and Jo. We stayed about an hour and then MU took us in his car back to my place where we stayed up drinking and coking till 5.15. Naughty.

Saturday, 20 November 1993

Up at 1.15, slightly hung over and feeling like a piece of shit. Just time to do one or two things before making it over to the Coliseum to join Kim and Al for the first night of *Lohengrin* by the ENO.†

They had borne up splendidly after the ravages of the night. The show itself was excellent. Not up to the *Meistersingers* at the ROH, but still excellent. Fascinating design by Hildegard Bechtler. Worked especially well in the First Act. Slight embarrassment in the third, when the front white curtain wouldn't fly out and they had to stop.

---

*Made Up (to protect identity).

†English National Opera Company, resident at the Coliseum Theatre, when not on tour with their English-language productions of the great opera repertoire.

Audience naturally laughed and sniggered. Still, fine night and excellent performances. Very cute young man played Gottfried (or Godfrey as they rather oddly called him). Still don't really go for the translations.

Supper afterwards at 2 Brydges Place, which was very pleasanty. Had sausages and fried camembert in front of the fire and Rod, owner with Alfredo, gave me a form to become a member, since (embarrassingly) I've never actually belonged.

Bed at midnight and a long, long, long, long sleep.

Sunday, 21 November 1993

A very very quiet Sunday. As placido a domingo as you could wish. Up round about one-ish: lots and lots of correspondence to sort out and plenty of television to watch. Retired early (well, twelve) and gazed at *The Parallax View* in bed. Part of BBC2's 'it was thirty years ago today . . .' Kennedy celebrations. Um, not sure celebrations is the word. Memorial. Oddly, C. S. Lewis died on the same day, but naturally his death was somewhat overshadowed. Interesting idea for a TV play or story: someone whose death, or achievement, or whatever, is completely cast in the shade by a massive, earth-shattering world event.

Monday, 22 November 1993

Voice Over this morning. Some training film with Griff as a manager. Only took fifteen minutes and then I taxied myself to South Kensington to pick up the Oscar letters. Marie Helene, the leading books and autographs popsy, was very friendly, as well she might be after being written a cheque for 18,997 bleeding quid. She also showed me Henry Blofeld's collection of P. G. Wodehouse firsts and unusuals. Simply wonderful. Simply, simply wonderful. But rather terrifying. They're going to be sold singly, rather than as a lot, which is a bore, since some of them will go for rather an amount I fancy. Poor old love has come unstuck as a result of Lloyd's* I gather. A lot of Names must be selling stuff: good for people like me and for Christie's and Sotheby's.

Back in time to do some writing with Hugh and then, at three thirty, off to Cambridge for a dinner. Paul Hartle's idea this. Paul was a young don at St Catharine's when I was at Cambridge: he's now Director of Studies in English there. Me, Nigel Huckstep (old chum from Cambridge, but a few generations older), Rob Wyke (ditto: currently housemaster at Winchester), Emma Thompson, Annabel Arden and Simon McBurney† all gathered to reminisce

---

*Lloyd's, the insurance organization, had suffered catastrophic losses, which were passed on to the Names who subscribed to various underwriting benches, in their jargon. Henry Blofield the cricket commentator (brother of the man after whom Ian Fleming named his most infamous Bond villain) sadly came out a loser.

†Simon is the much-praised founder and leading light of Théâtre de Complicité, a hugely successful company that has won more awards than any other of its kind all over the world. Annabel now mostly directs opera but collaborated many times with Simon McB.

and eat a good dinner in a private room in Cats. Partly to celebrate the fact that Annabel is spending this year as Judith E. Wilson Fellow at Cats. What a Judith E. Wilson Fellow is I never quite understood, but she teaches and lectures and seems to be enjoying herself enormously. Anyway, wonderful dinner, lots of wine and drink, in quantities that only academics know. Glen Cavaliero* showed up in Paul's rooms for the preprandials. Everyone cheery and on good form. Emma wearing her severely anti-glam Posy Simmonds round spectacles. Got highly squiffed and fell into bed in Paul's rooms at one thirty. Tomorrow I have to do this Camp Christmas thingy. Yuk.

Tuesday, 23 November 1993

Up at nine-thirty, a little hung over. Then I struggled over to Queens' to pop into an undergraduate's room for coffee. She had written disconsolately that I had done the Cambridge Union debate, but failed to do something or other for BATS† that she had asked me to turn up for. She and a knot of fresher friends stood around goggling at me while I tried to be cheerful and fun. Odd occasion. So squeaky clean and non-smoking and bright-eyed and lecture-attending. Escaped at ten-thirty and headed for

---

* Adorable old-fashioned English don at Cambridge. Great expert on those
  marvellous Powys siblings, John Cowper, Llewelyn, Philippa and T. F.
† Queens' College's drama club.

London. Was back by midday, where Hugh awaited. We wrote for most of the day and then I cabbed it to LWT (or *The London Studios* as the place now calls itself) for this Camp Christmas. Oh dear, oh dear, oh dear, oh dear. Horrid idea, why did I ever consent? Had to dress up as Santa and make up all my own lines, without rehearsal. Ghastly and under-rehearsed. Absolutely hopeless. Julian Clary sensibly an off stage voice. Everyone connected with it was gay. Lie Delaria was excellent doing her dyke act, but otherwise it was grim. Good Australian doing a Queen's Speech, Quentin Crisp filmed in New York, Martina Navratilova phoned in to say hi, Simon Callow and Antony Sher did something strange and then, at the end, I came on being dreadful. Completely hidden in a beard, so no one knew who the hell I was anyway. Lost steam and was simply very very bad. Christ, how embarrassing.

Zoomed straight off to the Groucho to recover. Bumped into Tim Roth of all people. Very fun to see him: he's over here filming something for the Beeb. Hung around chatting with him and his new wife. Don Boyd and Hilary turned up with Rufus Sewell and I was able to congratulate him on his excellent performance in *Arcadia*. Seemed a nice bloke, freakily handsome. Played some Perudo and escaped by 1.30. A highly drunken young man in a covert coat kept sitting too close to me . . . turns out he is the editor of the *Sunday Times* magazine or somesuch. Also the director Roger Pomfrey kept trying to score coke off me, which I find discomfiting. Relief to escape. On the way out, Greg from Channel 4 (can't think of his surname) told me that I had really opened a can of worms by writing in the *Spectator* and then saying on Clive Anderson that there were two gay men in the Cabinet. John Junor had written an article in the *Mail on Sunday* saying why didn't I have the guts to name them? This ignored the thrust of my argument, which was not to accuse them of a crime but to accuse them of hypocrisy in their insistence on telling us how to live 'core value', 'back to basics' lives. And in the *Standard* someone had written an article pointing out that Rory Bremner had done a sketch which had himself as John Major saying 'Portillo, Lilley* . . . don't think I can't see what you're doing at the back there.' On my return to the flat I wrote a note to Sir John Junor, but probably won't post it. No point really.

Wednesday, 24 November 1993

A day of quiet achievement. Ho, bloody ho. Started with a voice over for Intel processors. Stopped off at Fortnum's to buy sister Jo her birthday present for the day after tomorrow. Then round to Berry Bros and Rudd to order wine for Christmas. Simon Berry was in and I had a nice chat with him. Ordered some excellent stuff.

Back at the flat by lunchtime. Hugh was late: had a press screening of his series *All Or Nothing At All.* He was char-

---

*Who turned out not to be gay at all, for the record.

ismatic as ever, but I didn't especially like the script. One day Hugh will find the right material and emerge either as James Bond or something that will make him a world star. He has that star quality that I so noticeably lack. I just hope that people won't think I'm jealous when the day comes. Back to the flat at four-thirty in time only for an hour or so's writing and then he puddled off. He had time however, to speak to me man to man, as besto chummo, about *Bachelors Anonymous*. He put it to me as delicately as he could: 'Stephen,' he said, 'are you *sure* you want to have anything to do with it?' No sooner were the words out of his mouth (my *God* he is wise, that one) than I knew he was right. Secretly, inside (haven't even confided in you, Daisy Diary, dear) I have felt that a) the script is absolutely unrescuable tosh and b) Robin Hardy is not a man I can spend months and months with comfortably. Hugh pointed out that I was too modest or too flattered to realize that he had asked me to direct the movie simply because that put him in a position to be able to raise money for it. I should be aware of that and proceed only if it was the *right* project, not simply out of gratitude to a nice man who wanted me involved.

Heartrending conversation with Lo, who was wonderful and promised to ring him and pull me out. She rang back an hour later to say that she had succeeded, but that he was deeply distressed and angry. Gulp! So much easier to apply the surgeon's knife at the *inception* of these projects. Why am I such an arse?

Hugh said 'if you want to direct a film, then write one yourself: let it be as personal and as wonderful as you want it to be. If it's halfway decent an idea, money can be raised. Be aware that your name does mean something.' This has inspired me to be careful of Other People's Projects. About bloody time, Stephen.

Hugh popped off at 5.30 and I messed around till eightish, driving my own cab to Battersea/Wandsworth/Clapham, where Ian Hislop and his wife Victoria live. Quiet dinner *à trois*: strangely and comfortingly bourgeois house, rather like Dan Patterson's. Modish stencilled wallpaper and perhaps over-tidy faux antique chairs. No books that I could see or any life or mess or splendour. Odd compared to Ian's thrillingly disorganized *Private Eye* office, especially given how literary both Ian and Tori are. But a delightful dinner. I think Ian is all right, not untrustworthy: I think he knows the difference between a private dinner and usable gossip. For some reason I shot my mouth off about knowing Tristan Garel-Jones and talking to him about the age of consent and meeting Ken Clarke and all that. Hope he doesn't publish or I'll feel an arse. Back home by about twelveish. Crosswords and coke, then bed. Idiot.

Thursday, 25 November 1993

Just a plain old writing day. Hugh round at the usual hour and then a lot of chat, hysterical laughter and trying to get sketches out.

In the evening went off to the Groucho and played poker. Won a heap, snorted a heap. Also present Rory McGrath, Griff, Keith Allen. All the usual suspects. Bed at three. Twice damned villain. Watched the recordings of the Labour Party broadcast which had gone out at nine and ten. Seemed okay in my haze.

Friday, 26 November 1993

Hugh and I did a spot of work before zipping over to Holland Park for lunch with David Liddiment at the new Joe Allen/Orso restaurant, Orsino's. Liddiment is the man who's replaced Jim Moir* as head of Light Entertainment at the BBC. Tall, thin, glasses, Mancunian accent: seemed wildly unfriendly at very first glance. Turned out to be shyness, rather a decent sort really. Good that we touched base with him, I think. Decent grub.

Back home for me, and off to the dubbing studio for Hugh. More work on his Cellnet commersh. At seven-thirty I walked over to the Paris studios to record a couple of *Just a Minutes*. Think they went alright. I was against Peter Jones and Paul Merton. The first one had Pete McCarthy† as a guest, the second had Jan Ravens.‡ Jan excelled at her silly voices and impressions. Merton

---

*Not the same person as Vic Reeves.
†Comedian and writer, sadly taken from the world by cancer in 2004.
‡Fellow Cantabrigian: she directed our 1981 Footlights show *The Cellar Tapes*, voiced for *Spitting Image* and starred in *Dead Ringers*.

and Jones were splendid as ever. I my usual self, I suppose. In any case I won both games, for what little that is worth.

Then I had to walk very fast indeed to Le Caprice, for dinner with the Cleeses, Marilyn Lownes,* the Lauries and Bill Goldman. I had said I would be through recording by about eight thirty: it was actually 9.45 by the time I got there. Still, everyone on good form and enjoying the chance to use me as a friendly butt. Bill Goldman, as ever, spilling over with rich advice on how to proceed with the film business. I wish I had his *huevos*. Chucked it in at about twelve-ish. Ended on a sour note, though. There was a cluster of paparazzi outside the restaurant, Hugh did the sensible thing and zoomed out through the kitchens. I went ahead on my own and left John C. to do the same.

Saturday, 27 November 1993

Stayed in cheerfully most of the day, emerging at seven to cab it to Hammersmith. Ben (Elton) on at the Apollo. Saw him backstage first: Phil McIntyre† very sweetly had arranged a free bar backstage. Lots of dahlings present. Em and Ken, Hugh, Ade and Jenny, Bob Mortimer, Rik

---

*Better known as Marilyn Coles. Highly intelligent and deeply charming, she married Victor Lownes, the American boss of *Playboy*'s British operation.
†Ben's long-time manager. Still 'in post'.

Mayall ... all sorts. Ben on stunning form. Christ, those arseholes in the press who go on about him as if he is the quintessence of modern PC evil ... they haven't the faintest idea, they really haven't. If it weren't enough that he is the gentlest, kindest poppet in the world, he is also so much funnier and cleverer than they realize.

The party afterwards was just absurd. Too much voddie for the undersigned. And a whole deal too much of the old Bolivian marching powder too. X at one point, wanted a line, so I chopped him one in the loo. Y fully on the stuff too. I left at two and the joint was still jumping.

Sunday, 28 November 1993

Sunday papers and coffee. Norman Fowler is 'consulting his lawyers' after the Labour Party Broadcast had suggested that he had gone from privatizing National Freight to being on the board of the new company. 'They never mentioned that nine years passed between the two acts,' he (perhaps rather justifiably) complained. Oh dear, oh dear, oh dear. I feel a bit sorry about this as he's one of the few of that generation of Thatcher's cabinet I really admire. The AIDS epidemic landed in his lap when he was Health Secretary and, since retiring, he has continued to work and proselytize in the sector when he has no reason to other than moral decency.

To the Cleese's for Alyce Faye's son's wedding. A lot of the Nile holiday crowd were there. Peter Cook, Bill

Goldman, Ian and Mo Johnstone, Tomasz Starzewski etc. etc. Wedding went all right, rather chilly in the garden grotto. Good food and wine and, afterwards I made a small speech, as requested by Alyce Faye. Then a few rounds of Perudo with Peter C., Tomasz, Martin and Brian King. I skipped at three-ish, having arranged that Bill Goldman would come round at eight to examine my computer.

This he duly did. He's just bought a Mac and wanted to know how they worked. Not what you would call techno-phile, Bill, but he gasped and wowed appropriately when shown what a Mac can do. We then trotted off to Le Caprice again for dinz. I still have to rub my eyes and pinch myself to believe that I know the man who wrote *Butch Cassidy* and *Marathon Man* and who inspired me so much with *Adventures in the Screen Trade*.

Monday, 29 November 1993

A day working with Hugh, rather thrown off course by Emma Thompson arriving at twelve to have her script rescued. She had been writing her screenplay of *Sense and Sensibility* on a Mac, using Final Draft. Somehow it had all got corrupted. They saved it all, but lost the formatting and so on. I managed to get it all back in shape for her, but the defragging and so on took a very, very long time.

She is rather keen for Hugh to play Colonel Brandon and equally keen, so far as I can see, for me to play no one at all. Heigh ho, quite right, no doubt.

Off to Chris Beetles gallery at six. They were holding some kind of party and sale of illustrations on behalf of the NSPCC. All the usual suspects present, Cleese, Terry Jones, Terry Gilliam, Lord Archer, Frank Thornton* (all right, he's not really a usual suspect) and many others. Stayed for a while, signing T-shirts before the Terrys persuaded me out for a bite to eat. We decided on Groucho's.

Got very blasted on a lot of wine. The Terrys left and then I stayed behind, getting even drunker with Griff and Helen Mirren. Home at one.

Tuesday, 30 November 1993

An exciting day. I knew it would be my first evening in for ages. Galleys of *The Hippo* arrived. I *hate* the type-face they have chosen. What can I do? It's a Palatino, the most annoying feature being really irritating 'inverted commas' not curly like 'these', but naffly straight and horrid. In fact the type-face I'm using here is much better. Theirs is stark and clunky and just plain foul. Bollocks.

Hugh and I didn't manage to write much: we watched the Budget instead and started reading Emma's screenplay, which I had printed out for Hugh at her request. She's actually done a smashing job. It really reads well: I was in floods of tears, absolutely loving it. Such a great story, of course. Hugh would be excellent as Brandon.

*The immortal Captain Peacock in *Are You Being Served?*, of course.

But top marks to Emma, really brilliant work. The cunt of it is that she's right, there is absolutely *nothing* in it for me. Boo hoo. It could make Hugh a star, which he thoroughly deserves,* but yours truly is going to be a bit of a stay-at-home naffness, while Hugh jets off to Hollywood as Mr Big. I have always known that this will happen, but what will come hard will be everyone's sympathy for me . . .

Bed reasonably early and totally sober.

End of month, daisy, time for a print out.

And there, for good or ill, that passage of the diary comes to an abrupt end. At least it doesn't, but I seem to have lost the rest of it for the time being. Perhaps it is best to have offered you that excerpt and leave the rest to be published, when extricated from corrupted hard drives and no longer readable Zip and Jaz drives and floppy disks, after my death. No need then to protect the identities or habits of those I have protected here.

I have to be honest and say that reading the preceding pages gave me quite a turn. I have felt rather like someone groping forwards barefoot in an unlit attic, forever treading on unexpected lego bricks. Only twenty-one years have passed, but I feel as though I am peering into a wholly different world. I had no idea I was quite so busy, quite so debauched, quite so energetic, quite so irremediably foolish. To live that life and each day so studiously to

* Alan Rickman was cast as Colonel Brandon, and Hugh made do, hilariously, with Mr Palmer.

372

record it is something I do not even recall doing. I cannot even be certain who I was then. If I went back into the Groucho Club of 1993 and watched myself playing a game of snooker and disappearing every ten minutes to the gents, I am not sure I'd be able to hold back from massacring myself. How I managed to do so much working and so much playing without keeling over stone dead I cannot imagine. Believe me when I say, if you are younger than me, that you will not make it if you think you can imitate my wicked, wicked ways. Hold fast to the belief that I am a genetic freak who survived and that you are not. Do not test this assertion. *Verb sap.* as my old Latin master used to tell me – not that I listened. *Verbum sapienti sat est* – a word to the wise will do.

I have a very clear black-and-white memory of Michael Ramsey, Archbishop of Canterbury during my childhood, being sycophantically interviewed on a BBC Sunday-night programme.

'Your Grace, you are considered, I believe, by those who know you to be very wise.'

'Am I? Am I? Oh my goodness. I wonder if that is true.'

'Well, perhaps you can tell us what you think wisdom is?'

'Wisdom? Wisdom? Well now. I think perhaps wisdom is the ability to cope, don't you?'

I have never heard a better definition of wisdom since.

Certainly wisdom is nothing to do with knowledge or intellectual force. There are brilliant minds who can't sit the right way on a lavatory, and wholly uneducated people whose fortitude and humour in coping with lives that we would find unendurable shames us all.

The opposite of wisdom is generally considered to be folly, not a word much in use today. There are different kinds of fool of course. I fooled for a living in comedy shows on television, stage and radio. I became something of a licensed fool in palaces and private houses. I was a fool to my body – most especially to my brain and the linings of my nostrils, almost daring them to wave the white flag of surrender.

I often lie awake now, not for the old reason, not because my bloodstream is filled with that noxious, insinuating and wickedly compulsive stimulant, but because my mind is churning around and around wondering how as a young man I could ever have got myself into such a state. Where might my life have led me if I had not all but thrown away the prime of it as I partied like one determined to test its limits?

I do not remember that an unconscious whispered command to self-destruct drove me on, but looking back across the decades, reading the diary for the first time in twenty years, shaking my head in wonder at the reckless, impulsive, stupid, vain, arrogant and narcissistic headlong rush into oblivion that I seemed determined upon, I have to believe that a death wish was some part of the story.

And what possible excuse could I have to throw away the abundance of good fortune that at the time I could not believe I had lucked into and which today I still find unbelievable? Maybe that is where the answer lies.

It is such gimcrack armchair psychology that it may make you groan in dismay, but it is possible that I did not think myself worthy of that incredible luck and did all I could to dispose of it. Which takes me back to the world of my first book of memoirs, *Moab is My Washpot*, where I describe what I must hope and trust is a common feeling amongst many children: that of being watched and judged. When our race was young all humans felt it and called it God. Now, most of us call it conscience, guilt, shame, self-disgust, low self-esteem, moral awareness . . . there are plenty of words and phrases that dance around the rim of that boiling psychic volcano.

This very shame might paradoxically explain my bravado, in the way that the defenders of a crass, brash boor might explain that their friend acts in the way he does because he is 'so terribly shy'. It wasn't difficult for me to come out as gay, or later to be open about being afflicted with a mental condition that has led to attempts at suicide. I continue to this day unthinkingly to blurt out things which will get me slammed in the tabloids and cause embarrassment to my friends and family. A part of me truly believes that honesty is, as schoolteachers used to say, 'the best policy' in every way. It saves being 'found out', but it also – if this doesn't sound too self-regarding and sanctimonious – helps those who are in less of a position to feel comfortable about who they are or the situation they find themselves in. Without diverting ourselves about the nature of altruism and whether it really exists, I know that I write more or less the books that I wish I could have read when I was – oh, between fourteen and thirty I suppose.

Memoir, the act of literary remembering, for me seems to take the form of a kind of dialogue with my former self. What are you doing? Why are you behaving like that? Who do you think you are fooling? Stop it! Don't do that! Look out!

Books, too, can take the form of a dialogue. I flatter myself, vainly perhaps, that I have been having a dialogue with you. You might think this madness. I am delivering a monologue and you are either paying attention or wearily zipping through the paragraphs until you reach the end. But truly I do hear what I consider to be the voice of the reader, *your* voice. Yes, yours. Hundreds of thousands of you, wincing, pursing your lips, laughing here, hissing there, nodding, tutting, comparing your life to mine with as much objective honesty as you can. The chances are that you have not been as lucky with the material things in life as I have, but the chances are (and you may find this hard to believe, but I beg that you would) that you are happier, more adjusted and simply a better person.

If there's one thing that most irks my most loyal and regular readers it is the spectacle of me beating myself up in public. I try to fight it, but it is part of who I am. I am still a fool, but I have greater faith in the healing force of time. It is possible that age brings wisdom. The spectacle of many of our politicians and other citizens of middle age and beyond gives one leave to doubt that hope.

There is a fine legend concerning King Solomon, the wisest of all the Kings of Israel. You may know the story in another way. It hardly matters. It is a good story and worth remembering.

King Solomon was being visited by a great Persian king. During their conversation the Persian king said, 'You have much wealth and power and wisdom here, Solomon. I wonder if you have heard of the magical golden ring?'

'Of which ring?'

'They say that if you are happy it will make you sad, but if you are sad it will make you happy.'

Solomon thought for a second before clapping his hands for an attendant. He whispered into the attendant's ear. The attendant disappeared with a bow and the king clapped his hands again and called for dates and sherbets.

After the dates and sherbets had been consumed it was not long before the attendant had returned, bringing with him a goldsmith in a leather apron. The goldsmith bowed before both the kings and passed to Solomon a golden ring.

Solomon turned to his visitor. 'I have the ring that will make you happy if you are sad and sad if you are happy.'

'But that is not possible!' cried his guest. 'The ring is a

legend. It is not something you can command to have made in the twinkling of an eye.'

'Read it,' said Solomon.

The visiting king took the ring, still warm from the forge, and read upon it the words: 'This too shall pass.'

If days be good, they shall pass, which is a lowering thought. If they be bad, they shall pass, which is cheering. I suppose it is enough to know this and cling on to it for some small comfort when confronted by the irredeemable and senseless folly of the world; to be a little like Rafael Sabatini's Scaramouche who was 'born with a gift of laughter and a sense that the world was mad'.

But I know enough of myself and the instability that seems to be my birthright to be sure that I have not yet learned this lesson.

More fool me.

Postarse

Since there is no preface there must be a postarse. I have many people to thank. Literary parturition can be as messy and bloody a business as the obstetric kind. This book would not have been possible without all those who expend so much thought and energy clearing the thicket of my engagements and commitments in order to give me enough time to write. They include but are not limited to my writing agent Anthony Goff and my dramatic agent Christian Hodell. Most especially, of course, I owe everything to the book's dedicatee, my patient, efficient, kind and wonderful Personal Assister, Jo.

Everyone at Penguin Books has been sublimely professional, useful, wise, understanding and fun: above all my epically perfect editor Louise Moore and her stellar team: Hana Osman, Katya Shipster, Kimberley Atkins, Beatrix McIntyre, Roy McMillan and so many others. Once again David Johnson has taken on the task of organizing the author tour events, cinema streamings and those other oddities that constitute a book launch in the twenty-first century. His skill and experience have made that sluttish side of selling so much more enjoyable than it would otherwise have been.

Thanks to everyone mentioned in this book: some of you have read the manuscript and kindly corrected my memory, others have used the Search facility to jump from one mention of their name to the next and then 'signed off'.

It was the best of times, it was the worst of times.

Illustrations

Chelsea. Oh dear.

Chelsea – seems a waste of time to take trouble over tying a bow tie but neglecting to shave properly.

Kim Harris, Chelsea.

Kim in Draycott Place, taken by self (I solved that Rubik's Cube too but months after my father cracked it).

Kim Harris in our Chelsea flat.

My beloved parents . . .

My personal AsSister doing what she does better than anyone.

In 1986, I spotted a house for sale in classic west Norfolk brick. Reader, I bought it.

From P.G Wodehouse.

From P.G Wodehouse.

Chelsea: Pipes are hard work. P.G Wodehouse signed photograph evident. As is Rubik's Calendar, which is just showing off.

Chelsea flat, at work on something. You can just see the signed photograph of P.G Wodehouse on the left.

(All author's collection)

Rowan's inexplicable ability to find something more interesting than me.
Attempting a carol. Christmas Day, Norfolk, 1987.
(From the collection of Jo Laurie)

Chelsea – damn, I wish I still had that pullover.
(Author's collection)

All the details are on the clapperboard.
(Author's collection)

Quiet, dignified downtime. Eilean Aigas, Inverness-shire, 1995.
Everyone always anxious to sit next to me on the *Jeeves and Wooster* set.
(Author's collection)

Hugh, perfectionist as he is, always stays within his character: a drivelling poltroon from dawn to dusk while *Jeeves and Wooster* was being filmed . . .
(From the collection of Jo Laurie)

Official publicity still for *Jeeves and Wooster*. I remember it as if it were twenty-five years ago. (BBC photo library)

Filming *Jeeves and Wooster* at Farnham, 1989. Sister Jo visiting the set.
Giving Charlie Laurie his daily vodka and yoghurt smoothie. Christmas, 1988.

It's that butch look again. Christmas, 1988.
Newborn Charlie Laurie, adoring godparent, 1988.
My butch look, 1987.
My butch look, 1987.
(All from the collection on Jo Laurie)

Hysteria publicity show, 1991. (ITV/Rex Features)

Backstage at *Hysteria* benefit show. Sadler's Wells, 1989. (From
    the collection of Jo Laurie)
Reading at, I think, a *Hysteria* show. (Author's collection)

(*See over*) I know what you're thinking, and you're to stop it,
    January 1991. (Getty Images)

Self, Ben Elton, Robbie Coltrane, Griff Rhys Jones, Mel Smith,
    Rowan Atkinson. (Getty Images)

An idiot and an imbecile.
Ready to lay down their lives for my country.
A blithering idiot and a gibbering imbecile.
(All BBC Photo Library)

Radio Times 1988 Christmas edition: *Saturday-Night Fry* fea-
    ture. (Immediate Media)

Hugh, Jo and I. (From the collection of Jo Laurie)

With sister, Jo. (Getty Images)

A signing at a Dillons bookshop. London, 1991. (ITV/Rex Features)
Hugh's warmest, most approving look, 1991. (ITV/Rex Features)

A profile of a liar for the publication of *The Liar,* 1991, with sister Jo. (Tatler Condé Nast)

Tourrettes-sur-Loup – my best audience. (From the collection of Jo Laurie)
Tourrettes-sur-Loup – picking on someone my own size. (From the collection of Jo Laurie)

Hugh and I revealing our weekend recreational identities. (BBC Photo Library)

Mandela Birthday Concert, Wembley Stadium, 1988. About to perform in front of 80,000 people. Not in the least nervous. Oh no. (Getty Images)

I felt comfortable and ALIVE.
Incredibly, I still have that shirt. Haven't burnt it or anything . . . (BBC Photo Library)

Self and Hugh wining, dining and pointing at Sunetra Atkinson. (From the collection of Jo Laurie)

A bit more Fry and Laurie. (BBC Photo Library)

Cap Ferrat with Mrs Laurie.

Cap Ferrat, 1991 – Charlie Laurie, by this time, rightly, bored of my attempts to amuse.

Stripey me.

(All from the collection of Jo Laurie)

Self and self the National Portrait Gallery. Maggi Hambling's completed work.

Next to Maggi Hambling charcoal portrait of me commissioned by the National Portrait Gallery. Do NOT mention the hair.

(Author's collection)

Maggi Hambling's National Portrait Gallery picture of me.

(National Portrait Gallery, London)

Taking pleasure in red wellies: life gets no better, 1990. (From the collection of Jo Laurie)

The American *Peter's Friends* poster.

Peter's Friends publicity shot. From left: Emma, self, Hugh, Rita, Alphonsia – it's clear I'm thinking about the *Time Out* critic.

Full cast of *Peter's Friends*, 1992. From left: Rita Rudner, Ken Branagh, Alex Lowe, Emma Thompson, self, Alphonsia Emmanuel, Imelda Staunton, Tony Slattery, Hugh, Phyllida Law.

(ITV/Rex Features)

Publicity still for *Hysteria,* 1992. I have no words. (ITV/Rex Features)

Self. (Getty Images)

Labour Party fundraising gala. Beside Dickie Attenborough and Melvyn Bragg.
Sir Paul Fox, the Prince of Wales, self, Alyce Faye Cleese: premiere of *The Man Without a Face.*
With Alyce Faye Cleese at *The Man Without a Face* premiere. (Author's collection)

Publicity for Comic Relief, April 1991 – m'colleague, Hugh Laurie and Emma Freud, self, Jennifer Saunders, Tony Slattery. (Getty Images)

Note where I'm playing from. Total duffer. Inverness, 1994. (From the collection of Jo Lauire)

Jo and my third nephew, the most excellent George.
Carla Powell checking to see if my beard is real. It is. (Author's collection)

I can't quite explain why I'm sitting like that: I'm going to say in order to keep the jacket smooth . . . (Getty Images)